the Great Big Book *of* HOPE

Diane McDermott, Ph.D.
C.R. Snyder, Ph.D.

drawings by
Elizabeth Kelley

New Harbinger Publications, Inc.

Distributed in the U.S.A. by Publishers Group West; in Canada by Raincoast Books; in Great Britain by Airlift Book Company, Ltd.; in South Africa by Real Books, Ltd.; in Australia by Boobook; and in New Zealand by Tandem Press.

Copyright © 2000 by Diane McDermott and C. R. Snyder
         New Harbinger Publications, Inc.
         5674 Shattuck Avenue
         Oakland, CA 94609

Cover design by Poulson/Gluck Designs
Edited by Carole Honeychurch
Text design by Michele Waters
Illustrations by Elizabeth Kelley

ISBN 1-57224-212-4 Paperback

New Harbinger Publications' Web site address: www.newharbinger.com

02   01   00

10   9   8   7   6   5   4   3   2   1

First printing

To our grandchildren, Drew Rebecca and Danielle and Breanna Swenson. May you grow in hope and realize your dreams.

Contents

Acknowledgments

Producing a book is like having a baby. It takes at least nine months, and it consumes your thoughts from the first day that you decide to write it. It is also not a process one engages in alone. We have many people to thank for their support, encouragement, and ideas in the production of *The Big Book of Hope* and our families and students are at the top of the list. We also thank the elementary and secondary students who took part in our research. Several of the stories in this book were adapted from work originally published in 1997, titled *Hope for the Journey* by C. R. Snyder, Diane McDermott, William Cook, and Michael Rapoff. Our thanks, as well, go to the students who contributed stories to that work. And finally, our grateful appreciation goes to Carole Honeychurch, Kristin Beck, and all the folks at New Harbinger for their continued support of our ideas.

introduction

Hope for the Present— Hope for the Future

Welcome to *The Big Book of Hope*. You and your child are about to begin an exciting trip that will lead you through your past, present, and future. Prepare yourselves for an interesting and fun adventure as you work your way through the exercises that will teach you about hope.

As a parent, your major dreams for your children probably reflect some version of the following:

- "I want my child to be healthy."

- "I want my kid to be happy."

- "I want my child to be successful."

Parents everywhere share such aspirations. These hopes are within our awareness in many of our waking moments and perhaps even more so when we are jolted from a daydream by the telephone and immediately worry, "Could something have happened? Oh, please let her be okay!" Most parents can easily identify with this latter, worst case scenario. We all want the best for our children. And, of course, this desire involves somehow protecting them from the many harms that we know are "out there."

And so, we take on the grand assignment of seeing to it that our children are healthy, happy, and successful. This doesn't mean that you are some sort of Type A, hard-charging care-giving maniac who is going to orchestrate a perfect, station wagon–driven childhood, but it does means the same thing that it has for generation after generation of parents—*we want to provide our children with what they will need for successful and happy lives.*

It doesn't take too long after your child's birth (or adoption) to totally understand that you've taken on an enormous responsibility—one that dwarfs any and all previous ones. Sometimes people get a pet to "practice" caring for a child, but, oh, how that similarity pales in comparison to the real task! You cannot leave your newborn child in the garage; Alpo in a bowl will not do the trick for feeding; and so on. Those little pets are cute and cuddly, but raising them is so different from raising a newborn child. Indeed, the comparison becomes laughable to the couple who first "prepared" for parenting by getting a cocker spaniel.

Fathers can be seen standing at the hospital viewing window for newborns, overcome with excitement and wonderment about what lies ahead for that little guy or gal who is bundled up before them. The gurgles and coos are but a quiet prelude to the noises that you will hear for the next two decades. Nurses come and go, tending to the wee ones, and they seem to know what they are doing. But will you? Sure, there may be many grandparents, aunts and uncles, and other family members who are nearby at first, helping out and celebrating the birth. But suddenly, you find yourself driving back to your apartment without the familial entourage, and your child is under *your* care. Under the smiles of excitement, there is the unsaid question on the minds of both parents: "What are we going to do now?"

Life really can become a totally new ball game when your child arrives. In our work with new parents, one of their most common observations is, "I never was aware that I was going to become responsible for so many decisions that will shape my child's life." There is so much that you can provide, but we believe that there is a lasting, powerful gift without a price tag that can be dispensed any time you are with your child. That gift, of course, is hope. And while you are at it, take a full dose of hope for yourself.

Before you give in to the possible temptation to toss this book into the "giveaway pile" as some New Age psychobabble, consider the importance of hope in the lives of your children and you as a parent. The idea of "hope" may seem a little soft or dreamy at first, and we, as authors, started with exactly the same reactions. But a strange thing happened to us over the last two decades in our clinical work and research—time and again, the children and adults with hopeful thinking were the ones who prospered. Parents were reaching their dreams, and helping their children to do the same.

We remained skeptical, however, and would run yet one more study, recruit just one more sample. But, no matter whom we examined, we continued to see hopeful thinking deliver its benefits. So, time after time, our scientific cloaks of disbelief were shredded and we were left with a naked reality—*hope really does work*.

Accordingly, we could think of no better means of unleashing the power of hope than by applying it to what is arguably the most difficult and yet important task in our lives—raising our children. Simply put, we will argue that the lessons of hopeful thinking we provide for our children should be constant and unending.

Hope is an active, learned process—a way of thinking that activates an ensu-
ing set of behaviors. It's like a seed planted in a child's mind that will continue to
grow throughout the developmental process. Just as with the seed, there are environments in which the growth of hope can flourish; or, sadly, there are conditions
in which it can sicken and become stunted. Our work with children has been a
scientific search for the conditions that facilitate the development of hope. In this
book, we have translated our findings into workable, practical strategies that you
can quickly put to use, imparting hopeful thinking to your children.

We have used these strategies to enhance children's hope in schools, and we
also have seen the beneficial effects of these hope-inducing interventions when
applied at home, by parents. Although the strategies you will learn in these pages
are based on sound research involving many, many children, *we would emphasize
that they also are grounded in common sense and logic*. This latter point is crucial,
because if you as a parent don't resonate with the principles that underlie our
hope training, then you probably won't convey these to your children. This is just
human nature—people teach what they understand and believe.

As you move through these pages, you will see how these hope-raising
strategies may work for you and, in turn, how you can pass on what you have
learned to your kids. Before going any
further, however, we must ask you a
question, the answer to which should
determine whether you keep turning the
pages of this book. Namely, *do you sin-
cerely want your children to think hopefully—to have the self-confidence to reach for
their dreams*? An affirming answer means
that you will journey with us through the
following pages. Initially, we will be your
guides on this trip of hope, but our goal is
to eventually hand over the piloting to
you. If we can have you become the hope
guide for your children, then we will have
fulfilled our major goal in writing this
book.

The chapters in the first part of the
book are designed to give a thorough
understanding of the process of hope. We
will paint word pictures through
vignettes about high-hope children, as
well as their low-hope counterparts. We
will also describe how hope (or its lack)
permeates all aspects of children's lives.
We will describe children living in homes
where hope is low, if not nonexistent;

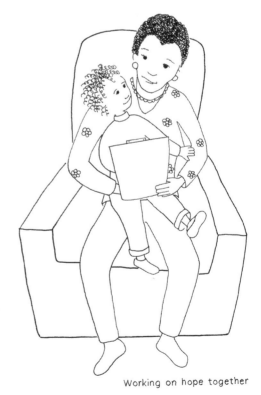

Working on hope together

conversely, we will take you to the environs of high-hope children. Along the way, you will begin to see how hopeful thought is affected by the atmospheres within families.

In this book you will learn what hope is and how to measure it. You will learn about the important domains of your children's lives, and see how hope can work to bring greater success and happiness in these areas. You will learn how to use many different strategies for instilling and enhancing hope in yourself and in your child. There are exercises and assignments that you and your child will do together, taking you on a shared journey and deepening your relationship.

Throughout this book you will read true stories of children who are struggling with familiar concerns. The way these children and their parents use hopeful thinking can serve as models for you and your child. Many of the stories feature children who lead average, middle-class lives. The final two chapters, however, focus on children who do not fit this model. Ethnic minority children often live in disadvantaged circumstances, thus they are especially in need of hope interventions and chapter 13 is just for them. The final chapter, "Hope for Children in Trouble," depicts two common but challenging problems—truancy and drug abuse. Children today experience a world fraught with dangers that we parents may not totally understand. Drug abuse and truancy are but two pitfalls that tempt young people, but they can serve as examples of how hope strategies can be used to help children through troubled times.

The focus of this book is on the strategies that instill and enhance hope. Because your child's world is so complicated, and because there is so much for you to learn if you are to be a good hope mentor, we have included a section filled with additional helpful sources of information. We have also listed books about high-hope children and adolescents that you and your child can share and discuss. For the development of your own hope, we recommend that you read our book titled *Making Hope Happen: A Workbook for Turning Possibilities into Realities*, published by New Harbinger Publications.

You also will notice that we have varied the use of the pronouns "he" and "she" throughout the book. Your child may be a boy, a girl, or you may have several of each. The hope-building strategies apply to both sexes and you may use them effectively with more than one child at a time.

We envision the work in this book to be fun as well as educational and hope-inducing. The exercises are suitable for the whole family and will produce hours of interesting conversation in which young and old alike can participate. Learn, increase your hope, and enjoy.

chapter 1

Promises and Premises

Hope is a thought process that facilitates goal setting and helps us work effectively to reach those goals—whether it is in the next five minutes or for the rest of our lives. Although hope is part of the normal development sequence in children, it's growth either can be stunted or can flourish, depending upon what is going on around that child—the environmental conditions and the attitudes of the significant people in the child's life. The good news is that parents can bring together favorable conditions so that the children can develop hopeful thinking. In fact, our goal in writing this book is to show you how to do just that.

To begin, we presume that you are a parent who wants to maximize the chances that your children will live successful and happy lives. Given that you are still with us, we also presume that you will invest the necessary time and energy to see to it that your children can think hopefully. If you are so dedicated, you can rest assured that your hopeful child will have increased chances of achieving their dreams and of being happy.

If our premises are correct, we can fulfill our promise to you and your children. Our promise is this: by using the strategies we describe in this workbook and following the steps we outline, hopeful thinking will increase in yourself and in your child. As a result of enhanced hope, your children will be able to set realistic and reachable goals. They will be able to find more ways to achieve what they want, and discover more ways to overcome obstacles in their paths. Finally, they will experience greater energy to work for their goals and, eventually, for their life dreams.

The strategies you will learn in this book will help you to establish a hope-enhancing environment. First, however, it's important for you to learn more about hope. We will describe the components of hope, and then, through vignettes, show you how hope looks in the lives of several children. As we discuss these stories, you will learn about goals, waypower, and willpower—the elements of hopeful thinking.

What Is Hope?

People use the word "hope" in many contexts. We are said to have "high hopes." We "hope" something will or will not happen. We say we are "hopeful" about the future. When we use the word "hope" in this manner, it is synonymous with "want" or "expectation." What we're really saying is, "I want something to turn out the way I would like." Used in this way, hope denotes a rather passive, "wait and see" approach to the desired object or outcome.

When you hear the word "hope" you also may think of the three virtues—faith, hope, and charity. Used in this sense, hope is a quality that imbues an individual with certain grace in the face of adversity. Again, however, such hope is experienced passively. In this context, therefore, hope isn't an active process used to reach objectives.

The concept of hope that we use in this workbook is dynamic—always involving an active pursuit of goals. Hope is a process, not a static state of mind. And, most fortunately, it's a process that can be learned.

Specifically, we define hope as three interrelated parts of thinking—goals, willpower, and waypower. Hope cannot occur without all three of these interacting components. We will describe each separately and then put them together to show how they work to produce hope.

Goals

Whether or not specifically identified as goals, every child or adult has mental targets for which they "aim" on a daily basis. For example, getting up in the morning, getting ready for school, eating breakfast, catching the school bus or walking to school—each of these constitutes goals with their attendant subgoals. When children go through these tasks without any problems, we rarely think of them as goals. Instead, they are just part of a daily routine that we take for granted. If, however, your child resists just one aspect of these necessary functions, then immediately it is elevated in awareness as being a salient target (sometimes also called "an outcome").

Whether your performance of a task is routine or very difficult to accomplish, it typically has a final goal that can be divided into a number of subgoals. Fortunately, we don't have to struggle in everything we undertake. Over the course of childhood, most life-sustaining actions become quite ordinary, even automatic, because we perform them countless times. If you think about it, making these actions automatic for our children is really our "assignment" as new parents. Namely, after a period of some eighteen to twenty years of "training," society expects us to deliver a highly functioning young adult who can perform many activities on "auto pilot." Indeed, as a society, we need to count on young adults going after their goals and doing so in a cooperative, nondisruptive manner. In short, our children are expected to become good citizens, however "good" is defined in a particular society.

These notions lead to some advice for parents. As parents and adults, our daily goal-oriented activities are habitual. Thus, it may be easy for us to forget that children and adolescents haven't yet mastered these goal-directed tasks to the point that they've become habits. In fact, we may sometimes be surprised to see how our kids *really must struggle* with such seemingly mundane tasks as tying their shoes. Indeed, good parenting means remaining patient and understanding when helping our children to set and accomplish seemingly ordinary tasks. If we become impatient and show this impatience to our children, we teach them to become restlessly impetuous rather than hopeful. We will return to this crucial point later in the workbook.

Waypower

After a goal has been identified, the next step in hopeful thinking is to determine how to reach that goal. This process, called *waypower thinking,* is the perceived ability to think of ways to reach our cherished goals. High-waypower people see themselves as being capable of coming up with many routes to their goals, whereas low-waypower people see themselves as being stymied in finding such routes. Or, even if a low-waypower person does find one pathway, she is truly lost if her first route doesn't get her to her goal. So, how do children come to truly see themselves as having the potential to produce "mental road maps" leading them where they want to go? The short answer is that they are coached by caregivers, and they practice, and practice, and *practice.* Through trials and errors in attempting to master small goals, they eventually understand that they can produce these mental road maps to get them almost anywhere they desire. For the successful instillation of waypower thought, the child should set goals that are small enough to be reached and yet challenging enough to intrigue them and sustain their interest.

Here is an example of waypower thinking provided by a child in one of our research groups. This child wanted to climb a particularly inviting tree. The tree had smooth bark and sturdy branches placed at intervals all the way to the top. The only problem was that the branches began far above the child's reach. As a high-hope child, she tried a number of ways to reach the first branch. At first, she tried jumping, but she couldn't jump high enough. She thought about nailing wooden boards on the trunk and using these for steps. But she loved trees and feared that the long nails would damage this one. Next, she looked around for something to stand on, but nothing was handy. Finally, she went into the house and asked her grandfather for a boost up. With his help, she was off to her goal, pausing to celebrate at the very first branch. Then, one by one, branch by branch, she was able to reach her goal—the top of the tree.

In this example, of course, the young girl learned tree climbing—but there are few grown-up jobs for professional tree climbers! But, what she did learn that will help her throughout her life is how to move from one pathways to another in order to eventually find one that works for her. And even more importantly, she learned something about her thinking—she could come up with a route to her goal if she kept trying, kept imagining alternative routes. This last lesson about her own creative, navigational capacities to a desired end is another that she will call upon (and count upon) for the rest of her life.

Contrary to the child who is high in waypower thinking, the children who are low in this type of thinking become frustrated and often quit when they encounter any obstacles to their desired goals. Asking for help with a problem is one path that such children may choose, but if this is always the first choice (and perhaps only option), they won't figure out their own routes for getting to goals. You will notice that our tree climber eventually asked her grandfather to serve as a friendly route to that lowest limb. Before that, however, this high-hope child had tried several of her own ideas.

We now have a good idea of two of the components of what we call hope. Goal setting comes first, because without a goal there would be no impetus to move forward. Once a goal has been formed, high-hope people use waypower thinking to set their course of action. The next component, will-power, is the motivational energy that sets the process in motion.

High hope girl

Willpower

The usual meaning for the term "willpower" is an individual's ability to stick to a resolution. One speaks of needing will-power to diet, or to maintain an exercise program. Willpower, in common usage, involves the passive resistance to a temptation of some sort. The individual needs to do nothing. We advocate a somewhat different, more *active* meaning for willpower. Will-power is a perceived wellspring of motivation that individuals can draw upon to work toward their goals. This mental energy is experienced as a belief that one will be successful in goal attainment, and a willingness to try even if success is not immediately forthcoming. High-willpower people frequently show enthusiasm for their work, and there is a positive tone to their thoughts and talk about their goals.

High and low willpower, respectively, can be very obvious in the demeanors of children and adolescents. Some children seem eager to try new things. They have an "I can do it" approach to life. Other children are hesitant, often saying, "I can't" even before they begin. Such children hang back, waiting and perhaps wishing that others will define the nature of what is to happen. High-hopers are children who are '"doers"; low-hopers are children who are spectators. As a parent, you're probably very familiar with the children at the ends of the spectrum we have described in this paragraph. Even though you're certain that a child could accomplish a task, is it difficult to convince him to break through self-defeating thoughts and to "give it a try"? Does your child have this low-willpower profile?

As may be obvious by now, we believe that both willpower and waypower are important components of goal-directed thinking. Very young children often express fanciful goals, because they haven't yet encountered many of life's limitations. First- and second-graders in our studies, for example, have told us about their dreams of becoming basketball stars, astronauts, and ballerinas, with seeming absolute certainty that these dreams will come true. Young children often report high hope, perhaps because they haven't experienced many limitations and failures. Older children are more realistic about their hopeful thoughts.

Willpower grows as children successfully reach their goals. The development of willpower depends, in part, upon the waypower a child can exercise, because the more options there are for achieving the desired end, the more chances there are for success. In turn, both willpower and waypower increasingly are based on realistic and reachable goals. When their efforts are successful, children come to see themselves as capable of achieving what they want, and thus both willpower and waypower flourish. This process, described in the next section, begins in infancy.

The Birth and Growth of Hope

Hope begins to develop immediately after birth. Even in reaching the simple, early goal of seeking food from the caregiver, the infant is learning that certain actions produce specific desired outcomes. We are not suggesting that very young infants are cognitively aware of causality, but as any parent can attest, babies learn quite early how to get what they need from their caregivers.

Where Goals Come From

As babies develop, they can use their small fingers to point to what they want. Some researchers believe that this occurs as early as three months, and it is certainly common by the time the child is a year old. When a baby points at a desired object, she is selecting a goal. For example, there may be many toys available, but the goal-directed baby will indicate the specific one with which he wishes to play. Our point here is that goal selection begins very young, first with the basic needs to sustain life, such as those involving food, protection, and comfort. When those basic needs are met, the infant seeks further stimulation and shows curiosity about matters going on around her. Selecting goals is a natural process without which the infant would not survive, let alone grow and develop into a healthy individual.

The formation of goals provides the underpinning of hope; moreover, goals are fundamental to both waypower and willpower thinking. In the process of goal selection and attainment, the infant becomes aware that specific actions lead to certain consequences. When he cries, for instance, a caregiver appears to attend to his needs. When the infant points to a toy, someone produces that toy for her amusement. Such linkages of action and reaction become the basis for waypower. It's unlikely that the infant has a conscious recognition of this process; nevertheless, it serves as groundwork for later waypower thinking.

Waypower in the Early Years

As infants become toddlers, their waypower thinking becomes more developed and conscious in nature. Consider the actions of a two-year-old who wants some candy that he's spotted in the grocery-store checkout line. First he points to it, but his mother says, "No." Next, he grabs for it, but he can't reach it. He tries in vain to stand up in the grocery cart, as his mother quickly puts him back in the seat. As a last resort, he begins to scream, either out of frustration, anger, or thinking that his cries might convince his mother to give him the candy.

As children grow, so, too, does their waypower thinking. Older children use reasoning skills to figure out various ways to get what they want. As our grocery-store toddler gets older, he probably will learn that fits of crying, screaming, and demanding simply do not get the candy; on the other hand, asking politely or suggesting that the candy could serve as his dessert may convince his mother to buy the candy for him.

Children develop waypower thinking by dealing with a "healthy" amount of frustration. Sometimes parents believe that they are caring for their children by removing all obstacles or sources of frustration. If that happens consistently, however, there is no need for the child to develop high-waypower thinking. After all, their parents are ready servants who will see to it that the child's wants are fulfilled. In our experience, this approach on the part of parents has resulted from their genuine belief in the equation "frustration = poor mental health." Unfortunately, such "perfect" childhoods leave young adults with no experience at dealing with impediments to their desires. They are in no way inoculated against life stressors and are totally lacking in the crucial waypower component of hope.

Antithetical to frustration-free childhood environs are children who undergo so much stress that they are literally swamped by it. If a child experiences a blockage of enormous proportions (e.g., the deaths of parents), or is repeatedly exposed to seemingly unending stressors (e.g., physical abuse by parent), then low-waypower thinking is likely to ensue. Children who live in fear, for example, are too terrorized to learn how to reach goals (save, perhaps, how to avoid the next parental outburst). We also know from a consistent body of psychological research that children will shut down their effort at goal attainment if success and positive rewards are not forthcoming.

In later chapters, we will explore goal-setting and problem-solving strategies that are designed to help children develop higher hope. From this brief discussion on the development of waypower, however, it is important to remember that children grow from their experiences of coping with the barriers they meet on the route to their goals. This process begins in infancy and continues to develop throughout life. With the proper conditions, that is, do-able goals, problems that can be solved, and caring guidance, waypower can flourish.

The Beginnings of Willpower

The third component of hope, willpower, also develops early, although not until infants are capable of recognizing that they are the initiators of actions. Such recognition is preceded by early inklings of selfhood, probably occurring in the first few months of life. By the time a toddler is one to two years old, selfhood is firmly established. One experiment that contributed to this conclusion is a fun one that you can do with your toddler. Place a dot of watercolor paint on the toddler's nose, and put her in front of a mirror. If the toddler looks into the mirror and touches her nose, then self-recognition has occurred (typically between twelve to eighteen months).

As further evidence for the developing self, listen carefully to the words used by toddlers as they assert their independence. A little girl dressing herself may proudly tell her mother, "I can do it myself!" A little boy trying to put together a complicated toy may spew out, "I can't do this." Sometimes children use their own names in referring to the initiator of the action. For example, the little girl dressing herself may say, "Suzy can do it." These signals of self-awareness are also the beginnings of willpower.

Willpower is the belief that one can reach a goal. If given the power to speak, it would say, "I can do it." *The Little Engine That Could* is an excellent tale of high willpower that can be read to young children. The Little Engine's positive self-talk is "I think I can, I think I can," as he struggles to reach the top of a very high hill. These are the types of messages that high-hope people, whether children or adults, give themselves when they want to accomplish a difficult goal.

You now have a basic understanding of the elements of hope, and the way that each relates to the other so as to produce hopeful thinking. Goals are the endpoints toward which waypower and willpower thinking are directed, and all three components function together as the process of hope. Willpower and waypower, although working together to produce hope, also are somewhat independent of each other. In measuring hope we find that people can be high in both willpower and waypower, low in both, or high in one and low in the other. The descriptions of children in the next section depict these variations.

Portraits of Hope—The Birthday Party

We begin our stories by visiting a birthday party given by Sandy Cottin for Jacob, her six-year-old son. The Cottins live in a large city on the West Coast, and the party is in the small back yard of the Victorian house in which they have a flat. As Sandy watches the children play, she wonders what their futures will bring. All are first-graders attending the same school. Though they live in the same neighborhood, they have very different home environments.

Sandy was a room mother for Jacob's kindergarten class, so she knew many of the children. As she watches them play, knowing that some of their lives are difficult, she wishes she had a gift to give each of them on her son's birthday—one that would enhance their chances for successful lives. The gift she is giving Jacob, because she herself is a high-hope person, is the gift of hope.

Sandy is especially interested in several children she particularly liked from the kindergarten class. There is Anna, whose mother died during the summer, and Cody, who lives with his grandmother because his parents are both in prison. Jared and Jamal Jackson, called "the JJs" by their friends, have parents who are eager to see their twin boys succeed in a world that is difficult for African Americans. From their stories, we can discern the challenges facing parents who are trying to build happy and fulfilling lives for their children—lives filled with hope.

✳ Anna—Little Girl Lost

The house was always dark, even on the sunniest of days. The shades were pulled because Anna's mother needed to rest. The apartment smelled like a mixture of medicine and urine, even though the visiting nurse did her best to keep the sickroom clean. Every evening, when he got home from work, Anna's father did housework, fixed dinner, and spent time talking with his wife. Every night the same question echoed through Anna's thoughts: Where did a little girl belong in this sad household?

Life was very different for Anna before her mother's illness. She and her mother explored the park, the zoo, and the museums almost daily. At night they told Anna's father about all the wonderful things they had seen, often acting out the funny antics of the animals and people. Every night, Anna's parents read to her for at least an hour, and she was allowed to run and play in the apartment all she wished. Anna was happy and exuberant. Each morning she looked forward to what adventures her day would bring.

After her mother was diagnosed with cancer, life began to change—slowly at first, and then rapidly deteriorating. Anna's mother began to tire easily, and their long walks together were shortened and eventually stopped completely. In the afternoons, when they previously might have played with toys or painted pictures, Anna now had to take a long nap and be very quiet so as not to disturb her mother's rest.

Anna's entry into kindergarten unfortunately coincided with her mother's ceasing all efforts to care for her active daughter. At first, kindergarten helped Anna to recover some of her previous joy in life—at least during the day. There were other children to play with, and there were new games, lessons, and activities. But always, like a dark shadow following her, Anna's thoughts would turn to her ailing mother and what she would find when she went home.

Over time, Anna's hope also began to diminish at school. She became frustrated easily when a lesson was difficult or a project didn't work for her, and she often refused to learn new games. At home, Anna watched television and tried not to bother her parents. Certainly she was sad about what was happening to her mother, but mostly she felt she had lost her place in the world. She was no longer the center of anything, and her role as a bystander to her mother's illness was confusing and upsetting.

During the summer before Anna started the first grade, her mother died. Two months before her death, Anna's mother had been in the hospital, where Anna and her father visited nearly every day. Knowing the emotional toll that the death of her mother was taking, Anna's father took her to see a child psychologist

Anna

who was a specialist in grief counseling. The weekly sessions helped Anna to express her feelings and to realize that she wasn't to blame for her mother's illness. By the time school started, Anna was ready to begin a new phase of her life. She still remained reluctant to try new things, however, and often quit when her plans didn't work out. At Jacob's birthday party, Sandy notices that Anna doesn't join the games as readily as the other children, and when it is time to break the piñata, Anna gives up after one rather feeble swipe.

Anna exemplifies low hope. Both her waypower and willpower began to decrease when her parents could no longer focus their nurturing attention on her. She also grieves the loss of her mother, and her low-hope thinking may be an impediment to her emotional healing. Sandy knows this child's recent history, and she is eager to help her in anyway she can.

✳ The JJs—Children of the Dream

Jared and Jamal have parents who are determined to give their boys all the advantages and protection they believe that African-American children need to be successful. They grew up on the dream of Martin Luther King, Jr., and they want to make it come true for their twins. They are strict parents and have high expectations for Jared and Jamal. The boys were enrolled in a private Montessori pre-school prior to entering kindergarten. They took extracurricular lessons such as swimming and tennis, and their parents are now inquiring about foreign language classes.

Either one or both of the JJs parents make it a point to watch how the boys perform in their classes. Although they are encouraging, they're also critical of mistakes. The twins know that their parents expect them to be self-confident and enthusiastic about their activities, which they are, until the going becomes difficult. Often, when it appears that they might not be successful, they quit trying.

On the surface this parental interest appears fine, but the fact that both boys show anxiety and apprehension when they encounter problems suggests that the parental interest isn't fostering high hope. Clearly, the boys are aware of their parents' expectations and they're fearful of not meeting them. This is a pattern often seen in children who have high willpower or motivation for attempting their goals, but find it difficult to cope with problems that might interfere with success (i.e., low-waypower thinking).

✳ Cody—The Surprising Survivor

When Cody was three years old his parents were arrested and subsequently sent to prison for embezzling money from the bank where they worked. Cody was sent to live with his maternal grandmother, who had just retired from a long and successful career as a middle-school teacher. Still a youthful woman at sixty-three, and a widow for the past five years, Cody's grandmother was happy to have him live with her. Even though the circumstances were unfortunate, Cody adjusted rapidly to his new situation.

The home environment that Cody's grandmother provided was perfect for a small, rambunctious boy. Having worked with children for years, she knew how to establish structure while at the same time giving plenty of love. She knew the importance of allowing children to struggle with problems so that they could experience the joy of solving them. She knew how to direct Cody toward goals that were appropriate and reachable for his age. And, perhaps most importantly, she encouraged Cody in his budding belief that he could succeed.

When Cody was four years old, he decided he wanted to learn karate. His grandmother enrolled him in a class, encouraging his interest by getting him the white uniform and watching his classes. Although she wanted him to progress through the various levels, she knew he was very young to be learning a martial art. She praised him for trying and complimented him on the moves he did well. She was careful not to criticize him, leaving the training to the instructor. At six years old, Cody has mastered three levels of karate, and impresses the other children with his ability to box and kick.

In Cody, we see a high-hope child who enters into most of what he does with enthusiasm. He greets problems as challenges to be overcome, and has the confidence that he can overcome them. He has the motivation to follow the paths toward his goals, and he often inspires other children with his positive outlook.

What you have seen in the stories of Anna, the JJs, and Cody, are three examples of how early life experiences affect the way that children approach life. Will they go after their goals, or will they give up easily? Will they be able to solve life's problems, or will they be stopped in their tracks? Parents convey messages to their children that have a powerful effect on the development of hopeful thinking from the cradle into adulthood.

Later in this book, you will examine the messages that you give your child, as well as the *messages you heard when you were young*. We have found that, as parents, we often pass on to our children the same self-talk we heard as kids. As you read the brief vignettes of Anna, the JJ's, and Cody, you could see the reflections of their parents attitudes in their approaches to life.

Anna's father, of necessity, focused on her dying mother. Throughout the ordeal, he tried to meet Anna's needs in the best way he could, but his own hope was drained with the death of his wife. Perhaps Anna's loss of hope was unavoidable under her given circumstances. At six years of age, Anna was ready to enter a new phase of her life, but she carried with her the tentativeness and self-doubt that had developed during her mother's illness.

The twins' parents are trying to help their children become successful by giving them all of the advantages that they never had as kids. In the twins' vignette, we see that very high expectations can create anxiety in children who develop a fear of disappointing their parents. These boys are eager to learn and ready to apply their mental energies to new tasks, because they know the importance their parents place on success. On the other hand, the pressure they feel has made them anxious when they encounter problems, and they often quit trying before they reach their goals.

In Cody's case, his parents took foolish risks that resulted in their loss of custody. His grandmother, however, was able to step into a difficult situation and create a home in which Cody could flourish. She is a high-hope person and understands how to raise children; moreover, she is able to convey her enthusiasm for life to her grandson.

The Configurations of Hope

In this chapter, we have presented several stories from which we can understand hope in children. In the next chapter, you will learn how to measure willpower and waypower numerically, and how to combine these numerical scores so as to attain an overall hope rating. Children can be high in both willpower and waypower, and thus be fully high-hope kids. They can be low in both of those components, and thus be truly low in hope. They also can be high in one element and low in the other. Such children will be lacking in hope.

With the three stories in this chapter, we have illustrated several configurations of hope. Anna was low in both waypower and willpower, hesitating to start toward her goals and ready to quit early. The JJs were high in willpower but low in waypower, beginning their projects with high energy, but quitting when they encountered problems. Cody was high in both waypower and willpower, ready to take on challenges with the belief that he could succeed.

At this point, we ask you to think about the children whose hope you would like to increase. As a parent, you might use hope-enhancing strategies with one or all of your children. As you think about the children with whom you will use the techniques, we suggest that you create a brief description of each child. You know your children well, but in writing this description you may discover a fresh perspective for seeing them more clearly. Perhaps you will be able to look at them through a new lens—one that will focus on their hope.

In the space provided on page 18, fill in the name of the child and his or her age and sex. In the space alongside each name, write a very brief description of the child in terms of his or her ability to set goals, solve problems, and then work toward achieving those goals. By using the scales in chapter 2, you can derive a hope score based on the child's self-report and on your observational report. By using these short descriptions, you should have a good picture of the way you view your child. Both the child's self-report and your impressions will be important as you apply the hope-inducing strategies in this book. An example of how to do this exercise is provided at the top of the worksheet.

Description Worksheet

Child's Name	Age	Gender	Goal Setting • Problem Solving • Work Toward Goals
Ryan	8	Male	He is able to set some goals when an activity is important to him. He doesn't set goals or follow through with everyday tasks. He is easily frustrated when he meets difficulties and often quits.

chapter 2

Measuring Children's Hope

Whenever we contemplate changing how a child acts or thinks, it becomes important to have some way to determine a baseline measure of the quality we wish to alter. As the child begins to think and act differently, it also is helpful to have a way to record how much change is taking place. In this chapter, you will learn about several scales that you can use to provide an indication of your child's current level of hope. The first two scales are self-reports; that is, the child filling out the form furnishes the answers. The second set of scales is similar to the first, except they are based on your observations of a child or children rather than their self-reports.

The Young Children's Hope Scale is appropriate for measuring the level of hope in children from about the first grade to the third grade, depending on the child's reading and comprehension level. The Children's Hope Scale can be used to measure hope in older children and adolescents from about the fourth grade through high school. The Adult Hope Scale that will be described in chapter 5 also can be used with older adolescents.

The observational hope scales, as you will see, use the same items as those on the children's self-report scales, but the pronouns have been changed to reflect an observer's perspective. By combining your observations with the brief descriptions you wrote for the exercise in chapter 1, you will have formed a clear idea of your child's hopeful thinking and be ready to implement some of the strategies you will learn.

In the last chapter, you learned that hope is an active thought process involving goals, waypower, and willpower. Remember that, although the elements of waypower and willpower work together to produce hopeful thinking, they can be measured separately. By having individual scores for each of these components, you can develop a more complete idea of where to focus your hope-enhancing strategies. In chapter 3, we will give you additional ways to pinpoint your strategies by measuring your child's hope in important life domains.

The scale you select in this chapter will be based on your child's age as well as their reading and comprehension level. Study the items on each scale to get an idea about which one your child will understand best. First, some instructions for giving the scales.

Giving Your Child the Scales

When you ask your children to take one of the hope scales, we suggest that you don't discuss the meaning of hope or what the scale is measuring right away. It is important to remind children that there are no wrong answers. Assure them that whatever they think and feel is true will be the "right" answer. Sometimes children anticipate what they think a parent will want, and their answers may not reflect what they actually think. You can minimize this by assuring them that you are not going to be critical or disappointed by their answers. There are times, however, when for some other reason you don't think a child's rating is what he or she really thinks. We will show you how to handle that situation later in the chapter.

When you're giving the scale at home, choose a quiet place where there are likely to be few distractions. *Be sure that there is no television or music to divert the child's attention.* If the child is young, read the items and the response choices aloud, being careful not to emphasize one possible choice more than any other.

The Children's Hope Scale

C. R. Snyder and his colleagues developed this simple, six-item scale to measure the will, ways, and total hope in children and adolescents. It has been administered to many thousands children of all ethnicities and socioeconomic groups. The items have been selected and refined carefully so that children and adolescents are able to understand their meaning and can respond easily. This scale meets the psychological criteria for a good measure, and we have used it with confidence in many classrooms and therapeutic situations over the past ten years.

The Children's Hope Scale can be given to children as young as eight years old, assuming their reading skills are reasonably good. By age nine, however, nearly all children can read and comprehend the scale, and it can be used well into adolescence. As we mentioned before, it is a self-report measure in which the child or adolescent taking the scale determines the answers.

The Children's Hope Scale

Directions: The six sentences below describe how children think about themselves and how they do things in general. Read each sentence carefully, and think about how you are in most situations. Place a mark inside the circle that describes *you* the best. For example, place a mark in the circle (o) above "None of the time," if this describes you. Or, if you are this way "All of the time," check this circle. Please answer every question. There are no right or wrong answers.

1. *I think I am doing pretty well.*

O	O	O	O	O	O
None of the time	A little of the time	Some of the time	A lot of the time	Most of the time	All of the time

2. *I can think of many ways to get the things in life that are most important to me.*

O	O	O	O	O	O
None of the time	A little of the time	Some of the time	A lot of the time	Most of the time	All of the time

3. *I am doing just as well as other kids my age.*

O	O	O	O	O	O
None of the time	A little of the time	Some of the time	A lot of the time	Most of the time	All of the time

4. *When I have a problem, I can come up with lots of ways to solve it.*

O	O	O	O	O	O
None of the time	A little of the time	Some of the time	A lot of the time	Most of the time	All of the time

5. *I think the things I have done in the past will help me in the future.*

O	O	O	O	O	O
None of the time	A little of the time	Some of the time	A lot of the time	Most of the time	All of the time

6. *Even when others want to quit, I know that I can find ways to solve the problem.*

O	O	O	O	O	O
None of the time	A little of the time	Some of the time	A lot of the time	Most of the time	All of the time

The Young Children's Hope Scale

This scale is an adaptation of the Children's Hope Scale with many of the items simplified and three rating choices rather than six. When we first began our research on measuring hope, we discovered that children who were in the first, second, or third grades had a difficult time understanding some of the statements on the Children's Hope Scale. Therefore, we rephrased these items into a simpler form, which became the Young Children's Hope Scale. This scale meets the requirements of a good psychological measurement, and has been used in classroom and family situations with many hundreds of young children.

The Young Children's Hope Scale

Directions: The six sentences below describe how children think about themselves and how they do things in general. Read each sentence carefully. For each sentence, please think about how you are in most situations. Place a mark inside the circle that describes *you* the best. For example, place a mark in the circle (o) beside "Never," if you don't ever think this way. If you think this way "Sometimes," check the middle circle. If you "Always" think this way, place a mark in the circle beside "Always." Please answer every question. There are no right or wrong answers.

1. *I think I am doing pretty well.*
   O Never   O Sometimes   O Always

2. *I can think of many ways to get the things I want.*
   O Never   O Sometimes   O Always

3. *I am doing just as well as other kids in my class.*
   O Never   O Sometimes   O Always

4. *When I have a problem, I can come up with lots of ways to solve it.*
   O Never   O Sometimes   O Always

5. *Things I have done before will help me when I do new things.*
   O Never   O Sometimes   O Always

6. *I can find ways to solve a problem even when other kids give up.*
   O Never   O Sometimes   O Always

Scoring the Hope Scales

Both of these scales can be used to determine waypower and willpower, as well giving a total hope score, which is a combination of the two components. Items 1, 3, and 5 on both the Children's Hope Scale and the Young Children's Hope Scale measure willpower. In those items, you will see that children are asked to report how well they are doing generally in their lives and how well they are doing in comparison with other children who are their age. One important aspect of willpower is the ability to learn from past successes and failures. In item 5, children are asked to rate how well they can apply what they have done in the past to future situations.

Older children are usually able to think more broadly about their lives than are younger children. Older children also have better developed concepts of past, present, and future. This doesn't mean that the scores you obtain from young children are not valid. It does indicate, however, that young children may be focusing on one specific goal, rather than considering a number of the goals for which they have worked. The domain-specific scales detailed in the next chapter will allow you and your child to examine hopeful thinking in a number of life arenas, thus narrowing the number of goals to be considered for each item.

Items 2, 4, and 6 measure waypower on both the Children's and the Young Children's Hope Scales. In each of these items, children are asked to rate how well they can think of ways to solve problems or get the things they want. As with willpower thinking, older children are able to consider a wider range of goals than younger children. One example of how younger and older kids think differently about goals is drawn from the first- and second-graders in our research. When we asked them to tell us what goals they were thinking about when they read the items on the scale, they mentioned such things as going to the circus, sliding down the water slide, or getting a new dress. On the other hand, sixth-graders mentioned several goals for each item. A typical response was "I thought about how I'm learning to play the piano and I'm making some new friends."

The Young Children's Hope Scale has three possible response choices. The "Never" response is scored 1 point; the "Sometimes" response is scored 2 points; and the "Always" response is scored 3 points. To determine a child's waypower score, sum the response choices for items 2, 4, and 6. To determine a child's willpower score, sum the response choices for items 1, 3, and 5. The total hope score is obtained by adding both the willpower and the waypower scores together.

The Children's Hope Scale is somewhat different in that it has six, rather than three, response choices, and some of the items are worded in a slightly more complex way. In scoring this scale give "None of the time" 1 point; "A little of the time" 2 points; and so forth through to "All of the time," which is given 6 points. As with the Young Children's Hope Scale, to determine the willpower score, add the points for the choices made on items 1, 3, and 5. The waypower score is determined by summing the points for items 2, 4, and 6. The total hope score is determined by adding the two subscale scores.

What Do the Scores Mean?

Through administering these scales to children and adolescents, we have found that younger children tend to score higher than older children and adolescents, and also higher than adults. We compared children's hope scores with teachers' ratings on the observational hope scale, however, and found that, for the most part, children who had the highest hope scores also were rated more highly by their teachers. Our point here is that, while young children may tend toward more grandiose notions of what is possible in terms of their reported hope, these beliefs about themselves are reflected in their work and are communicated in such a manner that their teachers can track them.

All young children don't report high ratings on the hope scales, however. We found that children who live in disadvantaged conditions score significantly lower than children in more affluent environments. For example, children living on an impoverished Native American reservation were low in both the way-power and willpower components of hope. Similarly, children of Mexican immigrants who hadn't been in the United States long enough to establish themselves economically also obtained low scores. Although these ethnic and economic differences will be discussed in greater detail later in the workbook, they bear keeping in mind as you use the hope scales.

If you are using the Children's Hope Scale and are examining the total hope score, a score of 29 or higher places a child in the top 15 percent. These children are reporting that they have the willpower and waypower to meet their goals "Most of the time." Children who score at or below 21 are in the lowest 15 percent, and are reporting that they have the willpower and waypower to reach their goals "Some of the time." Notice that even children in the lowest group are reporting that they can use their will and ways to some extent. Children rarely report that they have willpower and waypower "None of the time."

You will find it valuable to examine the willpower and waypower scores separately as you consider the best strategies to help your child develop hopeful thinking. If you are using the Children's Hope Scale, there is a possible range of scores from 3 to 18 for each of the two subscales. A score in either waypower or willpower of 15 or higher places the child in the top 15 percent. As with total hope, this score indicates that the child can use either willpower or waypower thinking "A lot of the time." Conversely, a score of 9 or lower places the child in the lowest 15 percent of either type of thinking. Here is a chart in which you can see the scale points and associated percentiles.

Children's Hope Scale Raw Scores and Related Percentiles

Total Hope Raw Scores

29–36	Top 15%
22–28	Middle 70%
6–21	Lowest 15%

Waypower or Willpower Raw Scores

15–18	Top 15%
10–14	Middle 70%
3–9	Lowest 15%

If you used the Young Children's Hope Scale, the scores will be based on a range with 6 as the lowest point, and 18 as the highest score for total hope. A score of 14 or above places the child in the top 15 percent, while a score below 11 places the child in the lowest 15 percent. Each subscale score can range from a low of 3 to a high of 9. A score of 3 to 5 on either of the subscales indicates low willpower or waypower, while a score of 7 to 9 indicates that the child uses waypower or willpower thinking at least "Some of the time." Here is a percentile guide for raw scores on the Young Children's Hope Scale.

Young Children's Hope Scale Raw Scores and Related Percentiles

Total Hope Raw Scores

14–18	Top 15%
12–13	Middle 70%
3–11	Lowest 15%

Waypower or Willpower Raw Scores

7–9	Top 15%
6	Middle 70%
3–5	Lowest 15%

In our research, we routinely give the self-report forms to the students and the observational forms to teachers or parents. Although there is usually a high degree of agreement between the children's ratings and the observers' ratings, there are instances when the child's self-report is quite different from that of the observer's.

Because you are in an excellent position to observe your children setting goals, working for those goals, and working around any impediments that they encounter, we encourage you to use the observational hope scales on page 27. Any large discrepancies that occur between your ratings and your child's self-reported scores first should be explored for the possibility that items were not understood by the child. We have included the observational hope scales in a checklist format for your use. We also have alternated gendered pronouns for the sake of readability.

Scoring and Using Your Observations

The observational scales are scored the same way you scored your children's scales. For waypower, sum the ratings you gave to items 2, 4, and 6. For the will-power score, add the ratings you gave to items 1, 3, and 5. The hope score is, of course, the sum of the two subscales.

Use these observations, along with the description you wrote in chapter 1, to add another dimension to the picture you have of your child's hope. Other important people in your child's life also can use this scale. We suggest that both parents, older siblings, and grandparents can contribute to a realistic view of your child's hope.

Does the score your child reported fit the description you wrote for him or her? Perhaps not, but that doesn't mean you were wrong in your conclusions. Children, especially young ones, often have an exaggerated view of what they can do. As we have pointed out, in all probability they have yet to meet many of life's difficulties. You should ask what goals they were thinking about when they selected their response choices. If you find that they thought about only one goal, ask them to consider their thoughts about other goals as well. You may find that their ratings change once they take a broader view of their lives.

It's important to be certain that your child understands each item. Discussing the ratings they have given can be tricky, because the child may be tempted to change his or her answers to please you. While they shouldn't change their answers when they believe you don't like the ones they have marked, their first answers may not truly reflect the way they think. Children who don't understand the items don't think long about their answers. They often will mark all the same circles or mark them far too quickly. If you notice your child doing these things, ask whether he or she understands the item. You also can ask what the child is thinking about as he or she marks a particular circle. Here is an example of the way you might do this.

Children's Hope Scale—Observational Form

Select the number that reflects your observation best, and enter it in the space to the right of each item.

1	2	3	4	5	6
None of the time	A little of the time	Some of the time	A lot of the time	Most of the time	All of the time

1. He thinks he is doing pretty well. ____

2. She can think of many ways to get the things in life that are most important to her. ____

3. He is doing just as well as other kids his age. ____

4. When she has a problem she can come up with lots of ways to solve it.

   ____

5. He thinks the things he has done in the past will help him in the future.

   ____

6. Even when others want to quit, she knows she can find ways to solve the problem. ____

Young Children's Hope Scale—Observational Form

Select the number that reflects your observation best, and enter it in the space to the right of each item.

1	2	3
Never	Sometimes	Always

1. She thinks she is doing pretty well. ____

2. He can think of many ways to get the things he wants. ____

3. She is doing just as well as other kids in her class. ____

4. When he has a problem, he can come up with lots of ways to solve it.

   ____

5. Things she has done before will help her when she does new things.

   ____

6. He can find ways to solve a problem even when other kids give up. ____

"I notice that you marked all the circles for 'Never' on all of the items. I'm not sure that you understood what each statement really means. Tell me what you were thinking about on the first item, 'I think I am doing pretty well.'"

You will probably be able to tell by the child's answer if he or she has understood the question. Here are two possible answers; the first shows a lack of comprehension, while the second demonstrates an acceptable level of understanding.

"I thought about when I couldn't fit that puzzle together today."

"I don't think I am doing very well because I don't get good grades on my spelling tests and I don't know how to read as well as my friends."

Notice that in the first example, the child has given only one reason for marking the "Never" circle, and that reason is based on a momentary failure. In the second example, the child is comparing spelling test grades and reading ability with other children in the same class. In the first instance, you might ask the child to reconsider the item and think of more situations. In the second instance, the rating is probably reflecting the true thoughts of the child.

Are You an Overinvolved Parent?

The fact that you have selected to read this book suggests that you want to help your children achieve their dreams. This choice indicates that you're a motivated parent—eager to see your child succeed. This is, of course, a desirable, even necessary, quality for good parenting. As the story of the JJs in chapter 1 illustrates, however, too much pressure on the child can do more harm than good. It's very important for you to be able to recognize when your child's hope is low *without feeling that you are to blame.* Many parents believe that they are responsible for all of the thoughts and feelings that their children have, especially if those thoughts and feelings are negative. Parents do have a great deal of impact, of course, but based on recent research, it appears that peers, teachers, and others in the child's environment also are very important.

When children are very young, parents are often the center of their worlds. As they get older, peers become increasingly important, until, by adolescence, some researchers believe that peers are the most significant influence. This shift has implications for both the measurement of hope and the implementation of hope-building strategies. Young children, because they are focused on parental reactions, can be influenced more easily to give false positive scores. They are, however, more malleable than older children in changing their thoughts and behaviors. The challenges for parents wishing to increase their children's hopeful thinking are different for each age group. In later sections, you will learn how to use the strategies with all ages of children and adolescents and how to focus the techniques on their specific areas of low hope.

Before moving on to chapters 3 and 4 and the domain-specific hope scales that will allow you to determine the areas in which your child or adolescent is most in need of hope building, let's take a look at some additional profiles of hope. In the first chapter, you were introduced to Anna, Cody, and the JJs through brief sketches of their lives. Now that you understand the components of hope and how they are measured, let's look at each hope configuration in greater detail as they appear in other children. In these vignettes, each child is pursuing a goal, but each takes a different approach depending upon his or her level of will-power and waypower. After each vignette, we discuss how their level of hope has influenced each child's life.

❋ Brooke—Low Will, Low Ways

Brooke was born when her parents were in their midforties. They had tried for years to have a child, with two miscarriages and one stillbirth preceding Brooke. She became the center of their lives. Whatever she wanted magically appeared. Whenever she had a problem, it was solved for her. Brooke's parents had enough money to provide the best home, a nanny, and all the toys a little girl could want. Material things were not all they lavished on Brooke, however. She was loved and treasured like a precious gem—protected and sheltered from the outside world.

In fact, Brooke's parents were so protective of her that it was difficult for them to see her struggle with even simple barriers to her desired goals. Because her parents gave her everything she wanted, setting goals was also difficult for Brooke. Whenever she mentioned a toy or an activity, her doting parents were willing to supply it—and did so quickly. Despite her indulgent parents and nanny, Brooke learned all of the skills necessary to begin school, such as dressing herself, tying her shoes, eating with utensils, and using the bathroom alone. It was in setting larger goals and solving more complex problems that Brooke's low hope began to show.

One afternoon, while Brooke and her father were walking through the park, they stopped to watch some young people playing tennis in the public courts. They were running and laughing, and it looked like so much fun that Brooke decided she wanted to learn to play tennis, too. Her father told her that it takes many hours of practice to play that well, but that she could have lessons if she wanted them.

The next afternoon, the nanny took Brooke to a tennis club where her father had arranged for a private lesson. Although Brooke said she wanted to learn the game, her teacher noticed that she seemed more interested in watching the people on the next court than following his instructions. When she did attend to his pointers and tried the serve, she became frustrated when the ball didn't even go over the net. After many failed serves, she was frustrated and wanted to quit.

At home that night, she told her parents that tennis wasn't as much fun as she thought, and that it was too hard for her to learn.

Disappointed, her parents agreed that she shouldn't do it if she didn't want to. Privately, however, they were concerned over her readiness to give up, as well as the fact that she seldom identified things she wanted to accomplish.

Brooke's childhood is at the extreme end of parental solicitude. She had most of what might have become goals handed to her without any effort on her part. This profile demonstrates that doing too much for children can inhibit their perceived and actual abilities to set and pursue goals, including solving any problems or impediments that arose. As we had written earlier and will repeat at points in this book, *children need some frustration in order to learn that they can figure out solutions for themselves.* You also will learn that they need to have their own desired goals for which to work.

✻ Tiffany—Low Will, High Ways

Twelve-year-old Tiffany is a perpetual dreamer. She loves to fantasize about how wonderful her life will be when she grows up and becomes a professional singer. She sits by the bay window in her parent's apartment, watching the boats on the river and imagining herself as the lead singer of a band playing on a cruise ship. She imagines every detail of the picture, from the costume she'll wear to the songs she'll sing. But the dreams are more fun for Tiffany than actually learning to sing.

A while ago, when Tiffany told her parents about her dreams they offered to get her singing lessons. They always thought that she had a lovely voice, and she could carry a tune before she learned to speak.

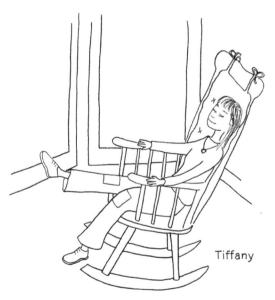

Tiffany

Each time they suggested lessons, however, she had an excuse for not wanting to take them. She usually said that she was too busy, yet she had plenty of time to daydream. Tiffany knows that she will need singing lessons if she's ever to become a professional singer. She believes that her dream can come true because she has read about girls who have become famous at an early age, but these facts don't motivate Tiffany to try. She knows the steps she will need to take to have a chance at stardom. In Tiffany's dreams she goes through each detail of her career. She even plans how she will solve such problems as getting an agent, or finding someone to record a demonstration tape.

Each time Tiffany thinks about taking lessons, she also thinks about the difficulty of finding a teacher, getting to her lessons on the bus, and the long hours of practice she'll have to do. Thinking about those things makes her tired, and it's so comfortable sitting in the window and dreaming about fame. She can see herself bowing to the audience and she practically hears the applause, but somehow she never feels the motivation to take the steps required to make her dream come true.

Tiffany's parents noticed that she frequently had good ideas, even makes plans for things she would like to do, but she seldom follows through. Her parents have observed that she can figure out the ways to get what she wants, and often she has good ideas about how to solve problems, but they have puzzled over how to motivate Tiffany to work for her dreams, whether or not she becomes a star.

Children such as Tiffany can be frustrating for parents. They see potential, and they often have small glimpses of what these children are capable of achieving once they are motivated. Equally frustrating are children, such as Eric, who has lots of enthusiasm for his projects, but seems to get bogged down when he runs into any sort of impediments.

✳ Eric—High Will, Low Ways

To look at Eric's room, you would say he has many interesting hobbies. His shelves are full of model airplanes, ships, and automobiles. He has several books for stamp and coin collections, and he has an easel in one corner with a partially completed watercolor on it. On closer examination, it isn't only the painting that is incomplete. Most of the models are in an unfinished state, and the stamps and coin books have very few contents.

Eric has lots of enthusiasm for his many hobbies—in the beginning. When he decided it would be fun to build models, he and his father went to the hobby store and selected several that appealed to Eric, even though his father thought they might be a little difficult for a beginner. Father and son set up a card table in the family room and began to assemble a replica of the *Starship Enterprise*, their first project. After an hour of trying to fit the pieces together and making a mess with the glue, Eric was ready to quit.

Recognizing that the *Enterprise* was a complicated project, Eric's father insisted they try something a little easier—a Model-T Ford. This went fairly well, but Eric's father did most of the gluing. When it was time to paint the model, Eric took charge. First the bottles were small and difficult to open. One of them was filled with dried-up paint, and then he spilled one bottle all over the card table. By this time, Eric was nearly in tears. Rather than cope with the problems, the models were placed, unfinished, on the shelves in Eric's room for some future time when he might have more patience.

Eric's parents had grown accustomed to his bursts of enthusiasm,  only to see his energy for the projects diminish when problems arose. They were very disappointed when he quit Boy Scouts after only three months, saying that it was "stupid to learn all that stuff." They were alarmed when he decided to quit the track team, and they very nearly insisted that he stay with it. In the end, his parents said nothing, and soon he eagerly decided to take up karate.

Eric

Many parents know the frustrations of having a child who begins projects with vigor, only to have the interest dissipate after a short time. Often they have invested in lessons and the requisite clothing or equipment, only to find that they've wasted their money. In Eric's case, his parents continued to invest in his interests and hobbies because they wished desperately for him to become committed to something. They wanted, as most parents do, to see Eric dedicate himself and to become involved in something meaningful.

By beginning projects with enthusiasm and then losing interest when the project became difficult, Eric was demonstrating low waypower. That is, he lacked the ability to figure out ways to solve the problems that made completing his projects difficult. When Eric spilled the paint, he might have simply cleaned it up and continued. When he found the dried paint, he might have gone back to the hobby store and gotten a replacement. While these solutions seem obvious to an adult, or to a high-waypower child, they can be invisible to a child such as Eric.

Eric and Tiffany are two very different types of young people, yet the effect of their behavior is the same. Neither of them will accomplish their goals until they have developed more of one of the two components of hopeful thinking. Tiffany is a great planner and problem solver, while Eric is brimming with energy for his goals. Putting the strong parts of each of the children together would produce a high-hope child—perhaps one like Cody, whom you met in the first chapter. Such a child would have enthusiasm for his or her goals, and would be able to figure out the solutions to the roadblocks encountered along the way. Let's look at another profile, this one of a high-hope child.

✳ Andy—High Will, High Ways

When Andy was twelve years old, he went to a rock concert with his parents where he heard the wonderful guitar music of Santana. At that moment, he knew he wanted to learn to play the guitar, too. When he told his parents what he wanted to do they were encouraging, but explained to him how difficult it would be to learn to play that well. As a teenager, Andy's father briefly had entertained dreams of being a rock star, but he wanted Andy to be more realistic. Nevertheless, Andy's parents told him that if he could earn the money for a guitar, they would finance some lessons.

Andy was an enterprising boy, so the first thing he did was to inquire at the local market about a job as a bag boy. He was disappointed when he was told to come back when he was fourteen, as the state laws demanded. If he couldn't work for any place of business, what could he do? He gave it some thought and realized that he could work for individuals, and that is just what he decided to do.

Andy's first step was to make a flyer advertising his skills. He could mow lawns, pet-sit for people going on vacation, baby-sit (although he didn't necessarily like to do that), and he could wash cars. Actually, he decided that there were many things he could do, so he called himself "Handy Andy" and left a flyer on every door in his neighborhood.

Soon the calls began to come with more jobs than Andy could handle. It seemed like everyone wanted to go on vacation at the same time and needed to have their lawns, pets, and house plants cared for. Andy had so many "clients" that he enlisted the help of his best friend, and the two of them were able to handle all the work.

Within a month, Andy had made enough money to buy an inexpensive electric guitar and an amplifier, as well. True to their word, Andy's parents enrolled him in guitar classes, and now they never even complain about the sounds emanating from his room.

Andy is a child who is able to pursue his dreams because he has both the confidence that he can work out solutions to the problems that might deter him, and the determination to work hard for what he wants. Andy's parents encourage him to work for his goal, and they allow him to discover his own ways to solve problems, even though they are always available to help. They praise him for his successes, and they help him see the lessons to be learned when he doesn't succeed. In Andy's family, trying is as important as winning.

In this chapter, you have learned how to measure your child's hope, and you have seen the configurations of hope in the lives of several children. The scales in this chapter measure hope in general life experiences. The goals are non-specific, and the child's thoughts are not focused in particular areas. In the next two chapters, however, the domain-specific hope scales will allow you to focus on the particular goals associated with important arenas of your child or adolescent's life. Chapter 3 presents life arenas that are frequently important to children between the first and sixth grades. In chapter 4, we focus on those areas that are important for adolescents.

chapter 3

Pinpointing Hope: The Life Domains of Children Ages Six to Twelve

In the last chapter, you learned how to measure your child's level of hope by using either the Children's Hope Scale or the Young Children's Hope Scale. You now know whether your child is low or high in overall hope, and you know how he or she scores on each of the hope subscales (willpower and waypower). This information provides an important starting point, but it's only one part of the total picture. In this chapter, you and your children will consider a number of life domains in order to determine where the use of hope-enhancing strategies might be the most valuable.

What Is a Child's Life Domain?

When we look at the flow of our daily lives, whether as adults or children, we can group our goal pursuits into a few major categories. As adults, we have such areas as home and family, work, social activities, and so forth. We know that each of these is important, and so we attempt to create a balance of time and energy allotted to each area in our lives. We also know that some domains are more important to us than others. We may not need to be highly successful in each area in order to be happy and fulfilled.

The life domains of children function in much the same way, although the categories are somewhat different. For young children, the important arenas in life include play and social activities, relationships with family, relationships with friends, health, safety, and schoolwork. Adolescents have these categories as well as others, which will be explored more fully in chapter 4. At different stages of a child's life, some domains are more important than at others. For example, a child of seven is less concerned with health and physical fitness than an adolescent of fifteen. If the seven-year-old is lucky, good health is a given and isn't of concern. An adolescent, however, is very concerned with appearances, and to be attractive, good health and physical fitness is a must. For this reason, we have presented the important life domains for each group, along with examples and profiles, in separate chapters.

Life domains may move in and out of prominence for both children and adults. A domain that was important at a younger age may become less important during our middle years, and then become important again in later years. For example, during the midlife developmental stage of adulthood, most people are concerned with the work arena—building a solid financial base and raising a family. During later life, in retirement, recreation or leisure may become as prominent as it was during childhood and adolescence.

Children also have shifts in the importance of life domains. Spirituality, for example, may be very important to eight-year-old Catholic children who are preparing for their first Communion. After this event, however, spirituality may not be salient until Confirmation, at age thirteen.

Our point is that while a general view of hope is certainly an important piece of the puzzle in order to understand and help your child, you will be more effective if you can target specific areas for your hope strategies. The domain scales we have included in this chapter are for you to use in developing a clearer picture of your child's hope. We have selected domains that are important for most children, but we recognize that they may not apply in every case. We advise you to discuss each of the domains with your children before deciding which arenas may or may not be important. We don't always know what our children are thinking, and some of their questions and answers may surprise you. The areas we have selected are important to most children. If your child shows no interest in one of these domains, we suggest that you use this as an opportunity to open up a discussion of that area of his or her life.

How to Use the Life-Domain Scales

You will notice that these scales are presented in a different format than the Children's and Young Children's Hope Scales. Instead we have used the same format as the observational hope scales. Older children who can read and comprehend well can take these scales by themselves. We recommend, however, that the scales be read aloud to children below the fifth or sixth grade. Ask if there are any questions about the meaning of the items as you read. Along with each item, we have provided an explanation that can help your child to understand. If the meaning of the item is clear, you may not wish to give the example, but, rather, elicit one from your child.

The six-point ratings are given at the top of each scale. It's a good idea to read the response choices aloud after you read the item, especially for younger children. As with the hope scale in the previous chapter, be sure you have a quiet setting to allow your child an optimum opportunity for concentration. It also is a good idea to give the scales at separate times. For example, give one or two scales on one day and another one or two scales several days later. Doing this will prevent a "response set," which is when an individual develops a pattern of giving the same (or very similar) answers to all items. Children often do this, especially when the task is challenging.

Scoring the Life-Domain Scales

There are six response choices for each of these scales, and each scale has six items—three for waypower, and three for willpower. Score the response choice for "Definitely False" one point, "Mostly False" two points, "Somewhat False" three points, "Somewhat True" four points, "Mostly True" five points, and "Definitely True" six points.

To determine your child's waypower for each domain, add the points recorded for the waypower items, and for willpower, add the points given for each of the willpower items. For the total hope score on that domain, simply add the points given to your child's responses on the entire scale.

Once your child has taken all of the domain scales that are relevant to his or her life, you will have a clear idea about the areas on which you wish to focus hope-building strategies. You will enter the domain scores, along with the hope-scale scores and your observational hope scores, on your description sheet in chapter 1.

Now you are ready to use the Children's Life-Domain Scales. There are six domains: schoolwork, play and recreation, relationships with family, safety, health, and spirituality. Prior to the scale, a description of the domain is given, and each scale will have explanations for every item. You can use these if your child doesn't understand what is meant by the statements on the scale. Each scale is followed by a story of a child who is working on developing high hope in that domain. These stories are meant to be read aloud to your child. At the end of the chapter, we will show you how you can use the stories to help your children understand the hope process.

What Is the Schoolwork Domain?

This domain encompasses the academic, rather than the extracurricular or social, part of your child's life. The items on this scale refer to how your child thinks about her capabilities to succeed with schoolwork. Having high hope in this area means being able to set realistic school goals, for example, turning in work on time, doing homework promptly, and maybe doing extra-credit work. High way-power in this domain means that your child knows that he can figure out ways to make good grades, or ways to learn difficult material. High willpower means that your child is willing and able to work hard to succeed with schoolwork. Notice that the items on this scale reflect the meaning of this domain.

The Schoolwork-Domain Scale

1	2	3	4	5	6
Definitely False	Mostly False	Somewhat False	Somewhat True	Mostly True	Definitely True

1. I can think of lots of ways to make good grades in school. (way) ____

2. I pursue my schoolwork energetically. (will) ____

3. Even if a subject is difficult, I can always find a way to succeed. (way) ____

4. I've been pretty successful in school. (will) ____

5. I can think of lots of ways to do well in subjects that are important to me. (way) ____

6. I get the grades I want in my schoolwork. (will) ____

Explanations

1. Thinking of ways to make good grades means doing such things as asking for extra-credit work.

2. Energetically pursuing your schoolwork means not putting it off until the last minute, and even doing extra work in order to do the best job you can.

3. Finding ways to succeed with a difficult subject may mean asking for extra help from your parent or teacher to figure out what you don't understand.

4. This means that you're satisfied with your grades and feel good about going to school.

5. Finding ways to do well in subjects you like means such things as asking the teacher how you can learn more about the subject, and participating in class activities.

6. This may not always mean getting an "A" or an "Excellent." There are times when getting a lower grade is still an achievement. It's very hard to be out-standing in everything, and it's the effort that counts.

✳ Sharon—A Love of Learning

Sharon, the fifth of six children, was definitely different from her brothers and sisters. They made average grades and were indifferent to their studies, although they had fun at school and were successful in other school activities. Sharon loved to learn. She learned to read when she was four, and her mother taught her how to add, subtract, and print her name when she was five. When Sharon started school, she was far ahead of most of the children in the first grade.

Sharon's parents feared that she would become bored and lose her love of learning if she were not challenged by the first-grade work. After a discussion with Sharon's teacher, they decided to take a "wait and see" approach. If Sharon started to lose interest, they would consider advancing her a grade, or even putting her in a private school. They need not have worried.

Sharon found that there were many new things to learn, even though she was more advanced than her friends in some subjects. When she already knew how to do something the teacher was explaining to the class, Sharon would listen patiently, and then ask privately for another assignment. When the class divided into reading groups, Sharon was in a group of her own, reading more advanced books quietly to herself.

But not everything came easily to Sharon. Although she could read well, and devoured books, she found that she was a poor speller. In the first and second grades, spelling wasn't stressed as important. In fact, the teachers were more interested in having students write expressively than learning the finer points of spelling the words. By the third grade, spelling tests became a weekly chore for Sharon. On her first test, she missed half the words, and when the same thing happened on the second test, she decided something had to be done.

Acquiring new knowledge had always been fun for Sharon, and her learning was based on understanding ideas. She found rote memorization to be tedious, and she resisted it at first. When it became obvious to her that committing the

Sharon

words to memory was the only way to learn them, she decided to find ways to make that exercise more pleasurable.

Sharon decided to set small goals for herself. The teacher gave the class twenty new words each week. They were given the words as the last thing on Friday, and then had a spelling test the first thing the following Friday. She figured that if she learned four new words each day, she would take Saturday and Sunday off. She knew she could memorize four words a day and, to be certain, she would have one of her brothers or sisters test her each evening.

The plan worked fairly well. The first week she only missed four, but she wanted to have a 100 percent. She thought about her plan to memorize four words each day, and discovered her mistake. She was only concentrating on the words she learned for that day, and she wasn't reviewing the words she had learned on the previous days. The next week, Sharon tried reviewing as she went along, and at the end of the week she made the coveted 100 percent.

Sharon's story shows a child who has a love of knowledge and desire to learn. Not all children share that enthusiasm, and not all children are able to learn as easily as she. Sharon's high hope helped her when she encountered a difficult subject for the first time. She was able to set small goals for herself and figure out how to make her plan work better when she wasn't as successful as she wished.

The Family Domain

The next domain is family relationships, an area that is vital to parents as well as their children. In the story following the explanations, we will meet Sharon's younger brother, Bobby, who is having a difficult time as the youngest member of a large family. But first, what is the family domain?

The part of a child's life that is encompassed in the family domain can be as small or as large as the number of people in the family. For some, the family may be only two people—a child and a parent. At the other extreme is the extended family consisting of parents, grandparents, aunts, uncles, and cousins. Godparents and old friends (honorary aunts and uncles) are considered family members among some ethnic groups.

High hope in the family domain means that the child is reasonably happy at home most of the time, and is able to communicate feelings in an appropriate way. There are usually some squabbles between children, but a high-waypower child can think of ways to resolve them. This child likes to have family involvement in his or her activities and thinks of activities the family can do together. The child with high willpower actively maintains good relationships with other family members.

The Family-Domain Scale

1	2	3	4	5	6
Definitely False	Mostly False	Somewhat False	Somewhat True	Mostly True	Definitely True

1. I can think of lots of fun things to do with my family. (way) ____

2. I work hard to keep my family relationships good. (will) ____

3. I can think of lots of ways to include my family in the things that are important to me. (way) ____

4. I have the kinds of relationships I want with my family members. (will) ____

5. There are lot of ways to tell my family how I feel. (way) ____

6. I have a pretty good family life. (will) ____

Explanations

1. This means being able to think of things you would like to do that your family also could do. Two such activities might be craft projects or baking cookies.

2. This means that you try hard to get along with your family, even when you don't want to. Perhaps you hold your temper when you are angry, or you do what you're asked to do.

3. This means finding ways to involve your family in your activities. A few such activities might be sports, clubs, or events where you perform.

4. Having the kinds of relationships with family that you want means that you're happy with the way you treat each other and feel about one another.

5. Telling your family how you feel means that if something is bothering you, you can let someone know. It also means that when you are happy, bored, afraid, or have any other important feeling, there is someone in your family with whom you can talk.

6. Having a pretty good family life means that you are happy with it, even though you may get mad at people in your family, and you may not get everything you want.

✳ Bobby—The Baby of the Family

Sharon's youngest brother is Bobby— number six in a family of six children. The first word most babies speak is either "Mama" or "Dada," but Bobby's first word was an emphatic "No." At first, everyone thought it was cute, but as the years went by and Bobby continued his opposition, his family began to get fed up.

Curiously, Bobby was only negative with his family. At school he was popular, and his teachers always had high praise for him. At parent-teacher conferences, Bobby's parents often wondered if the teacher had him confused with some other little boy. At home he simply refused to do what he was told to do if he didn't want to do it. He wasn't mean, and he didn't throw tantrums, but he steadfastly used his first word, "No."

The difference between Bobby's attitude at home and the way he was at school was so marked that his parents decided to have him talk with Dr. Lopez, a counselor. What he told Dr. Lopez provided some insights, but if Bobby was going to have a happier home life, some changes were going to have to be made. Bobby said that everyone at home always told him what to do and when to do it. He felt like he was at the bottom of the totem pole, and the only power he had was to refuse to obey. He said he felt angry much of the time, but because he loved his parents and brothers and sisters, he didn't want to be mean to them.

Bobby told Dr. Lopez about the kind of situation that made him the maddest. In the mornings, when everyone was running around getting ready for school and work, people kept telling him to hurry up and get dressed. He liked to take his time, playing or watching a little television while he put on his clothes, but they nagged at him to get dressed faster. The more they nagged, the madder he got, and the slower he went.

Bobby understood why he was negative at home; what he didn't understand was how to change. He said that everyone had bossed him around ever since he could remember, and that no one let him think for himself. Dr. Lopez explained to Bobby that each person in the family had learned a certain way to behave toward the others over the years, and that this way had been based on what they had come to expect. Perhaps they all tried to take care of Bobby when he was very young, and there were too many people trying to take charge. The point was, if the changes were going to be made now, they would have to be made by everyone—including Bobby.

A family counseling session was arranged and Bobby, with the support of Dr. Lopez, explained to his family how he felt. Initially, some of his brothers and sisters began listing their complaints against Bobby, but Dr. Lopez deflected these in favor of a more positive approach. The group decided that each person would change one bossy behavior toward Bobby, and Bobby's goal was to comply with at least two requests each day. This was to continue for one week, with a check-in on progress the following week.

During the course of counseling, Bobby and his family took a number of small steps toward getting along. They changed the way they thought about Bobby, and Bobby changed the things he told himself about them. Progress wasn't immediate, but the small changes that each person made were praised. In time, with patience and determination, Bobby took his place as a well-loved and loving family member.

Before Bobby saw a counselor and began to work on the problems he was having in his family, his score in this domain was very low. He didn't want to participate in family activities and never suggested that they take part in his interests. Bobby was fortunate to have good relationships at school, indicating that he knew how to get along with others. Dr. Lopez showed Bobby how to use the skills he already had in order to accomplish the small steps toward better family relations.

Bobby's parents sought the help of a counselor who applied some of the suggestions given in this workbook. Using the strategies we provide will help enhance the hope of children who are not operating at their full hope potential, but there are times when a counselor or psychologist is also needed. When there are a number of people involved in a family concern, an outside person often facilitates better communication, making sure everyone gets a chance to be heard and understood. In Bobby's case, this was an important part of the groundwork enabling him to begin making changes that would lift his hopeful thinking.

The Safety Domain

The next domain, safety, is especially important for young children. There are few truly safe havens left in our society, and it's important for your children to have high hope in this area. After you administer this domain scale, talk with your child about situations he or she thinks might be dangerous and discuss ways to stay safe. It isn't only important for your children to be safe, but it is also important for them to *feel* safe.

The Safety-Domain Scale

1	2	3	4	5	6
Definitely False	Mostly False	Somewhat False	Somewhat True	Mostly True	Definitely True

1. I think I am pretty safe most of the time. (will) ____

2. I can think of many ways to keep myself safe. (way) ____

3. I feel as safe as most kids my age. (will) ____

4. When I think I might be in danger, I can think of lots of ways to get safe. (way) ____

5. The ways I have stayed safe in the past will help me stay safe in the future. (will) ____

6. When other kids don't know what to do when there is danger, I know that I can find ways to be safe. (way) ____

Explanations

1. Feeling pretty safe means that you're not afraid that something bad will happen to you.

2. This means understanding the different rules that will keep you safe, such as not talking to strangers and wearing your seat belt.

3. Many children feel unsafe at times. Do you feel unsafe more often or about the same as other kids?

4. This item means that you know ways to keep yourself safe in an unsafe situation. For example, if you happened to catch fire, you would know to stop, drop, and roll.

5. This means that you think the safety rules you have already learned will help to keep you safe when you get older.

6. Sometimes when children are frightened and don't feel safe, they don't know what to do. This item means that when you don't feel safe, you can think of ways to get out of danger.

✳ Rosie—A Quick Thinker

When Rosie was ten years old, she had quite a fright. She lived with her parents and older brother on a large farm where the nearest neighbors were a quarter of a mile away. Her brother was on the high school basketball team, and on this particular evening, they had their playoff game. Rosie loved the games, and she was very disappointed when she caught a bad cold and needed to stay home in bed.

After a lengthy discussion, Rosie's parents decided that, since she wasn't very sick, they would go to the game and leave alone for a few hours. This decision was fine with Rosie because she didn't want her parents to miss the game and, besides, she often spent time by herself in the afternoons. The only difference was that this time it would be dark outside.

After her parents and brother left, Rosie snuggled up in a cozy quilt in front of the fireplace with her favorite book. She even made herself some cocoa, determined to have a good time. At first she felt safe alone in the house, but after an hour or so, she began to feel edgy. The house seemed to make noises she had never heard before, and even the cat looked tense and ready to hide. The real fright came when the horses began to neigh and the dog started to bark. He was a big dog, but friendly, and rarely barked unless a stranger came to the farm.

Rosie's first inclination was to scream with fright, but then she realized no one would hear her. She told herself to calm down and to think of what would be the sensible things to do. The house was large and there were many windows, but the first thing Rosie did was to make sure they were all locked and that the doors were bolted. She also closed the curtains in all the downstairs rooms, so that no one could see in. Then she turned on all the lights and the television, so that it would seem like there were other people at home.

The next thing Rosie did was to call the neighbor down the road, Mr. Kurtz, but unfortunately he wasn't at home. Next, Rosie called Mr. Brown, a neighbor who lived farther away. To her relief, Mr. Brown answered the phone, and Rosie quickly poured out her story in a breathless and shaky voice. Mr. Brown said he would drive over immediately and asked her to stay in the house with all the doors locked.

Rosie was relieved and grateful when she heard Mr. Brown's truck crunching on the gravel driveway, but she didn't move until he knocked on the door and identified himself. She recognized his voice immediately, but she was very surprised when she opened the door to find not only Mr. Brown, but also Mr. Kurtz, and a man she didn't know. Just then Rosie's parents drove up and were also surprised to see so many people at their front door.

Everyone went inside and everything was explained. Mr. Kurtz said that he had brought his friend over to see a horse that Rosie's dad wanted to sell, and when he saw the car was gone, he thought no one was home. Being familiar with the barn, Mr. Kurtz thought it would be all right if he let his friend see the horse. They were just coming out of the barn when Mr. Brown drove up.

Rosie told her story next, elaborating just a bit about the noises she heard, although now she knew that the horses neighed and the dog barked because they didn't know Mr. Kurtz' friend. She described all the things she had done to keep herself safe, even saying she wouldn't mind staying alone again—maybe. Everyone praised Rosie for her quick thinking and for staying calm when she was really afraid. She felt very proud because she proved that she knew how to take care of herself.

Rosie's story shows a child who has high hope in the domain of safety. It's likely that she learned good safety rules while taking care of farm animals and using farm tools and was able to transfer her knowledge when it came to taking care of herself. As you read this story to your child, stress how Rosie was able to calm herself so that she could think of things to do. Ask your child what he or she would have done in a similar situation.

The Health Domain

The health domain is just as important as the safety domain for the well-being of your child. Many children don't think about this part of their lives unless they're ill but it's increasingly important for children to have hopeful thinking in this domain in light of the increase in childhood obesity and the availability of poor-quality fast foods.

The Health-Domain Scale

1	2	3	4	5	6
Definitely False	Mostly False	Somewhat False	Somewhat True	Mostly True	Definitely True

1. I think I am pretty healthy. (will) ____

2. I can think of many ways to stay healthy. (way) ____

3. I think I am as healthy as other kids my age. (will) ____

4. When I don't feel well, I can think of ways to take care of myself. (way) ____

5. My past health habits will help me stay healthy in the future. (way) ____

6. I actively do things to keep myself healthy. (will) ____

Explanations

1. When you are healthy you probably don't get sick often and usually feel good.

2. Some of the ways you might think of to stay healthy are eating the right foods, getting enough sleep, and washing your hands frequently.

3. This means that you are sick no more often than most of the kids that you know.

4. This means that, when you don't feel well, you can think of some special ways to take care of yourself, such as going to bed and drinking lots of water or juice.

5. This means that you are learning ways to stay healthy now, and that these ways will help you grow up to be healthy.

6. Some of the healthy things you might do are getting lots of rest, brushing your teeth, and eating lots of fruits and vegetables.

✳ Jesse—Learning to Live with Care

Jesse was a spirited and lively eight-year-old. He played soccer, rode his skateboard, and loved action video games. He loved being active, and he never thought much about his health; he took it for granted that each morning he would get up eager to find out what would happen that day. What did happen, so gradually that he wasn't aware of it at first, was to change his life forever.

When Jesse was in the fourth grade, he started noticing that he felt a little different than usual. He wasn't as excited about soccer because he was so tired after a game. He often craved candy bars when he felt tired, and although they gave him more energy, he also felt ill after eating one. When he had to ask his teacher for passes to the drinking fountain many times each day, she became concerned about his health. His teacher talked to the school nurse, who called Jesse's parents.

The next few weeks were difficult for Jesse. He was in and out of the doctor's office, being poked and prodded, and having all kinds of tests. He was frightened by all this attention, but his doctor did her best to reassure him. Finally, when it was all over, he was told he had diabetes. He understood that there was a problem with the way his body used sugar. He learned that he would have to take a substance called insulin, because his body didn't produce its own. He understood all of this, but he couldn't anticipate how complicated his life was going to get.

Jesse's had to take insulin twice a day—morning and night. The insulin was injected, and the amount was determined by pricking his finger and then measuring the amount of sugar in the drop of blood that appeared. At first, Jesse's mother did the blood test, measuring the insulin, and giving him the injection. After a short time, however, Jesse wanted to learn to give himself the insulin and also to take care of himself the way his doctor had said. He could have some sweets, but no more huge candy bars or soda pop. He could eat foods with artificial sweeteners, but he always carried a few pieces of hard candy in case he started to get shaky. Also, Jesse had to eat nutritious foods and get plenty of rest.

Jesse knew that this regimen was for life. The carefree little boy who never thought about his health was replaced by a child who took excellent care of himself. With his parents' help, Jesse regained his health, and because he developed such good habits, he became the best soccer player in the whole league.

The story of Jesse is a good example of how a domain can move into prominence when it had previously been unimportant to the child. If your children are in good health, they may not know how to respond to some of the items on this domain scale; however, this will provide a good opportunity to talk with them about maintaining good health.

The Play and Recreation Domain

The next domain, play and recreation, is an important part of childhood. We know that children rehearse for adulthood through many of the games they play.

Playing with friends is an important part of social development, and childhood is a time to have fun.

The Play and Recreation–Domain Scale

1	2	3	4	5	6
Definitely False	Mostly False	Somewhat False	Somewhat True	Mostly True	Definitely True

1. I think I play with my friends pretty well. (will) ____
2. I can think of lots of fun things to do. (way) ____
3. I think I play and have as much fun as other kids my age. (will) ____
4. When a game doesn't work out, I can usually think of lots of other things to do. (way) ____
5. The games I have played in the past will help me with new games in the future. (will) ____
6. Even when my friends can't think of what to play, I know I can think of something. (way) ____

Explanations

1. Playing with your friends well means that you have fun and don't fight or argue too much.
2. This means you don't get bored easily. You usually have a number of things you would like to do.
3. When thinking about other kids you know, you spend about as much time playing and having fun as they do.
4. This means that you usually have ideas for other fun things to do when the first thing you wanted to play doesn't work out.
5. You have learned certain skills while playing, for example, jumping rope, throwing a ball, or skating. This items means that you can see how these skills will help you when you learn new things to play.
6. This means that sometimes, when your friends are bored and can't think of anything to do, you usually have some ideas of what to play.

✳ Tommy—Never a Dull Moment

All the kids love to play at Tommy's house. It isn't that he has so many toys or games; it isn't even that his mother makes the world's best snickerdoodles. Kids flocked to his house because Tommy can always think of something fun to do.

One rainy Saturday, when all the children in their separate homes were sick and tired of watching cartoons, they appeared one by one on Tommy's doorstep. The family room filled up rapidly as children from up and down the street came to see if Tommy could play. Of course he could! He liked nothing better than having a group of his friends ready to do something fun.

On this particular Saturday, the weather was really stormy. The simple drizzle had turned into a gushing electrical storm, and suddenly all the lights went out. Several kids screamed, alarmed by the loud crash as lightning hit close to the house. Certainly no one was going to go home in this weather, so it was up to Tommy to think of something to do. What was needed was something fun to distract everyone from the thunder and lightning.

The first game Tommy thought of was hide-and-seek. When everyone started to hide, however, Tommy's mother told him she didn't want kids crawling all over the house. They would have to stay in the family room.

Tommy's next idea was a little complicated, and this time he asked permission first. He wanted to get out the trunks in the basement where years of old and outgrown clothing were stored. His game was to have everyone dress up and pretend to be their favorite book character. Each person would take a turn acting out their character's role while everyone else had to guess who they were.

Tommy

Even though some of the kids didn't read much, everyone had some character they liked. Rummaging through the clothes was fun, and after a while everyone looked like someone else. By this time they had lit candles, and the dimness of the family room made the costumes look more real. Under Tommy's direction, each child took a turn attempting to portray his or her favorite character. Some of them, like Harry Potter, were easy to guess. Others, like Ozma of Oz, stumped everyone.

Tommy and his friends played until late afternoon, when his mother came in with a big tray of milk and her famous cookies. By that time the rain had stopped, but no one had noticed. The lights came on moments later, as if to signal that the show was over. After devouring the cookies, the children began to leave, each one saying thank you and that they had a wonderful time. The rainy afternoon had turned into a wonderful surprise party, thanks to Tommy and his good ideas.

Not all children can think of creative ideas on the spur of the moment as Tommy did. Many children have had their creativity dulled by watching hours of television or playing unimaginative video games. As you give your child this domain scale, ask what types of activities he or she likes to do. Using their answers to each item and the examples given, brainstorm with your child about creative ideas for play.

The Spiritual Domain

The last scale in this chapter measures the spiritual domain. While we recognize that many children don't have formal religious training, many other children are raised within a religious community. Even without a formal affiliation, your child may have a sense of spirituality and a personal definition of God. Spirituality is more than the tenets of formal religion. It is the belief that there is something greater than oneself, and most children have at least a rudimentary idea what that might be.

Children who are raised to believe in God usually can articulate their faith. In our research, Catholic school children showed the highest domain scores during the time of their first Communion at age seven, and then again at age thirteen, during Confirmation. When a religious rite of passage is eminent, children appear to be more aware of their spiritual domain.

You will notice that we have used the terms "religion," "faith," and "spirituality" interchangeably throughout this scale. Although there are fine discriminations that are understood by older people, children often think of these words as having the same meaning. Consider the terms with which your child is most familiar and then explain the items in his or her own terminology. The explanations listed at the end of the scale are also helpful to clarify the meaning of each item.

The Spirituality Domain Scale

1	2	3	4	5	6
Definitely False	Mostly False	Somewhat False	Somewhat True	Mostly True	Definitely True

1. I can think of many ways to express my spiritual beliefs. (way)____

2. I try hard to feel close to God. (will) ____

3. When I question my faith, I know that I can find ways to believe again. (way) ____

4. I get comfort from my belief in God. (will) ____

5. When other kids say they don't believe in God, I know that I can think of ways to keep my faith. (way) ____

6. I think my spirituality will help me through difficult situations. (will) ____

Explanations

1. Some ways you might express your spiritual beliefs are praying, being thankful for what you have, and taking care of nature.

2. Feeling close to God means developing a personal relationship with Him. Talking to Him is one way to do that.

3. Sometimes, when bad things happen, you might doubt that there is a God. But you feel that you can overcome your doubts by using the ways you know to express your faith (things like prayer, meditation, or talking to a spiritual leader).

4. You feel safer because you believe that God watches out for you.

5. Some other children are not raised to believe in God. When they tell you this, you can use the ways you express your faith to remove any doubts you might feel.

6. When times are hard for you, if you are ill or sad, you know your faith in God will help you pull through.

* Marybeth—Who to Believe?

Because the public schools in Marybeth's city weren't safe, her parents decided to give her a Catholic education, even though they were Episcopalian. Her parents thought that the teachings of both denominations were so similar that the religious education she would get would be consistent with their beliefs. If there were a few points that were different, they could teach her about those at home.

Marybeth enjoyed school, and she especially liked the religious education classes that were taught by Father Bill first thing every morning. Every Wednesday the whole school attended mass, and Marybeth participated along with the Catholic students. She even learned the liturgy and the responses better than many of her Catholic friends.

During the summer between the first and second grade, Marybeth was sent to live with her grandparents while her parents traveled in Africa. Marybeth loved her grandparents, and usually they agreed on everything and got along well. This time, however, Marybeth discovered a difference that upset them all greatly. Marybeth's grandparents belonged to a Protestant denomination that believed that Catholics were wrong and misguided in their beliefs. Most of that summer was spent in arguments between Marybeth and her grandparents as they tried to dispel her beliefs. It was a most upsetting time for all of them.

When school began the next year, Marybeth's mind was in turmoil. Who was right? Who should she believe? Her parents tried to explain why her grandparents were opposed to Catholics by telling her about the history of the different churches, but that wasn't the explanation she needed. She was hurt and confused because people she loved didn't accept what she had come to believe. Where could she go for answers?

Marybeth decided to ask Father Bill for his advice, and so she went to his office at the church and timidly asked him for a bit of his time. Many of the children thought all priests were imposing figures and were openly in awe of them. Father Bill was different. He was a jolly, loving, grandfatherly man who, in the right outfit, could have passed for Santa Claus. Marybeth loved him, and she knew she could trust him to be fair in her dilemma.

What Father Bill told Marybeth to do was to pray to the Holy Spirit for guidance. He didn't try to convince her that one set of beliefs was better, or right, while the others were not. In fact, he told her that, in the end, everyone wanted the same relationship with God, but different religions held different views about how to obtain that.

So Marybeth did pray. She prayed furiously, but no answers seemed to come to her. After a while, she simply stopped worrying about it so much and went on with her life as she had before. Her answer came when the other children were preparing for the first Communion, and she found that she wanted to take that step also. Although her parents had wanted her to become Episcopalian, they recognized that being in a Catholic school might cause her to decide to be Catholic. They knew also that decisions of that type were not set in stone, and that later she might choose another denomination.

When Marybeth told her grandparents about her decision, she explained it this way: "I asked God for an answer, and, because I feel like this is the right choice for me, I believe that this is the answer to my prayers." Marybeth's reasoning and spirituality impressed her grandparents, and even though they would have preferred her to remain Protestant, they gave their approval to her choice.

Marybeth's story shows a child who has a greater spiritual consciousness than many children her age. But, like lots of other kids, she is confused by the different beliefs around her. She has high hope in the spiritual domain, which helps her to resolve the questions for herself. Her beliefs may change as she grows older, but she has acquired some tools to help her resolve any future crises of faith.

Final Thoughts On Domain-Specific Children's Hope Scales

Now that you have given your child each of the domain hope scales, you have a clearer idea about where hope-enhancing strategies can be used to the best advantage. Be sure to add this information to the picture you are developing of your child's hope, for you will be referring to it in later chapters.

This chapter has contained domain scales created to fit the lives of children between the first and sixth grades. While the next chapter is designed for adolescents, some of the scales may fit the needs and interests of younger children. As a parent, you know which scales are the most appropriate to give. If your child is an adolescent, you can certainly use some of the scales in this chapter, if they seem to fit your young person's life. No matter which of the scales you use, be sure to discuss with your child the answers they have given. Use the scales as a way to open up a dialogue about the domains of your child's life. Take this opportunity to get to know your child better.

chapter 4

Spotlighting Your Adolescent: Life Domains of the Teen Years

In the preceding chapter, we focused on the important life arenas of younger children. The domains covered were schoolwork, family relationships, play and recreation, health, safety, and spirituality. In this chapter, we turn our attention to the domains that are important in the lives of adolescents. Some of these are similar to the children's domains, (e.g., academic and family relationships); however, the domains of health and fitness and romance, included here, are of more interest to adolescents than to young children.

Dealing with Adolescent Resistance

If you are a parent of teenagers, you know that enlisting their cooperation in any program that involves you (i.e., you participating *with* them) can be dicey. If you already have a good relationship with your adolescent that includes the freedom for him or her to tell you about important issues, then half the battle is won. Your teen probably tells you about friendships, schoolwork, boy- or girlfriends, and so on. From these conversations, you can gauge where his or her hope may be lowest and suggest taking the scales for those domains as a way to examine them further.

Here is one example of parents making use of the open lines of communication between themselves and their son. Ryan is a seventeen-year-old who has a close relationship with his mother and father. He tells his parents about most of what he does, and he even talks openly about his worries. Although he has attended both the junior and senior proms, he has taken girls with whom he was merely good friends. Neither of these girls showed any interest in becoming more than friends, however, and Ryan was left feeling like a "loser" in the romance department. In appraising his appearance, Ryan confides to his parents that he is too tall and skinny to be attractive.

We will revisit Ryan when we discuss the domains of health and fitness and physical appearance. The point here is that Ryan's parents can identify his need for hope enhancement in these areas because they have listened to his thoughts and feelings. Because Ryan expresses his low hope, his parents can introduce him to the hope-building process so that he can learn some strategies and help himself. Ryan already is asking for help, so he's likely to be receptive to his parents' suggestions.

At this point, many of you may be saying to yourself, "My teen and I sure don't communicate as well Ryan and his parents do!" What do you do if your adolescent child chooses to exclude you from many of the important parts of his life? During adolescent development, it is the norm for young people to turn away from their parents and identify strongly with their peers. In their need to become independent of their families, many young people become hostile toward any perceived intervention from their parents, no matter how wise the help offered is or how much it might be needed. There is no simple answer for parents who are wondering what went wrong. A formerly loving and compliant child can turn into a sarcastic rebel over a matter of months.

If your adolescent is rebelling against family intervention, clearly your suggestion that he could benefit from learning to think more hopefully won't be welcomed with open arms. There are ways, however, for you to covertly infuse some of these strategies into your adolescent's life. In the story accompanying the family relationship domain, you will see how the parents of an especially obnoxious young woman were able to bring about some important changes. They established small relationship goals along with a system of reinforcements that eventually brought peace to the family environment.

Preventing a situation from becoming lousy is always easier than correcting one that already is bad. For parents whose children haven't entered the difficult adolescent years, maintaining communication is central to good parent-child relationships. We've found that most parents want to have open, loving, and mutually respectful relationships with their children. The reality, however, is that many parents don't know how to produce and maintain such a positive relationship. These relationship skills aren't something you're born with—you have to learn them. There are numerous books available that will help you deal with young people, and if you feel that you could use some help, we suggest that you read some of those. In fact, in Suggested Reading at the back of this book, we have listed books that we believe can help you facilitate communication with children of all ages about difficult issues.

Although parent-child relationships are not the explicit focus of this book, we recognize that if you are to implement this hope-enhancing program with your adolescent children, you will need to be able to establish a receptive family environment. Therefore, we've listed some basic rules for improved communication in the following section. While these guidelines may not supercede the need for a good book on parent-child relationships, they should get you off to a good start.

Guidelines for Effective Communication

In order to give your communication a boost, here are some guidelines that, in our experience, will help you speak more effectively with your adolescent.

1. The first rule of good communication is *learning how to listen*. This means that you allow your teenagers to say what is on their minds, even if you don't like what you may hear. This means not interrupting and expecting not be interrupted, in turn. Sometimes parents just go through the motions, acting as if they're listening to their teenagers, while, in truth, their minds are on something that happened at work or some other "important" issue. Our point here is that listening to your child is one of the *most* important things you can do to improve communication between the two of you. And faking it simply won't do—kids can tell when you're not really present.

2. Adolescence is a time when emotions, along with hormones, run rampant. Learn to respond to emotional statements *objectively*, understanding that hyperbole is often used to get a rise out of you, rather than reflecting true feelings. One good way to respond to an emotional statement is to label the feeling, rather than trying to get the young person to calm down. For example you might say, "I can see how angry you are." Such a statement doesn't place you in agreement with what is being said, but neither is it critical or judgmental of the emotion. Instead of trying to directly negate your child's feelings, it's better to try to understand those feelings and, in the process, deflect their counterproductivity. This is analagous to certain martial arts moves where one uses the opponent's energy to deflect their force.

3. If there is a problem or an argument, *ask your adolescent how she would like to see the issue resolved*. You may not agree with her suggestions, but at least this approach offers a point from which to begin negotiating. Do *not* automatically negate her suggestions (see item number 2). Hear her out. If you cannot accept what she has offered, show your adolescent respect by expressing a willingness to discuss compromises and alternatives.

4. Learn to ask questions in such a way that conversation is encouraged rather than shut down. In the counseling field, these are called *open-ended questions*. They usually begin with the words "how" or "what," and are stated in such a way that a one word answer is very difficult. It can be very common for a sulking teenager to try to shut down conversations

with a string of monosyllabic replies, like "yes," or "no," or perhaps the sarcastic "fine" (uttered with just the right disgust). "How was your day?" is an example of such a question. If your teen says "Fine," ask him to tell you more about it. Of course, it's important for you to be genuinely interested and willing to listen in a nonjudgmental way. You may even try to recall how you felt at a similar stage in your teenage years.

5. Learn to *share your own feelings by using "I" statements.* When you say, "I feel angry when . .," you're communicating personal responsibility for your anger. If you say, "You make me angry," you are shifting the responsibility to your child. Research consistently shows that no one (from children to adults) likes to be around a person who often blames others. Learning to control one's emotions and becoming responsible for them is an important lesson in growing up. As a parent, owning your own emotions is one way you can model that behavior. Furthermore, by accepting the responsibility for your emotions, and especially admitting when you are wrong or could have behaved more appropriately, you model flexibility and a "humanness" that opens further dialogue.

6. The final suggestion isn't a skill, but rather an attitude. Try to be *open* to new ways of speaking, of dressing, new kinds of music, and the host of activities that constitute the popular, ever-changing culture. You don't need to embrace these fads, but do recognize that they are the badges of your adolescent's peers and, as such, deserve respectful consideration (assuming such fads are not hurtful of others or antithetical to other important core values that you and your ancestors have embraced across generations).

The best time to begin forming a good relationship with your children is when they are very young. These communication guidelines are effective for use with people of any age, from the very young to adulthood. If you begin using good communications skills with your children when they're small, it is likely that your children will be willing to tell you about themselves throughout their lives. If you currently don't have an open line of communication with your children or adolescents, using these skills will help you establish one. Remember, however, that if there have been years of poor communication, *it will take time for those patterns to change.*

For your part as a parent, some of these skills will take thought and practice if you are not accustomed to using them. Think about the situations with your teenager that are the most problematic for you, then plan how you will apply these communications skills. One helpful hint: If you find your emotions getting heated, leave the situation until you can think clearly again. In doing this, it's important to tell your teenager that you need a little time alone to compose yourself, and that you're not leaving as a means of expressing disrespect for them. You might even ask your teenager if you could broach the same topic at a later point when you can hear what they are saying better, rather than just "getting mad." Remember, you are modeling good communication as well as establishing the type of relationship that will allow you to help your adolescent develop hopeful thinking.

Introducing the Domain Scales

If you haven't yet asked your adolescent to fill out the Children's Hope Scale shown in chapter 2, we suggest you do that now. If you think the Adult Hope Scale in chapter 5 is more appropriate, have them fill out that instead.

Take this opportunity to discuss the active process of hope, and how hopeful thinking can help your kids achieve the things they want from life. Emphasize that the first part of learning hopeful thinking is finding their current level of hope and which of the four life domains (in this chapter) are most in need of hope enhancement. Most teenagers truly enjoy finding out more about themselves and, if the scales are presented as an easy way to do that, your adolescent may become intrigued.

Before introducing the Life-Domain Scales, try discussing how your adolescent thinks about the different areas of his life. Most young people live in the moment and may not have given much thought to how their lives are divided into separate domains. Being able to visualize these arenas, however, allows the teenager to make plans, set goals, and think about the future in an orderly way. It might help if you note that you have found it helpful to think about the various parts of your life.

The Academic Domain

The adolescent life domains will be presented in the same format as the children's domains were in the preceding chapter. First, we will describe the domain, followed by the scale. To clarify any ambiguities, examples will be given for each item. And finally, each domain will be illustrated by the story of an adolescent exercising hopeful thinking in that domain.

The academic domain for adolescents is more complex than the schoolwork domain for children. Beginning in middle or junior high school, students have a number of different teachers and move from class to class throughout the day. This pattern will continue throughout the rest of their education, regardless of how advanced they become. Furthermore, academic performance, while always important, becomes a predictor for future advancement in the educational system. During high school, this domain may become the major focus in an adolescent's life. A student will have a differing array of colleges to prospectively attend, as well as scholarships available, depending on her grades and entrance-test scores.

The Academic-Domain Scale

1	2	3	4	5	6
Definitely False	Mostly False	Somewhat False	Somewhat True	Mostly True	Definitely True

1. I can think of lots of ways to make good grades in school. (way) ____

2. I energetically pursue my schoolwork. (will) ____

3. There are lots of ways to meet the challenges of any class. (way) ____

4. I've been pretty successful in school. (will) ____

5. My past academic successes have prepared me well for future successes. (way) ____

6. I get the grades I want in my classes. (will) ____

Explanations

1. When you're able to think of many ways to make good grades, it means that you have good study skills, you are able to pay attention in class, and that you know what's required in order to make the grades you want.

2. Energetically pursuing your schoolwork means that you do your work when it is due, rather than putting it off. The opposite of this would be procrastination and avoidance of schoolwork.

3. Different classes have different requirements in order to make good grades. High waypower in this domain means that you can think of ways to meet those requirements.

4. Being successful means getting the grades you work for, and that doesn't always mean As. If a subject matter is especially difficult for you, a lower grade can mean great success if you worked hard for it.

5. By past successes, we mean all of your efforts as well as your achievements. You may not have gotten top grades in every class, but if you've tried to master the material, you will have a good background of information and study skills to support your future academic efforts.

6. This means that you are consistently satisfied with your performance and how your teachers judge it.

Not all students are interested in academics, of course, and many young people choose not to get a postsecondary education. Some may even drop out of high school before graduation. Based on our research, young people who don't finish high school are more likely to have a low level of hope in their lives, and low hope specifically in this academic domain. We have placed the academic domain first in the list of domain scales because obtaining an education is an important way for young people to achieve their dreams in the United States. The number of years spent in school is a predictor of both financial and social success. If you value these latter outcomes, then the academic domain is especially important arena to help your teen develop high hope.

✽ Dennis—Let's Make a Deal

Dennis' mother and father were divorced when he was in the first grade and, because his mother traveled extensively for her work, he went to live with his father. Although Dennis and his father got along well enough, he always thought that life with his mother might be more fun. Life with his father always was centered around work, whether it was schoolwork, housework, or work in the yard. Even play had to be educational, and somehow Dennis and his dad never got around to just having fun together.

Dennis' mother, on the other hand, loved to laugh and play. She didn't take life too seriously and was always ready to find something enjoyable to do. Sometimes this contrast between his parents was confusing for Dennis, but he made the best of it by trying to follow the rules of both households.

By the time Dennis was ready to begin high school, his mother had quit traveling and had purchased a new home in another town. Dennis decided that he wanted to live full time with his mother, not just on weekends, and told his father so. Dennis' father was full of doubts. Would there be enough discipline? Would she make Dennis study, or would she just let him watch television? What would happen to all his good work habits? Mainly, he was very concerned that Dennis' grades would slip, and that he wouldn't get into a good college.

Dennis decided to make a deal with his father. If he could move in with his mother, he would continue his

Dennis

good work in school and keep his grades high. If he dropped off the honor roll, he would move back to his father's house. Everyone agreed to this deal. Dennis then moved in with his mother that summer.

The next semester, Dennis found his new school to be much more difficult than he had anticipated. For one thing, it was four times as large as his old school. There were many more students in each class, and he didn't know anyone. The subjects Dennis signed up for were all considered difficult, and he found that he had much more homework than he had ever had before. He began to question whether he could actually do it all.

The homework was nearly overwhelming at first, but Dennis was well organized and he knew how to study because of all the years he spent under his father's supervision. The first thing he did was to begin using an assignment book that had a section in it for each class. He also talked to his teachers whenever there was material he didn't understand. The hardest time for Dennis was after school, before his mother got home. He knew he was on his own to do his homework and not play on the computer or watch television, so he planned one hour of relaxation and then forced himself to get to work.

That first semester took all his determination to stick to his plan, but, in the end, he made the honor roll. He was proud of himself for the grades, but he was also very proud of something else. In all the years he'd lived with his father, Dennis had always had supervision. What he found out was that he could be responsible for himself. He realized that he had the power to achieve his goals by using all the good habits he had already acquired.

The story of Dennis shows high hope in the academic domain. He was able to apply what he had learned in the past to help him succeed in a new school, he found ways to cope with the massive amounts of homework, and he pursued his work energetically. As a high-hope person, Dennis saw challenges as opportunities for growth and was able to quell negative thoughts by replacing them with positive ones.

The Family Domain

The next area we'll examine is the family domain. As we suggested in the first part of this chapter, adolescents often distance themselves from their families in an attempt to discover their own identities. Because they may experience lower hope when this occurs, it's important to offer them extra help to get through this difficult period.

The Family-Domain Scale

1	2	3	4	5	6
Definitely False	Mostly False	Somewhat False	Somewhat True	Mostly True	Definitely True

1. I can think of lots of things I enjoy doing with my family. (way) ____

2. I work hard to maintain good family relationships. (will) ____

3. Even when we disagree, I know that I can find ways to solve problems with my family. (way) ____

4. I have a pretty successful family life. (will) ____

5. There are lots of ways to communicate my feelings to family members. (way) ____

6. I have the kinds of relationships I want with family members. (will) ____

Explanations

1. Many teenagers only want to spend time with their friends. However, a person with high family-relationship hope finds satisfaction in family activities as well.

2. Working hard to maintain good relationships means sometimes putting family concerns before your own, listening to others, and cooperating with group decisions.

3. Finding solutions to problems is related to learning how to get along. It means that you're willing to compromise, and it also means that you are willing to apologize.

4. A successful family life is one in which you're generally happy and satisfied. There will always be a few arguments, but the high-hope person accepts some conflict as the nature of families and doesn't harbor grudges or resentments.

5. Communicating feelings in a family is an important part of having good relationships. A high-hope person knows appropriate and effective ways to share feelings and is able to listen to the feelings of others.

6. Having the kinds of relationships you want with family members means that you are willing to work hard to maintain good feelings. You don't let negative feelings fester, you are willing to be open and direct in your communication, and, most importantly, you can be forgiving.

* Betsy—Learning to be Tolerant

The McCanns were a large, close-knit family of five children, two parents, both sets of grandparents, aunts, uncles, and numerous cousins. They all lived within a few miles of each other, all attended the same church, and most of the children went to the same schools. On holidays, the entire family gathered at one home or another, and there was always loud singing, dancing, and storytelling, often stimulated by a bottle of Irish whiskey.

Idyllic as this picture was for most of the McCanns, sixteen-year-old Betsy was embarrassed by her family's antics. Betsy was a serious student and devoutly religious. She was even considering taking a vocation in the church. The raucous celebrations of holidays and feast days soured Betsy's mood and caused her to be highly critical, or even sarcastic, about her family's behavior. Although she didn't like feeling so negative, she thought her family was being sacrilegious and therefore needed her criticisms.

For her family's part, although they were pleased that she was devout, they thought she was being something of a wet blanket. They worried that her relationships with her siblings and cousins were suffering, because no one wanted to be around such an uptight person. Betsy's brothers, sister, and cousins made fun of her, calling her "Saint Betsy." They thought she considered herself better then everyone else.

At first, the teasing made Betsy mad, and she tried to ignore it. But when she was really honest with herself, as she always tried to be, Betsy had to admit there was a lot of truth in what they said. She didn't like feeling negative, and she didn't like being cross with everyone, but she didn't know what to do about it. She decided to talk about her feelings with her mother, which is what she'd always done when she was younger.

Betsy's mother was very happy that she was finally talking about her anger and said that she, too, was a little put off at times by all the loud celebrating. But Betsy's mother also reminded her that they had a cultural heritage that was passed on in songs, dances, and stories, and that this behavior was simply an Irish way of celebrating. Betsy didn't have to take part in all of it, but she could never stop being Irish. She could resent her heritage, but her mother hoped instead that Betsy would choose to be proud of it.

With this in mind, Betsy began to consider her family from a different perspective. She began to study about her family's history in Ireland, and she started to see the value of preserving its customs and culture. Betsy's natural reserve meant that she never became the center of activity at family gatherings, but she was able to encourage and appreciate the celebration around her. She became a more tolerant person, and family harmony was restored.

Betsy demonstrated both high willpower and high waypower in the family domain when she was able to be honest with herself and find a way to change the way she behaved with her family. Sharing her feelings with her mother and asking for advice was another way she exercised her hope. Many adolescents are embarrassed by their family's behavior, and even though Betsy claimed that devotion was the reason for her embarrassment, she was also going through the identity crisis of adolescence.

The Health and Fitness Domain

The health and fitness domain also is an important one for adolescents, and one in which parents can play a significant role. As you read about this domain, think about the role model you set for your children in this area of your own life.

Next to thinking about romance, teenagers probably think most about their appearance. Of course, the two subjects are related, because the main purpose of looking good is to attract a boy- or girlfriend. The changes in body chemistry during adolescence create challenges for the teen who is trying to adjust to his or her growing body and fluctuating hormones. Like clumsy puppies, these young people often seem out of place in their bodies. They must deal with voice changes, skin eruptions, and emotions that can slide out of control in unpredictable ways.

Few, if any, teenagers are satisfied with the way they look. Girls are often obsessed with diets and being thin, while boys struggle to develop their muscles. The striking differences in the developmental rate of boys and girls add to the agony often felt by young people. Watch as a high school lets out for the day and you will see boys who look like they belong in elementary school and girls who look like young matrons. All of this contributes to the stress and confusion of an already difficult life period.

The health and fitness domain is an important one for you to share with your teenager. The ratings on this scale can help you discover how your adolescent feels about his or her physical self and how much hope they have to modify what they may not like. Use this scale to begin talking about health and fitness with your teen, letting him know that you can be a good resource.

The Health and Fitness–Domain Scale

1	2	3	4	5	6
Definitely False	Mostly False	Somewhat False	Somewhat True	Mostly True	Definitely True

1. I can think of many ways to maintain my health and fitness. (way) ____

2. I actively work at being healthy and fit. (will) ____

3. Even when I am tired, I can usually make myself work out. (will) ____

4. I can find ways to continue my health and fitness routine in a variety of situations. (way) ____

5. I believe I can sustain my health and fitness as I grow older. (will) ____

6. Habits of health and fitness I am acquiring now will help me in the future. (way) ____

Explanations

1. Thinking of lots of ways to maintain your health and fitness means understanding the importance of good nutrition, physical exercise, and rest.

2. Actively working at your health and fitness means that you work out, watch what you eat, and try to get enough rest, even when your friends may be ignoring these important habits.

3. Actively working on this domain means that your health and fitness is a high priority for you, and that you will maintain your habits even if you would rather be doing other things.

4. When you're traveling or when your other activities seem to be taking precedence, you are able to find ways to eat right, get enough rest, and do some physical activity.

5. Young people often assume older people can no longer be fit. This item means that you can see yourself maintaining your health and fitness habits as you age.

6. You realize that what you learn to do now to maintain health and fitness will serve you well as you grow older. You can see that you are establishing valuable habits now.

✳ Ryan—Becoming a New Man

Between Ryan's freshman and sophomore year of high school an amazing thing happened. He grew from five feet, five inches tall to six foot, three—a total of ten inches! Needless to say, his jeans were always too short, as were the sleeves of his shirts. When he looked in the mirror, he saw his little boy's face sitting on top of a tall, gangling body, all arms and legs. To make matters worse, his weight wasn't keeping up with his height. When he finally stopped shooting upwards, he weighed only 145 pounds.

Everyone he knew teased poor Ryan, calling him a "beanpole" and a "bag of bones." By the time his sophomore year was coming to a close, Ryan was thoroughly fed up with the teasing and the way he looked, so he decided to change his image. He began to read magazines to learn better health and fitness habits, and he asked his physical-education teacher for advice.

Ryan made a lot of changes over the course of the summer between his sophomore and junior years, so that when he went back to school in the fall, people hardly recognized him. With the help of his parents and his own initiative, here is what Ryan did.

In order to build up his muscles, Ben started working out every other day on weight machines and free weights at a local gym. On the days he wasn't lifting weights, he swam several miles in the lake near his home. On the advice of his doctor, Ryan took nutritional supplements to help him develop some bulk, especially calcium to help maintain strong bones after his growth spurt.

Ryan

Ryan also made some changes in his personal style that helped him change his image. The horn-rimmed glasses he had worn since junior high school were replaced with contact lenses. Ryan's father took him to a hair stylist, who trimmed his lanky hair into a fashionable cut. And finally, just before school started again, Ryan's mother took him shopping for jeans and shirts that really fit.

When Ryan went to school that first day of the new school year, the girls couldn't help staring, and the boys joked with him about his new looks. Of course, Ryan was still a shy young man inside his new image, but this only made him more attractive. He knew how hard he'd worked to change the way he looked, and he was determined that the habits he'd learned over the summer would stay with him a lifetime. He was very proud of his accomplishment.

This true story shows how a young person can change his appearance and fitness with hopeful thinking. The growth spurt Ryan experienced was extreme, but similar changes happen at a slower rate to nearly all adolescents. Any young person who is unhappy with the way he or she feels physically can make substantial improvements by following good habits of health and fitness. Ryan had supportive parents, but he was also willing to consult his physical-education teacher and his doctor. High-hope people don't hesitate to use any resources they can to seek out ways to reach their goals.

The Romantic Domain

The next domain, that of romance, frequently is on the minds of adolescents. In the story for this domain we will follow Ryan as he struggles to become comfortable with girls and learns to date.

As hormones race through their bodies, adolescents become obsessed by thoughts of romance. In the normal course of development these thoughts prepare them for their later roles as sexually responsible adults. In the early throes of sexuality, however, many teenagers are confused and even frightened by their feelings. Most young people feel inadequate to the task of pursuing romance. Girls often believe they must wait for a boy to ask them out, while boys are terrified of that prospect, and everyone is afraid of rejection. A few adolescents seem to have a handle on dating, going steady from an early age and, perhaps, finding security in one special person. For the most part, however, learning to develop romantic relationships is a major and daunting task of the adolescent years.

Parents can help make this task smoother. It is important to listen to your teen's fears, and be willing to discuss sexual information. Too many young people learn about sex and romance from their peers, who themselves know very little. Initially your adolescent may be uncomfortable discussing these issues with you, but if you are relaxed and open, they will eventually learn to be open also. Use the scale for this domain as a way to open the discussion.

The Romantic Relationships–Domain Scale

1	2	3	4	5	6
Definitely False	Mostly False	Somewhat False	Somewhat True	Mostly True	Definitely True

1. I can think of many ways to get to know someone I find attractive. (way) ____

2. When I am interested in someone romantically, I actively pursue them. (will) ____

3. I've been pretty successful in romantic relationships. (will) ____

4. There are lots of ways to convince someone to go out with me. (way) ____

5. I can usually get a date, when I set my mind to it. (will) ____

6. I can think of many ways to keep someone interested in me. (way) ____

Explanations

1. A person with high hope in this domain would be able to engage the other person in conversation, sharing interests and topics they might have in common.

2. Actively pursuing someone in whom you are interested means that you're not afraid to get to know that person and ask them out.

3. Depending on your age and expectations, successful romantic relationships can mean anything from being able to talk with the person you are interested in to actually dating.

4. Knowing how to convince someone to go out with you depends on having fun and interesting ideas and the confidence to ask that person out.

5. Setting your mind to getting a date takes an attitude of high hope, as well as the ability to think of fun things to do and the willingness to risk being rejected.

6. Attracting a person you find interesting is the first step. After that, it takes both willpower and waypower thinking to develop a relationship. High-hope people know that relationships take work, and they are willing to put in the time and effort to keep the romance going.

* Ryan—From Dweeb to Dateable

With his small size, scrawny arms and legs, horn-rimmed glasses, and limp hair, Ryan was the typical high school dweeb. The fact that he played chess and was a top-notch student didn't help him where girls were concerned. Every girl he thought was cute just looked straight through him—he might as well have been a piece of furniture. Unless, that is, they needed help with a math problem.

During Ryan's freshman year, he underwent a radical change in his height, but his weight and the size of his muscles stayed the same. The ten inches he grew only seemed to stretch out his already skinny body. But Ryan had high hope in the area of health and physical fitness, and, as we have seen, he was able to transform himself into what most girls would consider a "hunk."

Unfortunately, the transformation was all on the outside. Inside, Ryan was still the shy, self-conscious boy he'd been when he was small and skinny. He wondered how it was that other guys seem so self-confident around girls. How did they always know just the right thing to say and do? Ryan didn't think asking his parents for advice on this matter would help; in his mind, they were just too old to know what kids did these days.

Ryan decided to watch and listen to how other guys behaved with girls. Locker-room conversation, which had never intrigued him when he didn't think he stood a chance with girls, became a steady source of information. From listening to the boys who were successful and had girlfriends, Ryan learned ways to start conversations, ask girls out, and even how to put on a few "moves."

Ryan never wanted to be a Romeo, however. What Ryan wanted was a relationship with a girl he really cared for, and who would care for him back. He decided that his approach would be to make friends with girls before he decided to explore romance. He found that getting to know girls wasn't as hard as he had supposed. It just meant having a genuine interest in them. In his junior year, Ryan met a very nice girl whom he dated throughout the rest of high school and into college. Together, they each learned the meaning of a good romantic relationship.

As we saw in Ryan's health and fitness story, he was able to use hopeful thinking to accomplish his physical transformation. In this story, we saw that he could apply waypower thinking to figuring out how to become more confident in his relationships with girls. As is characteristic of high-hope adolescents, Ryan was able to identify his goals, figure out solutions to the problems he encountered, and then stick to his plan to meet his target. Ryan used the technique of modeling to learn how to initiate conversations, but he was selective about using what he learned. Ryan wanted a meaningful relationship with a girl, and so he created his own style to develop romantic relationships.

Using Additional Domain Scales

The four scales we have given you in this chapter cover areas most relevant to adolescents. The domain scales in chapter 3 also may be useful for your teenager to complete. All of these scales can be used in several ways. First, in addition to the general hope score and the waypower and willpower scores, these scales help you to pinpoint the areas in which your child or adolescent may be most in need of hope.

A second and very important function served by these scales is that of opening the door to conversations about the specific domains. It is our observation that adolescents and their parents don't talk enough about these important subjects. In part, this is due to adolescent independence, when young people believe that their identities must be forged without the help of their parents. In large part, however, this lack of communication is also due to parents' reluctance to discuss potentially embarrassing issues with their teenagers. If parents ask what their teenagers are thinking and doing, they might actually find out—a risky proposition to some parents.

From our years as therapists, teachers, and parents ourselves, we know that good communication between parents and children is fundamental to the development of hope. Use the guidelines in this chapter to give your communications skills a boost, and then use the domain scales to find out more about your child's hope.

chapter 5

It Begins with You:
Parents Need Hope

Why is it important for parents to be hopeful thinkers? The answer is really quite simple. From your child's earliest awareness, you are the most important influence on her thoughts and behaviors. It is parents who say "yes" or "no," "you can" or "you can't." You're the ones from whom approval and permission is sought. It's your words that will be internalized and incorporated into your child's language, and it is those words that will become the low or high hope that contributes to the thinking of your child.

The Generational Influence

One of the most important actions you can take toward helping your child develop higher hope is to develop your own hope. Through the years in working with parents and teachers, we have observed that adults who have high hope transmit hopeful thinking to the children with whom they have contact. Conversely, low-hope adults tend to communicate negative messages to children and discourage their hopeful thinking. The following story illustrates this point.

✳ **Joleen and Me—The Power of a Mother's Words**

I first met Joleen when we were both students at a prestigious dance school in Los Angeles. I suppose that what drew us together is that neither of our families had much money, and we were both receiving scholarships to the school. Joleen and I were both sixteen, and we were talented dancers, but that's where the resemblance ended. Physically, we were opposites. She was short and stocky, and I was tall and thin. She was dark, and I was fair. But the biggest difference was in our attitudes.

In our dance classes, especially ballet, we had to perform complicated sets of steps in front of the rest of the class. Our teacher was quite strict, loudly tapping her hickory cane on the floor in time to the rhythm of the piano. In her Russian accent, she shouted the names of the ballet steps and other, less pleasant, names if we didn't perform up to her rigorous standards. We all found her to be intimidating, but Joleen was especially daunted.

As we waited in line to perform the steps across the floor, Joleen would whisper in my ear that she knew she would trip, or at the very least, be told that she looked like a plucked chicken. After every class, Joleen would complain that she would never be a great dancer, and that if it were not for her mother's insistence, she most assuredly would quit.

My attitude was much different than Joleen's. When it was my turn to perform in front of the class, I really believed that I could do it. Even when the teacher made unfavorable comments about my style, I took it in stride as part of the learning experience. Whether or not I ever became a famous dancer, I loved ballet, and no one was going to ruin the sheer pleasure that it brought me.

Our dance classes were held in a very large studio with mirrors on three walls, and glass doors on the other. Students' mothers sat behind the glass doors, knitting leggings for their sons or daughters and commenting to each other on the brilliance of their children. While my mother was seldom in attendance, Joleen's mother never missed a class. She also never missed a chance to find fault with Joleen's mistakes.

Like so many "stage mothers," Joleen's mother had wanted to be a professional dancer when she was young. In fact, the family had moved to Southern California from Idaho so that Joleen would have a chance at stardom. Her mother's efforts to push Joleen toward dance were having the opposite effect from what she intended. Even at my young age, I could see how my friend was being destroyed by the constant criticism. Rather than working harder and learning to believe in herself, Joleen was ready to give up. Between the sarcastic comments of our teacher and the criticisms of her mother, Joleen felt utterly defeated.

My mother, on the other hand, wasn't one to push me into something. Nor was she using me as an instrument for her own gratification. She thought it was nice that I wanted to dance, and when she attended my lessons she always seemed amazed that I could move so gracefully. As I look back on the messages my mother gave me, I can see how different they were from those that Joleen heard. My mother always said, "If you believe in yourself, you can do almost anything you set your mind to. The trick is to keep your thoughts positive." Quite the contrary, I often heard Joleen's mother say, "You're never going to be a star; you're just too lazy."

I guess Joleen believed her mother, because after a few years she moved back to Idaho and got married. I, on the other hand, danced with a company for a few years and felt successful. It was important to me that I could work hard and achieve my goal. As I look back on my short dance career, I see how important my mother's encouraging attitude was in how I thought about myself and what I have done with my life.

It's clear from the story that Joleen and the narrator received two clearly different messages from their mothers. The narrator's mother was a high-hope person, while Joleen's mother was a low-hope thinker. Without intending to discourage her daughter, Joleen's mother repeatedly told her that she wasn't going to succeed. No matter how talented Joleen may have been, it would have been exceedingly difficult for her to overcome such negative thoughts. As her comments to the narrator show, Joleen internalized her mother's words, increasing their hope-robbing power as she repeated them to herself. In this story, we can see how low-hope thinking is communicated from one generation to the next. Low hope is quite literally passed down through the generations to weigh down the lofty thoughts of youngsters.

Later in this chapter, we will more closely examine the lives of the two mothers in this story to show how low and high hope are developed through both family influences and personal experiences. The next step, however, is for you to measure your own hope using the Adult Hope Scale.

What Is Your Level of Hope?

The Adult Hope Scale has been administered to more than twenty thousand people in research and clinical settings in several countries, where it has been used in helping people to determine their levels of hope under many differing conditions. Research has been conducted to insure that the Adult Hope Scale measures hope rather than a different but related characteristic, such as optimism. Our studies also demonstrate that the scale is measuring a trait; that is, your scores probably will be similar each time you take the scale unless, of course, you engage in activities to purposefully raise your hopeful thinking.

Determining your hope score is essential if you are to undertake the program in this book to help your child develop higher hope. Your hope scores will serve as a guide for changes that you may need to make in your own thinking in order to be a more effective teacher and role model for your child. Your scores will reveal which aspect of your hope—willpower or waypower—may need more work. This scale is somewhat different than the children's hope scales described earlier. After you have taken the Adult Hope Scale, we will show you how to score it.

The Adult Hope Scale

Directions: Using the four-point scale appearing below, read each item and, in the blank, rate how true you believe the item content is of you. Remember, there are no right or wrong answers, and only your honest answers will be helpful to you. Please go ahead and fill in a number in the spaces at the end of each item.

1	2	3	4
Definitely False	Mostly False	Mostly True	Definitely True

1. I energetically pursue my goals. ____

2. I can think of many ways to get out of a jam. ____

3. My past experiences have prepared me well for the future. ____

4. There are lots of ways around any problem. ____

5. I've been pretty successful in life. ____

6. I can think of many ways to get the things in life that are most important to me. ____

7. I meet the goals I set for myself. ____

8. Even when others get discouraged, I know I can find a way to solve the problem. ____

Scoring Your Hope Scale

To derive your overall score, add up all the numbers you marked in the blanks to the right of the statements. Your score can range from a low of 8, meaning that you marked all of the items "Definitely false," to a high of 32, reflecting the fact that you marked all of the items as "Definitely true" for you.

As with the Children's and Young Children's Hope Scales, we have administered this scale to thousands of people. Consequently, we can give some norms about your score. A score of around 24 indicates an average amount of hope, which actually may be a fairly strong hope score. That is to say, in order to have obtained a score of 24, your typical response was "Mostly true" to the items. Such a pattern would indicate that you're a moderately hopeful individual. In fact, we have found that many people have this reasonably high level of hope, and this is a solid base of hopeful thought.

A score higher than 24 indicates that you usually think very hopefully, while a score lower than 24 indicates that you may not be consistently hopeful. To be a high-hope adult, it is necessary to obtain a high score on both the willpower and waypower components, just as is the case for children and adolescents. Conversely, when you or your children score low on both the willpower and waypower components, it is indicative of low hope.

To determine your willpower score, add your ratings on the odd-numbered items; for the waypower score, add the scores for the even-numbered items. If you scored 12 or higher on the willpower items, but 9 or lower on the waypower items, you may have difficulties taking action toward goals. That is to say, you may be stuck when problems arise, unable to think of a solution. If, on the other hand, you scored more than 12 on the waypower items, and less than 9 on the willpower items, you probably are stuck for another reason. You may have many goals and ways to achieve these goals, but lack the mental energy (willpower) to implement your plans.

Profiles of Hope

In chapter 2, we presented the profiles of hope for young children, older children, and adolescents using the two children's hope scales. Here are the profiles for adults. Examine the scores below to see which pattern fits you.

- Full High = Willpower score greater than 12 + Waypower score greater than 12

- Mixed-Low Way = Willpower score greater than 12 + Waypower score lower than 9

- Mixed-Low Will = Willpower score less than 9 + Waypower score greater than 12

- Full Low = Willpower score less than 9 + Waypower score less than 9

Now that you have taken the scale and scored it, you can compare your hope profile with that of your child. Often, parents and children show remarkably similar patterns of hope. It's likely that you will see your own approach to life, whether low or high in hopeful thinking, reflected in your children. In this chapter, we began with the story of two dance students whose ultimate success was influenced by their mothers' low- or high-hope messages. Let's examine the lives of those two mothers and how they developed the levels of hope that subsequently influenced their children. You will note the generational influences of hopeful thinking in these stories. These two mothers illustrate low- and high-hope profiles, while two additional stories will illustrate the mixed-hope profiles. Look for similarities between these stories and your own experiences. Then look for similarities between your hopeful thinking and that of your child. You probably will discover that hope is a family affair.

✳ Full-Low Hope—Carolyn

Carolyn's people settled in Idaho over one hundred years ago on what was called "hardscrabble" land. Times were difficult and dangerous. The territory was newly taken from the Indian people to whom it had belonged, and there were frequent skirmishes that ended in someone's injury or death. Settlers became grim and hardened, trying to eke out an existence in an unfriendly environment.

Carolyn's immediate family still told tales of hard winters and Indian raids, even though it was many generations later. There was family pride in having survived and homesteaded on that unforgiving land. But there was also a cynicism and a bitterness born from the difficulties and hardships they had endured. Some 120 years advanced from her settler ancestors, Carolyn still exhibited this attitude in her belief that success was nearly impossible to achieve, and when attained, tenuous, at best. Carolyn's philosophy was that by expecting something bad to happen, you won't be caught off guard when it does.

By the time Carolyn was in school, her family had moved to Boise, where her father had a store. Carolyn was given dance and singing lessons, showing a great deal of talent for both. In adolescence, Carolyn decided that she wanted to be a dancer in the movies, setting sights higher than any she had held previously. Carolyn's parents encouraged her dream, although they knew absolutely nothing about how she could make it come true.

Boise had a small dance company and a community theater where Carolyn performed regularly. After achieving a degree of success in Boise and graduating from high school, she decided to move to Los Angeles, thinking that she might find the fame she sought in the show-business capital. Life in Los Angles wasn't what she had expected, however.

Carolyn moved into a rooming house occupied by other aspiring dancers and actresses. She enrolled at a local dance studio, seeking the connections that would allow her to find auditions. Although those were the right paths to take, she didn't anticipate the large number of dancers or the high quality of their work. At every tryout, she was but one among many, many talented young people. After two months of dance classes and auditions, Carolyn hadn't found any work. To make matters worse, it seemed as if she hadn't even been noticed by the choreographers.

The fruitless auditions began to take their toll on Carolyn's energy and her attitude. Her movements became somewhat sluggish, and she began to lack the pep and charisma that the dance directors wanted. Her negative expectations showed on her face, and a friend had to keep reminding her to smile.

Slowly, she began to realize that the dancing skills considered superior in Boise couldn't compare to the dancers who were trained by professionals in Los Angeles. Because Carolyn had grown up with her family's "expect the worst" philosophy, she accepted her defeat as being the usual family outcome. She sadly determined that she had only two options—to take another type of job in order to survive, or to return to Boise. She called her mother to say she was coming home.

Carolyn returned to Boise with her dreams shattered but resigned to the thought that she probably would have failed no matter what she did. Shortly thereafter she met and married a young man who worked for her father. Within a year they had a daughter whom they named Joleen. And then the fantasy started—each time Carolyn looked at Joleen, she saw a future dancer—one who would succeed where she hadn't.

As a teenager growing up in a small town, Carolyn was successful in pursuing her dreams of becoming a dancer. She had talent and succeeded amidst the easy competition. The pathways to her goal were clear and seldom blocked. All she had to do was to take dance and singing classes, and perform in the yearly recitals and theater productions. She received praise for these activities because she was a far better dancer and singer than the other performers in Boise.

When Carolyn went to Los Angeles, however, she encountered her first real impediments. Her waypower was low, and she could only conceive of one way to break into show business—through auditions. When she was unsuccessful using that route, she chose to go home rather than finding an alternative route to her goal. If Carolyn had been a high-waypower person, she would have identified what she needed to learn in order to improve her dancing. She would have found another type of job while she took the required dance classes to make her a better dancer—one who might even successfully compete amidst the stiff competition in Los Angeles. Carolyn's low willpower, illustrated by her negative attitude and her visibly low energy, didn't produce the necessary drive to succeed in such a highly competitive environment. She expected the worst and, when it happened, she didn't have the energy to fight it.

When Joleen was born, Carolyn decided that her daughter would fulfill her own unsuccessful dreams. Unfortunately, Carolyn never realized that her lack of success stemmed from her low hope. Although she gave Joleen dance classes and even moved to Los Angeles, where her daughter could have the best, she also delivered the negative and defeating self-talk that that would, in time, diminish her daughter's chances of success.

The next story illustrates a mixed hope profile—low waypower and high will-power. As you read this story, notice that, even though this person has goals, his limited ability to think of ways to achieve them minimizes his chances for success.

✳ Low Ways, High Will—Justin

As an assistant manager in a large department store, Justin had attained some success. He enjoyed chatting with customers and employees, and he was known throughout the store as a "good guy." Justin's goal was to become a store manager, perhaps even moving up through the administrative chain in the larger organization. But each time a promotion was announced, it never went to him. In fact, it had been five years since he had been promoted from a sales clerk to an assistant manager.

Justin was frustrated and didn't know how to approach his dilemma. He was loyal to the company, believing that the store offered good merchandise at fair prices, and he was willing to do whatever the manager asked. He thought he had all the qualities of a good employee and couldn't figure out why he was consistently overlooked. Justin decided to discuss the issue with his superior, Robert. He wanted to know if he could plan on advancement, or if he would do better to look for another job. What Robert said surprised him and made him examine other areas of his life.

Robert said that, in his view, Justin was easily frustrated, unable to cope with the problems that arose in his department. He gave as an example the way Justin handled the scheduling of sales clerks. When a clerk called in sick, and Justin wasn't immediately able to locate a replacement, he simply allowed the department to be short staffed. This, of course, caused customers to become annoyed when no one was there to wait on them. Occasionally, Justin would fill in, but this took time away from the paperwork that had to be finished.

Robert also said that Justin had very few ideas about how to improve sales and motivate the clerks. Although Justin's stated goal was to increase sales for his department, when he was asked for suggestions as to how this could happen, time and again he came up short. Justin was a hard worker, as Robert readily acknowledged. He came to work early and stayed late; he even worked through his lunch hour many days. But Robert let Justin know that, while hard work and dedication is important to success, they aren't all that counts.

What Robert had told Justin made him realize that his inability to find routes to his goals didn't affect him only at work. Justin thought of all the times he had set goals, such as building shelves in the basement or creating a rock garden, and then he thought of all the times that he had given up because something went wrong. Justin also realized that this wasn't a new problem for him. He could remember many instances when, as a child, he relied on his parents to solve his problems or to pick up the pieces from his shattered goals. He could still hear his parents telling him not to get upset or worry, that they would handle it.

Justin was beginning to realize that he lacked a component that was essential to realizing his life goals. He was unable to sustain his goal-directed efforts, no matter how good his intentions, because he could think of few paths to take or ways to overcome obstacles when trying to reach his objectives. In trying to keep Justin happy, his parents had not allowed him to find ways to cope with difficulties. As an adult, when problems arose that were not easily solved, Justin was more than ready to tell himself not to worry, that somehow it would all work out.

The next story depicts another mixed hope profile, this time one of low willpower and high waypower. Notice that in this story it is the lack of mental energy, rather than either a paucity of goals or ways to achieve them, that diminishes the protagonist's chances of having the career that she wants.

✳ Low Will, High Ways—Marcie

Ever since Marcie was an adolescent, she had dreamed of being an interior designer. When other girls were reading fashion magazines, she was reading about home decorating. It wasn't that Marcie was exceptionally artistic—in fact, she couldn't draw anything recognizable. Marcie's interest in interior design came from her love of homemaking. She was good at matching colors, fabrics, and wallpaper, and she could always pick the right accessories to decorate a room. She often was asked to advise her friends and family about the style of their homes.

Marcie began college with the intent of majoring in design. During her first year, however, she met a young law student, and they decided to get married. Marcie quit school and took a secretarial job to help support her husband. As soon as he graduated and had a good job, the children started coming—three, in all.

At age thirty-two, Marcie now looks back at her life and wonders what happened to her dreams. Certainly she was busy, and she has enjoyed the things she has done. But, as wonderful as it has been, being a mother and homemaker, Marcie still feels an empty place where her dreams once were.

Now that all of her children are in school, Marcie wonders if it's too late to become an interior designer. What would it take? How difficult would it be? Each morning, after the children are on the school bus and her husband has left for work, Marcie gets out her magazines and studies the ads for design courses. She has called the various colleges and art schools in her city to get information on programs. She has planned how she can fit the coursework into her homemaking and mothering responsibilities. She knows it's possible, and she has it all figured out.

But day after day she doesn't take the necessary first steps toward her goal. Even though she knows which school she can attend and which courses she needs to take, she allows other activities to take up her time. In the afternoons, when she finds herself watching soap operas, she berates herself with negative thoughts. She tells herself that she is lazy, and that she really has no talent after all.

Marcie vaguely remembers that her parents used to criticize her for having such impractical goals. They told her that she was unrealistic to think she could succeed in a design program. They thought it was frivolous, and so, in time, Marcie stopped trying and let the course of events determine her life.

With such critical parents, Marcie may have been uncertain about applying her mental energy to many of the goals she had as a child. We see that, as she became an adult, it was easier to let the needs and desires of others determine her actions than to pursue her own dreams. Eventually, even though she knew exactly how to get the training she needed to become a designer, Marcie found it easier to continue the life she had settled for rather than create a new and exciting career.

In the last story of this chapter, we describe a full high-hope person. This individual has both high willpower and high waypower that, as you saw in the story about the two dancers, this mother communicated to her daughter. As you read this description, you will see that high-hope can flourish even in the face of difficult life experiences.

✳ Full High Hope—Virginia

Growing up in near poverty conditions in a small midwestern town may not seem like an auspicious start for a young girl who wanted to do something interesting with her life. For Virginia, however, personal pride served as a motivator to excel in all that she did.

Virginia was the oldest of three daughters, born to a retired railroad worker and his homemaker wife. Her father had retired early due to an accident that left his right arm paralyzed. Although her mother brought in some money doing sewing and alterations, the family lived on her father's small retirement and disability checks.

The tiny house in which the family lived was always spotless, with flowers growing in the front and vegetables in the back garden. Although the home was sparsely furnished, everything was neat and well cared for. The girls took pride in their appearance also, and were always well groomed. Although they often wore clothes donated by wealthier families that had been altered to fit by their mother, they held their heads high in the knowledge that someday their lives would be better.

Virginia's parents fostered the belief that goals were attainable, and they were neither bitter nor depressed by their economic conditions. They made the best of their situation and encouraged their girls to set and work for goals that would lift them into more rewarding lives. Virginia's mother used to speak of being from pioneer stock. Times were hard in the early days, but their ancestors had survived and prospered by envisioning their dreams and working hard.

Virginia's dream was to become a writer. Her idol was Willa Cather, who was also from a small town in the Midwest. Throughout her childhood, Virginia scribbled poems onto scraps of paper and wrote extensively in a personal journal. By her senior year in high school, she was a rather accomplished writer and was having small pieces published on a regular basis in the local newspaper.

A turning point came when Virginia entered a short story in a statewide high school contest and won first prize. She was awarded a scholarship to the college of her choice as well as public recognition from the famous journalist, William Allen White. But Virginia wanted to write stories, not newspaper articles, and so she chose to go to a college that was out-of-state but recognized for its English program.

The program that Virginia chose was in California, in the same town in which her aunt lived. She would be able to live with her aunt, work part-time, and get her college degree. Virginia was a planner, and she had everything worked out in advance. She also was energetic, and with hard work and determination, she received her degree. After college, however, came the question of how to support herself and still find time to write.

Virginia had made many friends in college, and one of them was a secretary for an influential judge. Not only did Virginia find work in his office, but after a brief courtship she married the judge. Their daughter was born one year later, and Virginia finally felt that her life had settled into the prosperity and security that she'd always wanted. At last she had time to write, which she did until, after four years of marriage, her husband died.

Thrust back into the world of work, Virginia again relied on the influence and advice of friends. This time she was able to work doing what she loved. She obtained a coveted story-analyst position at one of the major film studios, for which she would read and write evaluations of prospective scripts. Her income was excellent, and she was able to give her daughter a good education, including the dance lessons she loved.

Material advantages were not all, or even the most important things, that Virginia gave her daughter. Through her example, she demonstrated that it was possible to achieve even distant goals—those that others might have thought were unrealistic. She set a model for strategizing ways to reach objectives, and she demonstrated consistently high energy and hard work.

When things went wrong, even when tragedy struck, Virginia sought ways to cope rather than retreating into self-pity. She expressed her positive self-talk openly with statements such as "I know I can do this," and encouraged her daughter to do the same. It wasn't easy being a single mother, and there were many barriers to overcome. In part, however, it was through seeing her mother cope successfully with life that Virginia's daughter also became such a high-hope person.

In Virginia's story, we see that having high hope doesn't depend upon wealth or an easy life. If anything, Virginia's hope was strengthened through adversity. As a child born into poverty, she focused her mind on goals that may have seemed unrealistic to others but were encouraged by her high-hope mother. Virginia was taught that she was from strong and adventurous stock, and that she could cope with hardship just as her ancestors had. She was nurtured on a mental diet of positive words, and offered those same messages to her daughter. They have served both women well as they lead productive and fulfilling lives—high-hope lives.

What Hope Messages Do You Send?

We have now come full circle through the possible profiles of hope. Did you recognize yourself in any of the stories? Although your hope story will be unique to you, there may have been characteristics described in the vignettes with which you could identify. All individuals hold in their minds a set of personal messages about their prospects for achieving their goals. These statements become most obvious when people are faced with problems, or when they undertake difficult projects. Here are some examples of statements that fit each of the profiles.

High-Hope Agency Statements

- Yes, I can.

- I can easily get started on a project.

- I don't give up easily.

- Problems make me try even harder.

- I'm full of determination.

- I really go after what I want.
- I'm excited about my future.
- If I'm down, I'll bounce right back up.
- I really look forward to tomorrow.
- I get very psyched up about things I want to happen.
- Sure, I can do it.
- I finish what I start.
- I'll certainly make it.
- I'm going someplace in my life.
- I'm not easily defeated.

High-Hope Pathways Statements

- I can find ways to get what I want.
- There are solutions to my problems.
- I definitely know how to solve problems.
- I'm not concerned about making mistakes.
- I learn something from my mistakes.
- It's very easy for me to come up with ideas about how to get things done.
- I'm good at planning.
- There is usually more than one path to get what I want.
- I see a barrier as a challenge.
- If I'm stuck, I'll find a way out.
- Solutions usually are available to me.
- I break a big goal into small steps.
- I typically can find out how to do something.
- I'm rarely at a loss for options.
- I'm full of strategies for reaching my goals.

Low-Hope Agency Statements

- No, I can't.
- I can't get started on a project.

- I give up easily.

- Problems make me want to quit.

- I lack determination.

- I have trouble going after what I want.

- I'm discouraged about my future.

- If I'm down, I stay that way.

- I don't look forward to tomorrow.

- I can't get psyched up about things I want to happen.

- I don't finish what I start.

- I'll never really make it.

- I'm going nowhere in my life.

- I'm easily defeated.

Low-Hope Pathways Statements

- I can't find a way to get what I want.

- There aren't any solutions to my problems.

- I don't know how to solve problems.

- I'm very concerned about making mistakes.

- I don't learn from my mistakes.

- It's very hard for me to come up with ideas about how to get things done.

- I'm lousy at planning.

- There rarely is more than one path to get what I want.

- I see a barrier as a defeat.

- If I'm stuck, I can't find a way out.

- Solutions usually are aren't available to me.

- I can't seem to break a big goal into small steps.

- I have trouble finding out how to do something.

- I don't seem to have many options.

- I lack strategies to reach my goals.

As you read these typical statements, do you see any that you use? Is the self-talk that you use what you want your children to learn? Through the example you set, you're teaching them how to talk to themselves. Are these messages encouraging? Or, are you inadvertently giving them discouraging messages? You may have decided that your self-talk simply reflects reality. We suggest that, on the contrary, your self-talk determines your *interpretation* of reality. The messages you tell yourself lay a foundation for your perception of whether or not you can find routes to your goals and have the energy to pursue them. These perceptions influence the goals you identify and whether or not you are willing to attempt to actualize your dreams.

In order to identify the messages you are teaching your child, we suggest that you keep a personal record for a few days in which you note your self-talk. For a more comprehensive program that will increase your own hope, we also recommend our book, *Making Hope Happen* (1999). One of the best ways to identify what your children are learning from you is to listen as they attempt a task. Are they repeating your own words back to you? If so, and they are not high-hope messages, it is time to set a new example.

chapter 6

Family Stories: The Roots of Hope

In the last chapter, you measured your own hope and learned that your self-talk can have a powerful influence on your child's hopeful thinking. In order to determine the types of thoughts you may be conveying to your child, we suggested that you keep a record of the self-talk you use for a few days, especially when you're facing a difficult problem or are about to begin a daunting task. You may find yourself using old, well-rehearsed negative messages about your prospects for success. Some examples of such statements were given at the end of chapter 5.

The profiles of hope in chapter 5 were described through various stories. In each story, you could see how one of the possible combinations of willpower and waypower scores appeared in the lives of a particular individual. In this chapter, we will continue to illustrate ideas with stories, but we will focus on the stories that are unique to your family have influenced your, and your child's, hopeful thinking.

One of the best ways for you to explore the messages you learned growing up, as well as the similar ones that you are communicating to your child, is to closely examine your family stories. These tales are the legacies of your family history. And, instead of simply detailing facts, they often convey important messages. These messages, often covert in nature, become incorporated into a sort of "family wisdom" that can set a pattern of negative or positive scripts for future generations. The stories you read in chapter 5 were good examples of this process. Consider the story about Carolyn and her daughter, Joleen, both of whom wanted to be dancers. In spite the fact that her family, decades ago, had succeeded in homesteading in hostile territory, Carolyn had received a negative family attitude that she communicated to Joleen. On the other hand, Virginia's family was filled with hopeful thinkers, even though their lives had been very difficult. This family's high-hope "wisdom" was communicated to Virginia, who then passed it to her daughter, both of whom were able to achieve their dreams. Thus, the ripples of low or high hope touch generation after generation.

In this chapter, we will show how to recognize and examine your family's stories—to discover the roots of your hope, so to speak. Storytelling and writing narratives are extremely effective routes for discovering where one's self-talk originates. Armed with that insight, you then are better prepared to develop and transmit messages filled with high hope. Children and adults both love stories, and by choosing family stories full of hope and emphasizing high-hope messages in each of the stories, you can bolster the legacy of hope in both yourself and your children.

The Benefits of Developing Family Stories

Many children today spend more hours watching television than they do in any other activity, including the time spent in school. While there are many excellent educational and entertaining programs, the fact remains that watching television is a passive and uncreative activity. And with the seductiveness of television, many children don't read books, and fewer still write about their thoughts, feelings, and experiences.

Counselors and therapists have long deplored television, in part, because it has a negative impact on family communication. Let us describe an all-too-typical evening at home. The television is turned on, the family members in attendance are all "tuned into" the screen. Those who don't wish to watch the show that's on the large family television are likely to be in their rooms working or playing on their computers, or fixated on another television set playing video games. Our point is that, all too often, *family members are not attending to, or focusing on, each other*. Through the suggestions we make in this chapter, we aim to increase your family communication and, indeed, to place more of an emphasis on the family than may presently be the case.

Several benefits flow from writing stories about one's family history, in general, and family members' experiences, in particular. Your children and you will get to know each other on a deeper, more personal level. You will discover the high- or low-hope messages that have been handed down through your family history. And most important, this story exchange can become a family project in which you'll be communicating with your children about a topic of shared importance and interest. In addition to these family benefits, the bottom line is that you will be helping your children build their hopeful thinking.

The Storying Strategy

Stories can be told or written. They can be about the family history, the adventures of recent and distant ancestors, or about personal experiences of the storyteller. In our observations of other parents, as well as through our own parenting, we have found that children are truly fascinated in hearing about parents' past experiences. Because you will be using these stories to explore hope, we suggest that you also write them down to make it easier to uncover the hope messages within each.

Telling stories is an activity that can be done by folks of all ages, from very young children to adults and seniors. Writing stories takes somewhat more skill, and may be beyond the ability of some in the family. For elderly family members, who may have more problems with poor vision, a tape recorder can be very handy. If at all possible, try to include the oldest living ancestors in this storytelling project, because it can help show children how familial roots extend back, giving kids a greater sense of continuity and connection with the past. Family histories often are peopled with intriguing individuals. It may well be that one's low- or high-hope family messages have developed because of the thoughts and actions of one key ancestor. Tracing the course of an attitude or belief is enlightening, and knowing where it came from provides greater insight for helping your child to make positive changes in her hopeful thinking.

Stories about your own or your child's personal experiences provide vivid insights into hopeful thinking in the present. In our research program, we have asked children and adolescents to write about the goals they had set, as well as how they solved the problems that arose in reaching those goals. We found that the contents of these stories paralleled the children's scores on the hope scale; moreover, by examining children's stories, we gained insights into what they thought about themselves and their lives. In chapter 7, we will show you how to identify negative and positive self-talk, as well as what we can do to change it. In this chapter, however, we will concentrate on helping you to identify your own family stories.

Where to Find Family Stories

All families tell stories about past events. In our work, we typically have found that family members are truly surprised at the number of such tales. Perhaps you never considered such tales worthy of repeating or as having any value at all. On the contrary, we believe these family stories carry crucial messages for your child. Here is one very brief example. When my mother (McDermott) was about twelve years old, she wrecked her father's horse-drawn wagon. She had been racing a neighbor boy when the wagon turned over and broke into many pieces at the bottom of a steep hill. No one was hurt. Even Nancy Hanks, the horse, came out of the accident unscathed. But my mother was in big trouble. When I was young, I loved to hear that story because I was a tomboy, and my mother's antics were so similar to my own adventures. When you share your stories and the stories of past generations, you are promoting an important link between your child, you, and the past. Through this bond your child is given a place in the family history. Just as importantly, however, the family history carries some crucial messages for how your child will live in the future.

Grandparents are a wonderful source of family stories. Many older people enjoy relating past experiences, and often their memories of these events and their participants are quite clear. The older generation has much to teach children (and us, as parents), and a richly detailed family story conveys a message in a far more interesting way than a lecture ever could. We suggest that you encourage your children to spend time with their grandparents and make storytelling a focus of their interactions. You also may need to tell the grandparents that you not only approve of their telling stories, but that you view these stories as family treasures. For many grandparents, this may come as welcome and surprising feedback, because they may have experienced societal prejudice and criticism for talking about the "old days."

As we have noted previously, your own life experiences also provide good stories for your children. Too often, however, parents use their experiences in contrast with their child's, pointing out how well off the child is compared to the childhood of the parent. "When I was a child, I had to walk two miles to school, and you're complaining about taking the school bus." This is typical of the "poor me–lucky you" type of statement to which most children will pay no attention. If you want your children to learn about your life growing up, it will be important for you to describe your experiences in an interesting way and *avoid the moralizing.*

Another source of family stories are those from the distant past. Many people have cultural roots that are rich with legend, and often these are high-hope tales. For example, African American people may be able to speak of ancestors who survived slavery and flourished afterwards. Individuals whose families immigrated to the United States, whether a long time ago or more recently, have a great heritage of which they can be proud. Native American people also have a compelling history that should be handed on from generation to generation. All of these brave people often suffered great hardships in order to create better lives for their children and grandchildren. The ethnic and racial identity of each of these groups can be celebrated by its children. Whatever your social and ethnic history, however, it's up to you as a parent to help the past come alive in the mind of a child.

The first step in developing family stories is to begin recording them in written form. You may wish to interview the oldest members of your family in order to hear the stories they tell of the past. What a loss if these elders die without telling the family story. In the next chapter, we will examine the high- or low-hope messages that are communicated in the stories you have collected. At this point, however, it is important for you to begin the storytelling process.

Tips for Developing Your Stories

When you get together with your siblings, parents, and grandparents, do you play the "remember when" game? Nearly every family has events in its past that can be turned into interesting stories for children. We often become so caught up in our daily lives that we rarely think about those recollections until another family member stimulates us. To begin your story development, we ask you now to remember some of those events. We also suggest that, at first, you just write down the various aspects of the event and don't worry about correct punctuation and grammar. Here are a few simple ideas that you can use as you document your experiences and those that are part of your family. In making these suggestions, we're focusing particularly on issues that may make such stories interesting to your child.

1. Select an event with some action in it. Children today are used to fast-moving stories, especially those with an element of suspense.

2. Describe the characters in vivid, colorful terms. Be sure you give the ages of the main characters and describe their physical appearances. You also can describe the kinds of clothes they may have worn, their living arrangements, and any other details that may be interesting and relevant to the story line.

3. Describe where the event took place, so that your listener can visualize it. You may wish to use a world atlas or globe to orient your child if the event took place in a far away or unknown location.

4. Describe the event in simple but clear words. Take your child's vocabulary into consideration. If there are words or phrases that typify the characters and times of your story, be sure to include these.

5. In order to maintain you credibility as a storyteller, make sure that the essential details of the story are the same each time you tell it. You may wish to embellish it with greater detail or more vivid descriptions as you become a more experienced narrator. Such embellishments, however, should be based on what you believe to be historically plausible for the times, people, and place you're describing.

6. If your story involves objects or events unfamiliar to your child, be sure you explain what they were. This is likely to happen when you tell stories about your ancestors, especially if these tales take place in another country and the clock is turned back to a previous century.

Here is an example of the first step, which is to remember one incident that you might like to make into a story. The narrator of this story is a middle-aged man thinking back to his childhood.

Incident: When my sister was six years old, she got frightened on Halloween by a neighbor who was dressed like Frankenstein's monster. She hit him with her toy broom.

This event has the potential to become a story that would appeal to children because it's rather unusual, and it involves the actions of a child. Let's see how it looks with more description and detail, following the guidelines for developing a story.

✳ My Sister, the Witch

There was one family on our block that went all out on Halloween, both in their decorations and in the amount of candy they handed out. Of course, they had a head start on scariness. Their house, being a large, yellow-brick Victorian complete with turrets and wrought iron fence, already looked as if it might be haunted. On Halloween, according to neighborhood kid gossip, the man who lived there turned into a monster. If you were brave enough to come to his front door, he gave you a dozen candy bars, but then you had to run fast to escape.

Every year my little sister wanted to trick-or-treat at that scary house, but at the last minute she was always too afraid. She had seen the delicious candy I had gotten "from the monster," and wanted to be brave enough to get some, too. That year, because she was six years old and had started first grade, she thought she was finally big enough to give it a try.

Mother made her a wonderful witch costume. She had a black dress and cape, a black peaked cap, and she even had green hair made out of yarn. To complete the outfit, she had a child-sized broom, which she carried along with her candy sack.

On Halloween, my sister went trick-or-treating accompanied by my mother. I was off with my buddies and didn't want a little sister tagging along, but my mother has told the story so many times, that I feel like I was there.

The night was especially dark, because the moon was tucked behind clouds. Although there were streetlights, it had been raining, so there was a slight misty halo around each one, lending an eerie cast to the neighborhood. As my mother and sister approached the frightening house, they could hear moans and screams coming from inside. There were cobwebs on the iron fence and a greenish light coming from the open front door.

No one seemed to be in sight, and my sister almost turned back. At my mother's prompting, however, my sister summoned her courage and went up to the door. To her surprise, an ordinary looking man who was dressed in a silk bathrobe greeted her at the door. He invited her into the foyer, telling her to wait just a bit while he found some candy. He turned his back to her while reaching into a large trunk, supposedly to get the candy bars. But when he turned back toward my sister again, his face had changed into that of Frankenstein's monster, complete with suture marks and electrodes embedded in his head.

My sister was terrified. He growled ferociously, and she screamed. She swung her toy broom with all the strength she could muster, hitting him hard across the face. He went down on one knee, and my sister took that opportunity to run—but not before picking up the candy bars he had dropped. My mother said that as my sister ran out the door, she heard him yelling, "Come back here, you little witch!"

Notice the way the story guidelines are used in this vignette. Although the narrator doesn't discuss himself, his sister and the "monster" are well described. The scene is set with a description of the night and the house, and suspense is heightened as his sister walks into the foyer. The action comes at the end of the story, when his sister hits the monster with her broom, grabs the candy bars, and runs away.

Some very good stories come from the family heritage, but it takes some creativity to make them interesting to children. Here is an event from the past that can be elaborated upon to make a good tale.

Event: Your great grandmother came from Ireland because the poverty and hardship there left few opportunities for a young woman. She came alone to the United States in search of a better life.

Although this is a common scenario for Irish Americans, and similar stories have filled whole books, its uniqueness for a given family is important for the child to whom it is told. By casting events with one's ancestors as the primary actors, children can understand their own roots of hopeful thinking.

❋ Eileen—A Story of Hope and Courage

The year of 1918 in County Kildare was a time of trouble. The world had been at war, and Ireland had its own problems in the fight between the north and the south. There was high unemployment and the earth refused to yield the crops that would feed the people. Young men and women saw such dark futures that courtship, let alone festive dancing and singing, seemed a thing of the past.

Sixteen-year-old Eileen was small, with fair skin, black hair, and bright blue eyes. Pretty as she was, she faced a future taking care of her aging parents and never getting to experience the pleasure of having her own family. For some period of time she considered becoming a nun. But she felt such a spark inside her that eventually she decided she wanted to experience as much of the world as she could.

Many of the young men she knew were setting sail for America, the land where dreams supposedly came true. None of the girls, however, would even consider such a dangerous plan—unless they had a husband waiting for them! Eileen had no one waiting for her. For that matter, there was no one even encouraging her to go. Her parents were against her leaving, her friends were against it, and even her parish priest voiced strong opposition to the idea.

Eileen had a stubborn streak, however, and she believed that she could handle whatever happened. She had courage that some said was foolishness, but she was determined not to live out her life in a dreary existence. Eventually, her parents agreed that there was little for a young person in Ireland, and that perhaps America would offer her more chances for happiness.

Eileen had very little money, and what she did have she wanted to leave for her parents. She decided that she would need to work her way to America, perhaps as a cook or maid aboard one of the steamers that came to Dun Laoghaire on the journey to the United States from England.

Obtaining a job, and thus passage to America, proved to be easy enough. Irish girls had a reputation for being obedient and willing to work extremely hard, and so Eileen soon found herself crammed into a tiny cabin with eight other girls. It was as if she were in a sardine can with these eight other "little fishies" who were on their way to the land of their dreams.

Eileen's first sight of the Statue of Liberty sent chills through her, shivers of fear, joy, and anticipation. Her experience on Ellis Island, however, quickly revealed the stark reality that America wasn't going to be an easy place to live. The immigration authorities were cold and pushed her around physically. They exuded a dislike for Irish immigrants, calling them "Paddy," "potato eaters," and much worse. When she finally boarded the ferry for Manhattan, Eileen thought the worst was over, but she was sadly mistaken.

After renting a tiny room in a cheap boarding house in the Irish section of the city, Eileen set about finding a job. She could cook, clean, and care for children, but everywhere she went she encountered the same phrase, "No Irish need apply." Apparently, Irish girls' reputation for hard work hadn't spread as far as New York. Saddened and distraught, Eileen went to the church near her rooming house to seek help. There she encountered a priest who embodied all of the warmth and love that reminded her of family and friends in Ireland.

Father William was from Ireland himself, and he had seen many young men and women in Eileen's situation. He was the best person she possibly could have found to help with her problems. Father Bill, as his parishioners called him, knew the Irish community well and had connections with many influential people. He worked extensively with Catholic organizations, including a charity hospital. He suggested that Eileen expand her skills to caring for the sick, and he said that he knew just the place for her to find work.

In those days, the nursing profession was still new, and most often hospitals were staffed by untrained, but good-hearted, women. The pay was low, but it was enough for Eileen to pay her rent and eat. Besides, she reasoned, she would be receiving valuable training in the healing arts.

Eileen learned her new job very quickly, and before long she had made herself a valued employee. The hospital was understaffed and filled with patients, so she worked long hours and often slept on a cot in the hallway rather than wasting the time it took to get back to her room. On one such occasion, she awoke to find a young doctor looking down at her with concern in his eyes. After he realized that she wasn't ill, only very dedicated, he asked her to go to breakfast with him.

Eileen's story had a happy ending. She married the doctor and continued her nursing job until their first child was born. After eight years, she was able to pay for her parents move from Ireland to the United States. She also did the same for a number of cousins, nieces, and nephews. Eileen never forgot the kindness of Father Bill. Without him, her life would have taken a very different route. But whatever road she may have taken could have led her to success. Eileen was a woman of hope, determined to make her dreams come true.

Eileen's story shows how one individual in the stream of a family history can be vividly described for the children of today. Her story is an excellent example of high hope. Her goal was to experience a life with far more opportunities than were available in Ireland at that troubled time, and she was inventive in devising plans to fulfill her dreams. Eileen was also a hard worker, focusing her mental and physical energy on the ways that would lead to the achievement of her goal.

When you create a story from your family history, you will need to learn about the time period and the place in which the story took place. If your child is old enough to understand what you are doing, this detective work can be an interesting activity that the two of you can share. The great granddaughter who heard the story of Eileen, for example, was fascinated with the details of the story and set about learning more about Ireland—the land of her ancestors.

Both of the stories in this chapter so far are about high-hope people. If your hope level and that of your child are low, however, it is likely that many of your family stories don't reflect high hope. The following story with a low-hope theme portrays a grim picture of struggle and hardship. Unfortunately, this story line cast its shadow on generation after generation.

✳ Fred—A Life of Disappointment

There were so many setbacks and so many regrets. Fred felt that very little in his life had turned out the way he'd wanted it to. To begin, his dream career had been halted just as it was beginning. As far back as Fred could remember, he had wanted to be a soldier. So, when the United States got into the Spanish-American War, Fred dreamed of riding to fame and glory as a dashing cavalryman. At sixteen, Fred ran away from home and joined the cavalry. He was an excellent rider, and because of his skill he was sent to Texas to train to be a Rough Rider under the leadership of Teddy Roosevelt, who later led the famous charge up San Juan Hill. Unfortunately for Fred, however, he became ill with malaria and had to spend many months in the hospital. When he had recovered sufficiently to go back on active duty, he was no longer eligible to fight in any battles. Instead, he was sent to be a guard at Ft. Leavenworth, in Kansas. A prison guard! This was a far cry from the excitement he envisioned as a dashing soldier riding on a strong horse.

Young Fred cut a handsome figure in his uniform, however. With his blond hair and blue eyes, he attracted the attentions of many a young woman. Indeed, he met a pretty schoolteacher named Jenny, and before long, they were married. When Fred's service commitment was over, he decided to try his luck staking a homestead in the Oklahoma Territory. Despite the fact that they already had one child and another on the way, Fred and Jenny set out for the "Wild West" with all their possessions loaded into a horse and wagon.

The Oklahoma Territory was a dry expanse of land where red grit constantly got into their hair, eyes, and mouth. Streams were few and far between, and few trees broke the flat landscape. They staked out their land and began to plant the crops that would be their livelihood. Unfortunately, Fred wasn't much of a farmer. He planted his wheat too late in the year, and his crop never developed the large golden heads that could be harvested.

In addition to Fred's other problems, it turned out that Jenny really hated Oklahoma. She longed for the green, rolling hills of eastern Kansas where the rest of her family still lived. During their second year in Oklahoma, Fred capitulated to Jenny's wishes, and the small family loaded their possessions into a wagon and moved back to Kansas.

Fred never found a job that he really enjoyed. Instead, he spent his days as a handyman, doing odd jobs for the other townspeople. He built his family a two-room frame house on some acreage at the edge of town. They lived there until Jenny inherited a larger home from an aunt who had died. The family survived on the small amount of money that Fred took in through his handyman labors. Jenny pitched in by gardening and raising chickens.

None of the family remembers Fred as being a happy man. He usually wore a scowl on his face and walked with a stoop. He spoke crossly to his children and criticized them for the smallest offense. Jenny turned to religion for comfort and stayed out of Fred's way. Her children remember her as being quiet yet kind and patient. Perhaps that is why, even though they were influenced by Fred's low-hope thoughts, they didn't completely give in to low-hope thinking. Fred and Jenny's children went on to lead moderately successful lives, but they carried with them a persistent sense of disappointment—a melancholy that spread over all of their relationships.

Stories such as that of Fred and Jenny are frequently found in families whose forebears settled the United States. Such stories frequently were filled with low hope because the times were hard, both physically and economically. The point we wish to make here is that the low hope of one person—the would-be dashing solider who turned into the scowling Fred—can seep through layers of generations, perhaps settling in what you and your children may experience today.

If we were to put Fred's mental orientation into words, he would probably utter such statements as, "Don't expect too much out of life" or, "Life is hard, and then you die." If this story is told through the generations in order to point out how difficult and disappointing life can be, it will strengthen the low hope that already exists within the family. On the other hand, even a story as depressing as this one can be told to make a high-hope point. In the next chapter, we will show you how to change potentially low-hope messages into stories illustrating the power of high hope.

Stories of Cultural Roots

The United States is fortunate to have many ethnicities and races. The stories you have read so far have been about people who are members of the Caucasian culture. If your family is part of another racial group, you may have a different but excellent source of stories to share with your children. We suggest that all children should learn about their cultural and ethnic roots. This is an important part of forming a strong and healthy identity—a hopeful one.

The following story, as told to a granddaughter, illustrates both the humor and pathos found in this family's history. It also shows the stoicism and determination that is found in much of Native American culture.

✳ Jim Returns from Boarding School

When your grandfather Jim was a little boy, the government took children away from their families and sent them to live at boarding schools. They don't do that now, of course, but at that time White folks didn't understand the customs of Indian people, and they believed that we should not teach our language or our customs to our children. So, as soon as children were old enough to go to school, they were sent away from their homes to boarding schools to be taught how to blend into the White culture.

The boarding school where your grandfather was sent was a long way from his parents' home—so far, in fact, that he could only visit them two or three times a year. Each time he went home, he longed to stay and be a member of his community. The law, however, dictated that he must remain at the boarding school until he was sixteen years old. But, instead of turning your grandfather into a White man, being taken from his family made him even more determined to return to his tribe and help them fight those unfair laws.

Finally, the day came when he could return home and stay. He hadn't been home to his tribe for six months, and because letter writing was prohibited, he hadn't even been in contact with his family since then. When the bus let him off at the place where his home used to be, he found only an empty piece of ground. There was no wooden house, no animals, nothing. Only the familiar trees and bushes remained. Where had his family gone?

The reservation was huge, and his family could have moved many

Jim

miles away. Your grandfather decided to sit on a rock outcropping and wait. He saw no point in walking somewhere, because he didn't know what direction to take. And so he simply sat quietly, enjoying the birds and small animals that had taken over the area and waiting until someone came along.

He waited for two days. He got hungry and cold, of course, but he wrapped himself in a blanket he had brought from the school. To blot out the hunger pangs in his stomach, he concentrated on the stars at night and the clouds in the day. On the afternoon of the second day, Jim's father came looking for him. "We knew you must be here," his father said, "because all the other young people have come home."

"I knew you would come to find me," Jim said, "but why did you move the house?"

Jim's father, your great grandfather, explained that everyone decided to move closer together so that they could share their resources more easily. He also said that the tribal council was becoming more active and wanted everyone to have a say in their decisions. Jim was pleased to hear this and, as you know, he eventually become the chairman of the council and made some important changes for the tribe.

There are several important cultural and historical aspects to this story. It's a fact that young Indian children were taken from their homes and sent to boarding school, yet this detail is related without rancor. Similarly, the other facts of infrequent visits home and the prohibition on letter writing are important for children to know in order for them to understand the conditions in which their people lived.

When Jim found his home was missing, his reaction was one of stoic acceptance and patience. His attitude is in contrast with the dominant culture that values taking action no matter what. Appreciation and respect for nature, another cultural value, is shown when Jim watches the animals, stars, and clouds. The child to whom this story was told had her culture reinforced, as well as having an excellent model in her Grandfather Jim. In a low-hope family, this tale could be seen as signifying the terrible things that happen to Indian people; moreover, the story could be used as a reason to remain mired in debilitating self-pity. In this high-hope family, however, it simply was considered humorous that Jim found the family house "missing."

Try Your Hand at Creating Your Story

Now that you've read a number of stories written about real people and events, it's your turn to write a story. Perhaps you've never tried to write a story, nor ever considered that you could. We firmly believe that everyone has stories to tell, and we have been treated to some remarkable and interesting ones created by the children and adults in our hope research groups. Earlier in this chapter, we provided some guidelines on story writing. Here are some additional steps to help you, followed by a worksheet with which you can create your first story. We urge you to include your children in this project. They, and you, will gain something very valuable from this activity.

1. Think of an incident or a family tale that you know. Write out the bare details of the story. If you cannot think of such a story, ask other family members if they can share any tales.

2. Write the incident as the first step on the worksheet. Don't worry about your grammar or punctuation. No one is going to criticize your work—this is for your child and you.

3. Briefly describe the people involved in the story. If you don't actually know what they looked like, you can use literary license and make a good guess about their appearances.

4. Jot down the time the event took place, as well as its location. As we stated earlier in the chapter, you may need to do a little research to flesh out these points. Use an encyclopedia, if you have one, or you can ask for the help of a reference librarian. Should you have access to a computer that is connected to the Internet, learn how to use a search engine (if you don't already know this skill) to find out more and more about a topic. The Internet can literally connect you with a "world" of information to help in your detective work.

5. If you first produce an outline, you probably will find that the story is easier to write than you might have imagined. Here is an outline of the story in this chapter about Grandfather Jim:

    (a) Set the scene—laws governing Indian children
    (b) Jim is sent to boarding school
    (c) Effect on Jim of home visits and school
    (d) Jim returns, finds house gone
    (e) Jim's reaction to missing house
    (f) Cultural lesson and outcome

6. Now you are ready to write your story. Follow the outline you have made and elaborate on each point. When you have finished, you will have your first story.

In the next chapter, we will teach you how to identify high- and low-hope messages in the family stories that you have written. You also will learn to help your child write stories, and then you can examine these tales to deduce their messages. We conclude the next chapter with suggestions for changing any negative, low-hope messages into ones that encourage high-hope thinking. You already are on the track of instilling hope in your kids (and yourself), so stick with us as we continue to share our hope lessons.

Story Worksheet

1. Incident:

2. Description of the people involved:

3. Description of the time and place:

4. Outline of story:

5. Story:

chapter 7

Once Upon a Time: Using Stories to Create Positive Messages

In the last chapter, we focused on stories that came from your family history. You learned that these stories often convey the low or high hope that travels form one generation to the next. You saw that hope is learned, and that a crucial arena for the instruction of hope is the family. Your attitude about goals, roadblocks, and your eventual success or failure is demonstrated through the statements you make to yourself, and much of this self-talk originates in the messages given to you by your family.

Now, you've started writing the stories you learned from your family. Some of these stories may be historical, such as those Fred, Jenny, and Eileen described in chapter 6. Some of your stories may be current, that is, about you or your immediate family. But in each of these stories, a message is conveyed about hope. In this chapter, you will learn to identify those messages as well as how to reframe the low-hope content into high-hope themes.

Although your child was peripherally involved in the assignments of the previous chapter, he or she will need to be an active participant in this chapter. You and your child will be developing stories and searching for the hope messages contained in them. Together, you will learn to spot and change low-hope self-talk.

Identifying Your Family Hope Messages

If you have completed the story-writing assignment in the last chapter, you are ready to begin your analyses of the generational hope messages embedded within it. Let's begin this process with a brief story that may be similar to the one that you've written. This story is about an important event in a father's childhood, one that he has often told to his children. As you read this story, pay attention to the words and phrases that have been underlined. These convey either low or high hope to the reader or listener. At the end of the vignette, we will list the high- and low-hope words that have been underlined and show you how they can influence the tone—positive or negative—conveyed in the story. These words and phrases are the carriers of hope.

✳ Ben—A Problem Reader

Reading was very important in Ben's family. His father read the Torah every day, and Ben, at eight years old, was expected to attend Hebrew school once a week. He was <u>having enough trouble learning</u> to read *Dick and Jane* books in English, so that learning to read the prayers in Hebrew <u>seemed quite impossible</u>. <u>Ben was so frustrated</u>. How was he to get it straight? In English, the words go from left to right; in Hebrew, they go from right to left. In English there are vowels right in the words, and in Hebrew these vowels are separate. <u>To make matters worse, he never could remember</u> what sounds went with the different letters—letters that all looked alike to Ben.

Clearly, <u>Ben was not doing well</u>. Therefore, his father spoke to the Rabbi about what could be done, and Ben was brought to him for a lecture.

"You have to try harder," the Rabbi said, "or <u>you will never learn</u> the laws or the prayers."

Ben explained that even reading the English words <u>was extremely difficult</u> for him, and that the other children in his class could read aloud with no problem. At that point, Ben's father began to wonder if Ben might have a physical problem that hadn't been detected. He knew that <u>Ben felt like a failure</u>, yet <u>he knew his son was intelligent and could have a successful life</u>—if they could figure out what was wrong.

Let's leave Ben's story for a moment to examine the messages underlined. With the exception of the last observation, that Ben was intelligent and could have a successful life, the other words and phrases are all oozing with low hope. If the story ended there, and if it were told by Ben to his children, it would pass on a gloomy message about the negative effects of what was later determined to be dyslexia. Fortunately, the story doesn't have to end at that point. Let's explore the words and phrases in the conclusion to this story to understand how Ben was able to think hopefully in order to cope with his learning disability.

In the late 1960s, little was known about learning disabilities. The term "dyslexia" was just beginning to work its way into the language of educators, and it certainly wasn't familiar to most people. When Ben's father took him to see the family doctor, their physician referred them to a learning specialist. At this point, <u>they were concerned and yet relieved</u> that perhaps something could be done to help Ben.

Ben was told by Dr. Glass, the learning specialist, that he had a condition known as dyslexia, which meant that he had trouble seeing words as they were written. Indeed, people with dyslexia reverse many words and letters. Dr. Glass also told Ben that, because of this problem, he was having a <u>hard time</u> remembering how words sounded and that reading aloud in class would be very <u>difficult for him</u>. What Ben remembered most from his first visit to Dr. Glass, however, was that there was a new treatment that seemed to be effective. If Ben practiced the exercises he was given, <u>he could learn to read</u>.

More than anything else, Ben <u>wanted to read more easily</u>. <u>He knew he was smart</u>, but he also <u>knew he had a problem</u>. He was <u>willing to work as hard as it would take</u> to overcome his disability. The method he was to practice involved making letters in sand and tracing letters with his fingers on sandpaper. This seemed strange, but if there was a chance that it could work, <u>Ben was going to give it his all</u>.

Ben's treatment required that he had to practice making his letters for several hours each day. At first he was tempted to cut his practice short so he could go outside and play with his friends. With his mother's prompting, however, as well as <u>his determination to succeed</u>, he decided to give up some of the fun stuff he was used to doing with his pals. He continued working at the treatment, and <u>it paid off</u>. After several months of hard work, Ben began to notice that he could recognize and remember the letters that had been really

Ben

difficult for him—"p," "b," and especially "q." In addition, words that he used to reverse, like "saw" and "was," <u>he began to read</u> correctly.

   <u>Ben and his parents were pleased</u> with his progress, and they knew <u>he had worked hard to succeed.</u> <u>The only disappointment</u> came when Dr. Glass told them <u>not to expect</u> Ben to be able to learn Hebrew in addition to English. He could, however, memorize the prayers and rules in Hebrew, even if he couldn't learn to read them. Ben and his parents <u>were satisfied with this,</u> and Ben <u>proved to be an excellent auditory learner</u>. Even though Ben would have liked to learn Hebrew, he knew that <u>he already had accomplished a big goal</u>, and <u>he was very proud of himself.</u>

   In the second part of the story you can see that there are many more positive statements. Had Ben's father not believed that his son was intelligent and sought expert advice, Ben's life would have turned out differently. He may well have slipped into pervasive feelings of failure and inadequacy that are often driven by low-hope thinking. Ben can tell his children this story and know that he is living proof of what high hope can accomplish.

   To help you understand the low- and high-hope statements that have been underlined in each segment of Ben's story, examine the following list in which each statement is placed in either a low- or high- category.

First Story Segment

Low-Hope Statements	High-Hope Statements
• having enough trouble learning	
• seemed quite impossible	
• Ben was so frustrated	
• to make matters worse	
• he could never remember	
• Ben was not doing well	• Ben wanted to read more easily (goal statement)
• you will never learn	
• was extremely difficult	• his son was intelligent (will)
• Ben felt like a failure	• could have a successful life (will)

Second Story Segment

Low-Hope Statements	**High-Hope Statements**
• they were concerned	• yet relieved (will)
• caused him to have a hard time	
• difficult for him	
	• he could learn to read (will)
	• he knew he was smart (will)
• knew he had a problem	
	• willing to work as hard as it would take (will)
	• was going to give it his all (will)
	• determination to succeed (will)
	• it paid off (will)
	• Ben and his parents were pleased (will)
	• he had worked hard to succeed (will)
• the only disappointment	
• not to expect	
	• were satisfied with this (will)
	• Ben proved to be an excellent auditory learner (will)
	• he already had accomplished a big goal (will)
	• he was proud of himself (will)

Notice that we have identified each positive statement as willpower or a goal (in Ben's case, he had no high-waypower statements). Keeping the elements of hope in mind will help you to recognize and pick the high-hope statements. Low-hope statements will be those that indicate a poor view of self and a lack of belief in either the ability to find ways to reach the goal (waypower thinking) or the ability to begin and continue one's effort.

Having seen one example of how to identify low- and high-hope words and phrases, you should be ready to go over your story, highlighting the low-hope words and phrases with one color of marker and the high-hope ones with a different color. When you've finished, see which color predominates. If you have used a yellow marker for high hope, and your pages are mainly yellow, then your story probably reflects goal setting, problem solving, and hard work. These would be aspects of high hope.

If, on the other hand, you marked the low-hope statements in blue, and this color predominates, it's likely that your story has a more negative tone. Perhaps your character failed to achieve the goal, was unable to solve problems, and generally felt bad about the situation.

Even though you have highlighted the words and phrases in your story, it's important to list them as either low or high hope, just as we have done in the previous example. Later in the chapter, we'll show you how to rephrase your messages, and you will need to refer back to these statements. Use the worksheet on this page for your entries.

Hope Category Worksheet

Low-Hope Statements   **High-Hope Statements**

Assuming that you have an idea of the types of words and phrases you habitually use, you can tell whether you, as a parent, tend toward low or high hope. At this point, we ask that you put several of your assignments together to help you understand how your self-talk is influenced by the stories you have heard in the past. In chapter 5, we asked you to keep track of the kinds of statements you make to yourself when you are beginning a difficult project. In chapter 6, you wrote one or more family stories. In this chapter, you took one of your stories and highlighted the low- or high-hope messages that emerged. To give you a glimpse of where we're going, at the end of this chapter you will learn how to turn those messages into ones that communicate hopeful thinking.

As you examine the different statements you've identified, you should notice that a general pattern is emerging. There will be a positive relationship between your self-talk when you're engaging in a difficult task and the messages you highlighted in your story. Likewise, there is often, although not always, a relationship between the general tone, positive or negative, of both family stories and personal ones. We have found that, because hope is learned, it often is communicated via the tales that are told from one generation to the next. Before we discuss how to change the negative messages, we want to focus on your child and his or her stories. After you have identified the negative or positive messages your child is using, we will show you how to enhance hopeful thinking for both of you.

Engaging Your Child in Story Writing

Depending upon the age of your child, writing stories can be an easy or a quite challenging project. Very young children often have active imaginations but not the skills to formulate narratives. Older children and adolescents, on the other hand, often have the ability to create stories but may lack the motivation to do so. Let's tackle one age group at a time.

Young Children's Stories

Young children tell tales all the time. Researchers think that children as young as two years old are capable of telling stories about themselves. Clearly, although children that young cannot understand the items on the hope scale, you nevertheless can record some of their tales so as to get a sense of their level of hopeful thinking. Children like to talk about real and imaginary friends, about pretend adventures, and about the things they've done and want to do. All of their stories have value, and we encourage you to listen to them as much as possible. Remember that good communication starts with your being an attentive listener to your child's thoughts and feelings. In fact, based on our cumulative sixty years of clinical experience in helping children, we believe that listening carefully to your child is one of the best parental insurance policies that you can use to help your child with future problems.

Even though children seemingly talk almost endlessly about many things, their stories about their future activities are the most important ones for the purposes of enhancing hope. Here are nine tips to help you get started.

1. Unless you have a very precocious young child, he probably doesn't write yet. Get a good, easily operated tape recorder. Let your child play with it, recording his or her voice until the novelty (and giggling) wears off. You want your child to be very natural and comfortable in recording themselves.

2. Select a quiet and private place to have your child record their story. Try to eliminate possible interruptions and definitely make sure that hand-held games, as well as television and telephones, are out of sight and earshot.

3. To get started, ask your child a few open-ended questions. Open-ended questions are those that cannot easily be answered with a crisp "yes" or "no." Here are some suggestions.
    *   "Tell me about what you did today."
    *   "What kinds of things would you like to be able to do?"
    *   "What new thing would you like to learn?"
    *   "What do you want to do when you grow up?"
    *   "Tell me about something that you had a hard time doing, but that you managed to do."
    *   "What were some of the problems you ran into?"

4. Once your child is talking, try not to ask too many questions. Instead, use minimally encouraging responses. These are very brief utterances such as "uh huh," "yes," or "tell me more."

5. You also can try clarifying responses, especially if there is something you don't understand. By using clarifying responses, you're feeding back to the child what she has said, sometimes in your words, but often in the words that she has used. This response allows you to be certain that you really have understood what your child said and shows your child that you have been paying attention.

6   You may wish to direct the story back to the original topic if your child loses their train of thought, or if he begins to focus too much on someone other than himself.

7. Notice that the suggested questions are geared toward having the child tell about goals, accomplishments, difficulties, and dreams. All of these are the material in which the elements of hope are to be found. You will

probably have to go through this question-and-answer process a few times before your child begins to formulate stories. You will get better at asking the right questions and, in turn, your child will get more precise about answering them.

8. Once your child has told several stories, spend some time transcribing them. We have found that a written transcript makes it easier to identify words and phrases that are indicative of low or high hope.

9. Highlight both the low- and high-hope phrases in your child's stroy as you did with your own stories.

Children who can write fluently may not need the tape recorder, but they may still choose to use one. Frequently children become so concerned with the handwriting style, spelling, and grammar that they find it difficult to be spontaneous. Using the tape recorder is helpful in the storytelling process because it can help free the child to focus solely on the story. In our research, however, we have found that children in the sixth grade and higher have had no trouble writing brief narratives about problems that they had solved.

If your child is in the fifth grade or middle school, you can use the same questions as you would for young children. Be sure to listen carefully, don't interrupt, and avoid making negative and judgmental comments about what you're hearing. Remember that the purpose of these stories is to enhance your child's hope. The best way you can learn what she is thinking is to be open and accepting of what you hear. Before we proceed to adolescent story writing, here is an example of a child and her mother developing the child's story.

Lisa is a very self-confident and popular eight-year-old who is in the third grade. Although her family is a large and active one, she and her mother have found a quiet place at the desk in Lisa's room to work on Lisa's story. They have told the other children in the family that they are going to be busy for a while and don't wish to be disturbed.

Mother: Because this is going to be a written story, and I know you are just learning to write, do you want to tape record it at first, or try to write it yourself?

Lisa: I think I would like to try the tape recorder. What should I tell about?

Mother: Well, what's the most important thing you have tried to learn to do recently, either at home or at school?

Lisa: Hum, I'm not sure what you mean. Like, what was something that was hard for me?

Mother: That would work. Tell me about that.

Lisa:	There is this girl at school, and she was pretty mean to everyone. No one liked her. She is really big and the boys tease her a lot.
Mother:	How is that related to something that was hard for you. It sounds like a story about her.
Lisa:	Because I sort of felt sorry for her. I have a lot of friends and I thought that maybe I could make her nicer, if I got to know her a little.
Mother:	That's a really kind thing to do. How did you plan to go about it?
Lisa:	I thought the first thing I would do was stand next to her in the lunch line and start talking to her. But I told my friends what I was going to do—you know, about trying to get her not to be so mean.
Mother:	And what happened when you did that?
Lisa:	My friends thought I was crazy. They didn't want me to talk to her. But I did it anyway. I'm not afraid they'll stop liking me
Mother:	What was she like? What did she do?
Lisa:	She was pretty surprised that I talked to her, but we just talked about the book we're reading in class. Actually she seemed pretty smart.
Mother:	What else did you try in your effort to make her less mean?
Lisa:	Out at recess, I asked her to play tetherball with us. My friends got a little mad, but she turned out to be really good at it. After a while, they forgot about being mad and tried to beat her. But no one could.
Mother:	Did you try anything else?
Lisa:	When I got to be captain of the kickball team, I picked her first. A few kids didn't like it, but she turned out to be good at that, too. I guess because she's big. You know, I think my plan is going to work.
Mother:	How are things with her now? Does she still seem mean?
Lisa:	She is a lot nicer to my friends and me, but she still hates the boys. I guess that's okay. Sometimes I hate the way they act, too.
Mother:	It sounds like you accomplished your goal.
Lisa:	I did, and we're all happier now. Without all that meanness, she seems happier, and I feel pretty good about it.

In this story, we can see high-hope thinking in action. Lisa has a goal, to help another girl become nicer, and she tries different ways to accomplish it. A low-hope child might have been put off or stopped by her friends' displeasure, but Lisa followed through with her ideas. It took courage and energy to accomplish her goal, but she was willing to expend the effort—and it worked.

Notice that the mother mostly used open-ended questions, and she was able to redirect the story to focus on Lisa's goal, rather than the mean child. The mother's comments were positive, both about what Lisa wanted to accomplish and in pointing out that she was successful. Lisa is a high-hope child, and so her positive statements are easy to discern.

In this next dialogue, the child's messages are more negative. We ask that you try your hand at identifying the low- and high-hope statements by underlining in pencil as you read. Check at the end of the chapter to see how many words and phrases you identified and how well you did in correctly categorizing them as low- or high-hope statements.

> Sean is in the fourth grade, and he probably is the smallest kid in his class. His whole family is small, but that doesn't mke him feel any better about it. He wants to do everything the bigger boys can do—especially play basketball. Actually, Sean has some skills that would make him a valuable player, if he had more confidence. He can make baskets from a long distance if no one is in his way, and he moves around the court like lightning.
>
> Sean's father is working with him on the story. They are the only ones at home, and so they have the quiet house all to themselves. Although Sean can write, they have decided to use a tape recorder.

Father:	Tell me what you want to do most, Sean.
Sean:	I want to be able to play basketball on the junior high school team, but I know they'll never let me.
Father:	Because you're small?
Sean:	They just won't give me a chance. But I know I can score more points than a lot of the other kids, and I really am fast.
Father:	What have you thought about doing so that you can play on the team?
Sean:	Well, I talked to Mr. Rollins; you know, our gym teacher? He said I would have to grow about a foot in the next year. So, no way I can do that.
Father:	Are there some other things besides basketball that would be as much fun for you?
Sean:	No way! If I can't play basketball then I'm not going go out for any sport.
Father:	You know, everyone tells you how fast you are. How about trying track—maybe sprinting?

Sean: I'm just too short to do anything well. Might as well just sit on the bench.

Sean is demonstrating low hope through his inability to consider options or new goals. High-hope people are able to change their targets when they realize their first goal is unattainable. Furthermore, even though it's likely that Sean won't ever be tall, he has allowed the gym teacher's answer to block any further efforts he might make to play basketball. After all, he does have at least two important basketball assets—he's very fast and can shoot baskets. He just might find a niche on the junior high school team, but his low-hope manner of thinking undermines his chances.

After recording the dialogues in the two examples, either the parent or the child can transcribe the story using the child's description of the event. It is important to use the child's exact words. For example, in the previous dialogue, Sean expressed low hope when he said, "No way I can do that." On the other hand, Lisa expressed high hope when she said, "I think this plan is going to work."

These two conversations were with young children who were not able to compose and write their own stories. They chose to use a tape recorder that allowed the parents to transcribe their statements into story forms. In the next section, we explore story writing with adolescents.

Adolescents' Stories

By this point, you will have engaged your teen in the process of discovering and enhancing her level of hope. In chapters 1 and 2, we discussed the resistance that sometimes is encountered when parents ask adolescents to participate in family activities. Unlike writing stories with younger children, this assignment is an activity that can be done by your teenager without your assistance. If you're going to use the stories for hope enhancement, however, they can't be private, such as a journal or a diary would be.

Here are the directions that we use in our research with adolescents and adults when we ask them to write about themselves. We usually don't refer to this task as writing a "story," because that sounds complicated and imposing. Instead, we give them the following instructions.

Write about a goal you have set for yourself recently. What were the ways, if any, that you thought of trying to use to reach your goal? What problems did you encounter? What did you do about those problems? How did you feel and what did you think while you were working for your goal? What was the outcome?

Young people usually write two or three pages about a wide variety of things. When we review their stories for indicators of hope, we look for the goals they discuss, the number of ways they think of to reach them, and how they handle the problems they encounter. We are also interested in the words they use to describe their actions and outcomes. Are they positive words? Or do they indicate negative thoughts?

This story is typical of the ones written by high school students. Based on the story, the writer appears to have moderately high hope, although she could benefit from increasing her hopeful thinking even further.

✳ Consuela—Fitting into a New Schoool

My name is Consuela, but my friends in my old school always called me Connie. I liked that better, because it's easier to pronounce. A few months ago we moved to Minnesota, where there aren't many Mexican people, and it seemed like teachers and kids were always tripping over my name. I loved living in Arizona, where so many people speak Spanish—it was comfortable. It also was warm and dry there, and up here it's always cold and wet.

My father moved us up to Minneapolis because he got a job transfer. I know it meant a promotion for him and more money for the family, but for me it meant having to start in a new school just at the beginning of my senior year in high school. I worried that I couldn't make new friends easily because, by this point in school, everyone already had their cliques formed.

I knew I had to adjust to the situation, but I didn't like it and complained a lot. In the evenings, I shut myself in my room and wrote e-mails to my friends in Arizona. During the day at school, I didn't try to talk to people, which meant I had to eat lunch by myself. Well, I figured I could stand anything for a year. I planned to go back to Arizona as soon as I graduated.

Something happened a few weeks ago, however, that makes Minnesota look better. I was walking down the hall at school with my arms loaded down with books. A group of rowdy boys slammed into me and I dropped everything all over the hall. All of a sudden, there was a great looking guy helping me pick them up. He was so polite, and after he helped me, he asked me if I wanted something to eat. Of course I said "yes."

Since then, Donny and I have been going out a lot. As it turned out, his family just moved here from California, so we're sort of in the same boat. I have to say, Minnesota is looking better and better.

This adolescent's story is moderately hopeful, but we would add the cautionary note that she relies on another person to pull her out of her doldrums. If she were a full high-hope young woman, she would perceive effective ways to cope with the move "on her own." High-hope people often do turn to others, but it's usually for advice or brainstorming, not as saviors.

Identifying the Messages

As a parent teaching your child or adolescent how to use their stories to identify their personal messages, you will want to have a large sample of their narratives. Encourage your child or teen to write a number of brief vignettes about their life. Ask them to write about the goals for which they've worked, the problems that they've encountered in pursuit of those goals, how they managed to sustain their efforts, and what happened in the end. It also is instructive to have them write about goals and plans they may have for the future, how they plan to reach these goals, the problems they anticipate, and how they will sustain their efforts.

At this point, you should have several stories or narrative samples from you child. Your task now is to go over the writing with your child, highlighting the high- and low hope words and phrases. Make a list, as you did earlier in this chapter, placing the statements in either the high- or low-hope categories. There may be phrases or words about which you're in doubt. When you encounter those, ask your child more about what the statement means. Once you understand it better, you will probably know whether the thoughts behind it were high or low in hope. Neutral statements, for example, "I think I'm about average," may actually reflect low hope. Many people don't wish to be average; thus, such statements actually may be negative. Ask your child to tell you about what the neutral statements mean.

To illustrate this process, here is a brief vignette written by a thirteen-year-old boy. The statements that were highlighted by his mother have been underlined.

✳ Caleb—A Big Boned Boy

My name is Caleb, and I just started the seventh grade. The most important thing you should know about me is that I'm sort of big— well, <u>I'm too fat</u>. I know it's because <u>I eat too much</u>, but I love to eat and <u>I don't know if I can stop</u>. <u>I'm going to try</u> to eat less, though. That was my <u>New Year's resolution</u>.

Here's the problem: I start out with a bowl of cereal that Mom says is okay. But by the time we are ready for lunch, I could eat a horse. I just cram in as much food as I can, and sometimes <u>I don't think I can stop.</u> I just get so hungry that <u>it seems impossible</u> for me not to eat. And when I get home from school I'm starving again, so I eat some more. <u>I think I'm a desperate case.</u> <u>Nothing can help me.</u>

The school nurse told me I need more exercise, which <u>I hate to do.</u> <u>I really hate gym class</u> because when I have to run the guys laugh at the way my fat jiggles. <u>I'm going to show them</u>, though. I'm <u>signing up</u> for wrestling, and <u>I can hardly wait</u> to sit on one of those smart mouth kids. But I really think <u>I could wrestle okay</u> using my weight.

Caleb's Hope Worksheet

Low-Hope Statements
- I'm too fat
- I eat too much
- I don't think I can stop
- it seems impossible
- I'm a desperate case
- nothing can help me
- I hate to do (exercise)
- I really hate gym

High-Hope Statements
- New Year's resolution (goal)
- signing up for wrestling (way)
- I'm going to try (will)
- I can hardly wait (will)
- I could wrestle okay (will)

Notice the types of statements that Caleb's mother underlined. Usually statements that use words such as "too" or "should" are cues that the person isn't satisfied with the situation, and they are using self-defeating language. In this case, Caleb says that he is too fat and that he eats too much. While those are descriptions, they indicate that he views himself negatively. Descriptions, unless there are indications that the individual is unhappy, would not ordinarily be considered low-hope statements.

Some descriptions are indicative of high will or high ways. For example, when Caleb says he can wrestle, that is a positive thought about his abilities. Other examples would be such statements as "I'm smart," "I can score points," or "I'm a fast runner." All of these statements indicate that the individual has positive thoughts about him- or herself.

The other underlined statements in Caleb's dialogue clearly are reflections of his negative outlook. At this point in his life, he doesn't think he can do anything about his weight, and he is an unhappy kid. The positive statements underlined are not quite as obvious. At first it appears that Caleb's desire to wrestle is to get back at the mean boys. It also seems, however, that he thinks wrestling is a sport he can do, and that his weight will be an advantage. This shows waypower thinking, and his New Year's resolution does show that Caleb has set a goal for himself (although such New Year's resolution goals are notoriously poor in terms of being realistic).

Caleb and his mother have now gone over his story, highlighting and listing his low- and high-hope statements. If you are following the assignments and models in the workbook, you also will have highlighted and listed the messages found in your child's story. You are ready now to learn how to change low-hope statements into those reflecting higher willpower and waypower thinking. In short, you are ready to use these stories to enhance your child's hope.

Changing the Message—You Are What You Think

To introduce you to the process of changing low-hope thinking, we are going to continue with Caleb and his mother. Their interaction about the story will show how you can work with your child to reframe the negative thoughts into more positive ones. Let's look at how they talk about the story.

Mother: Now that we have read your story together, we can go over some of the words and phrases you've used that tell us about how you feel and think. Let's take it one part at a time.

Caleb: Okay, but I'm not sure I understand why we're doing this.

Mother: Remember the test you took that told us about your hope? We're working on ways to help you feel more confident about doing the things you want to do. For instance, right now I know you don't feel good about the way you look. In your story, you say you think you're too fat.

Caleb: I am too fat, but I don't think I can do anything about it!

Mother: That's what I mean. By thinking that you're stuck, you're making it harder to achieve your goal. Let's start at the beginning of your story and look at the things you're saying to yourself.

Caleb: Well, here goes. I guess this says that being fat and eating is what's most important about me.

Mother: When you really think about it, are those the things that are really the most important? Is that all you are?

Caleb: No, I'm also pretty smart. I'm good at a bunch of things, like chess, computers, and stuff like that.

Mother: So maybe the first thing to do is for you to start telling yourself that you're not *just* fat. Every time you tell yourself how fat you are, you have to say, "I may be heavy, but I can do a whole lot of things really well." There was something else in that paragraph—do you see what it is?

Caleb: My New Year's resolution? We talked about hope always having a goal, so I guess that's my goal.

Mother: Yes, it is, and it's a good one. Remember that it's always important to keep your goal in mind. Now let's look at the next part of
the story. What do you see there?

Caleb: I talk about how hungry I get, and I say that I don't think I can
stop eating.

Mother: Yes, and those are pretty negative, self-defeating things to say,
aren't they? Let's highlight those too. Let's also think about how
to change those so that you will feel encouraged, rather than
discouraged.

Caleb: I guess I could just reverse them, but that wouldn't sound like
the truth. Like if I just said, "I think I can stop."

Mother: How about something like, "I get really hungry, and sometimes
it feels bad. I think I can stand it, though. It's hard to stop
myself from eating, but I can do it." If you admit that it's hard,
but that you can try, you are telling yourself the truth. When
you say that you are a desperate case, though, that simply isn't
true. You can stop saying untrue things about yourself, but you
will have to remember to stop yourself.

Caleb: I'll try to do that, but it might be hard for me to remember.

Mother: We'll make a little list to remind you. But let's go on to the next
part now.

Caleb: I talk about what happens in gym, and how I get teased. I hate
that so much! It also really makes me mad. So mad that I want
to get even.

Mother: It sounds like you might have found a way to "throw your
weight around," and that it could be good exercise for you, too.
Let's highlight some of those phrases. Now we're going to put
all the words and phrases into low- or high-hope categories.
What do you see when we do that?

Caleb: I see that there are more in the low-hope group than in the high.

Mother: What we're going to do now is take some of the low-hope statements and change them into things you can say to yourself that
will be encouraging. We'll make a list that you can put in several
places around the house, and that you can carry in your notebook. You'll have to look at it a lot and remember to say the
encouraging statements when you start to say the low-hope
words.

When you reframe the negative statements in your child's story, it's important to recognize that he is used to saying them, and that drastic changes cannot

be made immediately. The long-range goal is to teach your child to use high-hope statements consistently, but these would be very different from his usual thoughts. It may be difficult to change the thoughts right away, so it's necessary to take small steps, just as it is when working for any large goal.

Here are the changed statements that Caleb and his mother developed for him to use. He agrees that these are believable, and that he will try to use them instead of the negative words he has been using. His mother will copy them and place them in key places, such as on his bathroom mirror, on the wall beside his bed, near the refrigerator, and inside of his school notebook. She has asked Caleb to read them at least ten times a day.

Caleb's Positive Statements

- There are a lot of things that are good about me, and I'm *not* just fat.

- I am fat now, but I can do something about it.

- It's hard not to eat too much, but I can eat less, if I try.

- It is possible to lose weight.

- I can help myself lose weight.

- There are some exercises I like, such as wrestling.

In the space below, write some of the negative words and phrases you highlighted from one of your child's stories. In the space next to that, write the changed message, using Caleb's changed messages as an example.

You will notice that Caleb was asked to read his high-hope statements at least ten times a day. That is one method of restructuring a child's thinking. In the following chapters, we will expand our discussions about techniques and strategies that can help your child change.

In this chapter, you have learned how to help your child or teenager write stories, and you've also identified and then highlighted the high- and low-hope words and phrases in these stories. You also have begun to guide your child in rephrasing their negative self-talk. Another essential ingredient in your child's success in raising their hope and getting what they want in life is the ability to set goals and use small steps to reach those goals. Goal setting is discussed in the next chapter, where you also will learn more about instilling positive self-talk.

Message Worksheet

Low-Hope Message   **Changed Message**

chapter 8

On Your Mark, Get Set, Go for the Goal

We have mentioned goals throughout this workbook, but up to this point, they haven't been the focus of our attention. Everything you've done with your child so far has led to this basic and critical component of hope—goal selection. In previous chapters, you have learned what hope is and how to measure it both in yourself and your child. You've learned about important life domains and have measured your child's hope in these areas.

Personal and family stories have been another important feature of this workbook. It is through these stories and dialogues that you have learned how to tap into your child's hope as well as your own. You have seen how stories can communicate low or high hope over generations, and stories also have been used to demonstrate ways to put hope strategies into action. These hope-building stories provide a step-by-step model for you to use while you enhance your child's willpower and waypower.

In chapter 7, you identified the low- and high-hope words and phrases that your child used in stories. You have seen how negative thoughts can be changed into positive, encouraging messages; and as we proceed with goal selection and hope-enhancing strategies, we will continue to employ message rephrasing. The self-talk used when embarking upon goals determines children's perceptions about attaining those goals. If those perceptions are self-defeating and low in hope, the probability of success is clearly diminished even before the child has started to pursue the goal. Conversely, if children begin with positive perceptions about finding ways to reach their goals, as well as strong beliefs in their capabilities to overcome problems, they establish conditions that are favorable for success. It is for these reasons that we'll continue to use a thought-restructuring process along with other powerful strategies.

What Are Goals?

Hope begins with goals. Without goals, there would be no reason to perceive ways, or to experience the will to apply effort. Without targets, there would be no directed activity, only random movement. As you learned in chapter 1, even tiny babies show goal-directed behavior when they cry to be fed or are uncomfortable. Nearly everything we do involves a goal, whether it is small and habitual, or long-range and large. This is an especially important point for children to understand, because often they don't believe they can accomplish goals. If they can be helped to see that each thing that they do actually constitutes a goal, then their feelings of accomplishment will increase.

Let's look at a few of the accomplishments that children may not recognize as goals. For example, most children select their clothes for the day and dress themselves. Many children prepare their own breakfasts, fix their lunches, and manage to get themselves to school on time. These are substantial accomplishments for a child, and many adults don't do well with similar tasks. When these activities are routine, however, we may not think of them as achieved goals. Nevertheless, each of these activities is a goal, the accomplishment of which deserves a pat on the back. If your child does these things, do you show how proud you are of him?

Recognizing your child's many past achievements provides a foundation for her belief in future successes. Following on this point, the first assignment in this chapter is for you to introduce the subject of goals to your child by taking an inventory of the goals that she has accomplished. Do you recall Caleb and his mother, whom you met in chapter 7? Below we give some examples of goals that Caleb has reached in the past few years.

Caleb's Recent Accomplishments

- Learned to play chess

- Learned to ride a bike

- Taught himself to use his computer

- Learned to identify the constellations

Caleb didn't add all of the things he has taught himself to his list, but he focused on those achievements that required significant effort. Caleb's mother put this list alongside the one they made of positive statements concerning his weight loss. When he feels discouraged about reaching his goals, he can read this "accomplished goals" list so as to gain a mental lift.

Goals can be short- or long-term, and they can be small or large. They can involve everyday matters, such as those we have mentioned, or they can be activities requiring special efforts. Goals can be objects we wish to acquire or skills we want to learn. In short, goals can be anything we can conceive of in our minds. Helping your child to identify and select goals is critical to the development of hopeful thinking.

Selecting Goals for High Hope

Children love to dream and fantasize about the things they will do in their lives. When we asked a group of seven-year-olds what they planned to do, we got answers ranging from being professional basketball players to being a famous ice skater. None of the answers was mundane, and most of them were unrealistic. It is fun to dream about grand ambitions and even to pretend in games that they are true. Perhaps some of those children will go on to actualize their early wishes, especially if they also develop truly high hope.

As much fun as dreaming may be, it isn't the type of goal identification that leads directly to the development of hopeful thinking. While we encourage parents to discuss fantasies with their children, it is most important to discuss kids' immediate short- and long-range goals. What new skills do they want to learn? What material things do they want to acquire? What do they want to reach for in their schoolwork? In this latter regard, good friends, good grades, and having fun are the goals for many children. From questions such as these, you can help your child to formulate goals along with the associated willpower and waypower thoughts to increase their levels of hope.

Characteristics of Hope-Enhancing Goals

There are shared characteristics of hope-inducing goals. First and foremost, such goals should be clear and well defined. Some goals are phrased as general statements, such as "I want to play ball better" or, "I want to dress more like the popular girls." When your child expresses a goal in general terms, ask her for further definition of what she means by "playing ball better." A more precise definition would include making four baskets in each basketball game, or perhaps stealing the ball twice and blocking at least one shot. "Dressing more like the popular girls" might mean wearing particular sweaters or jeans. Whatever the goal may be, make certain that you and your child have it clearly defined. A vague goal, unfortunately, only begets vague success in realizing it!

It also is extremely important to make sure that long-range goals are clearly defined. Most major achievements in life are long-range in nature. Because our children don't have the advanced cognitive development of adults, they may not be able to envision the future in the same manner we parents do. To children, the future is a *long* time away, and their lives seem to stretch forever. Thus, it truly is difficult for most kids to visualize long-range goals. Accordingly, we parents need to help our children clarify their goals from early on.

Hope-enhancing goals must have feasible and realistic paths to their attainment. Some of the fantasies expressed by children in our research program were so fanciful that there appeared to be no way that they could be achieved. For example, the little girl who wanted to be a famous ice skater lived in a town with no ice-skating rink. We advise you as a parent to be cautious, however, when determining that your child's dreams or aspirations are unrealistic. History is full of examples of children who have achieved great accomplishments against tremendously difficult odds.

When your child tells you his goals, your own parental hope takes on special importance. In the early chapters of this workbook, you learned that it is difficult for low-hope parents to teach high hope to their child. When helping your child to discover pathways to goals, for example, your own hope is crucial. If your hope as a caregiver is low, you are likely to discourage your child from pursuing goals *that seem difficult to you.* Here is an important point to remember: Goals that seem impossible to a low-hope parental role model may appear reachable to a caregiver with high hope.

When your waypower is low—perceiving that you are incapable of coming up with ways to reach goals—you'll probably have difficulty helping your child find pathways to actualize her dreams. Similarly, if your willpower is low, you will find it almost impossible to give the encouragement your child needs to initiate and sustain goal-directed energy. *We cannot give what we do not have, and we cannot teach what we do not know.* If your hope score is low, and you haven't done the work in order to learn how to think hopefully, we suggest that you go back and begin that process now. You will find that your child is as much a beneficiary of your hope enhancement as you.

Another characteristic of hope-enhancing goals is that they can be broken down into smaller steps. Sometimes in the United States, adults and children alike seem to want to reach their goals immediately and in one, simple step. This attitude is captured in the words of a young boy who was heard speaking to his mother, "I want what I want, and I want it now!" Remember here that *patience is an ally of hopeful thinking.* Large and long-term goals absolutely must be divided into smaller, more do-able steps, the accomplishment of which also become goals. Furthermore, small and short-term objectives usually can be divided into even smaller parts that make it even easier for them to be reached.

As you help your child define goals, it's important to think in terms of the small steps that, when taken together, lead to eventual success. If a goal cannot be broken up in this manner, then it probably is not a feasible objective for your child. Waypower thinking is related to a child's ability to come up with the small steps that lead to the accomplishment of any goal. With low waypower, the final target remains a distant idea without visible pathways leading to it. High way-power enables a child to see many different routes, or smaller steps, that will lead to success. A twelve-year-old boy in our research program captured this notion beautifully with his insight that "Waypower thinking is my bridge to what I want."

A final quality of a hope-enhancing goal is that it must motivate your child into action. Your child should really want or need the goal. Without a strong desire for the goal, the mental energy required to achieve it will be low, and this low willpower almost certainly will consign a child to failure. Willpower thought is not all "fun and games," however. In fact, many a child's long-range goals involve taking steps that they don't necessarily enjoy. Two such examples are going to school or wearing braces. Children often complain about such goals, although their outcomes (a diploma and straight teeth) are certainly desirable. To encourage high willpower thinking, frequently remind your child about the benefits of attaining their goals.

Ask your child the following questions when she is considering a new goal. Be sure to discuss each answer, asking your child to thoroughly describe the goal, the will, and the ways. Through this exercise, you are teaching the active process of hoping.

Goal Questions

- Is the goal clear and well defined?

- Is it a long-range or a short-range goal?

- Is the goal large or small?

- Is the goal do-able?

- Can the goal be broken down into small steps?

- Can your child (with or without your help) identify the large and small steps to the goal?

- How much does your child really desire the goal?

Here is a vignette in which we illustrate the goal-selection process. Read this with your child, and then see if she can answer the goal questions for the child in the story.

✳ Molly and Friends

Molly was seven years old, and she lived with her parents in an apartment house in a very large city. Although there was a park with a playground across the street, Molly's parents didn't have much time to take her to play. There were no other children in the entire apartment building who were her age, and Molly was very lonely. After thinking about loneliness, Molly came up with the idea that she needed a puppy to keep her company.

When she first told her parents she wanted a puppy, they both said, "Impossible! We don't have time to take care of an animal." But that didn't stop Molly; she was determined to have her puppy. She knew exactly what type she wanted and even where to get it. She wanted the type of dog that would not need much space and that she could teach to do tricks. She knew that the Humane Society had more than enough puppies for adoption, and that they all needed good homes. The problem was that she had to convince her parents that her idea was a good one.

Sometimes, when she really wanted something, she cried and threw a fit until she got it. This time, knowing that she had to convince her parents that she could take care of a dog, Molly thought that she had better act as grown up and responsible as she could. The first steps in her plan were to check out a book on puppy care from the school library, along with a book that described all the different kinds of dogs. She couldn't read all the words, so she asked her teacher for help.

In a few days, Molly had a huge amount of information, and was ready to tackle the big hurdle—asking her parents. She had learned that some breeds are smarter and quieter than others, and that a big dog often is better in an apartment because they are calmer than a small one. She also discovered that most dogs can learn to do tricks.

Molly

Molly had also learned about taking the puppy outside to go potty and get some exercise. At last, Molly felt well prepared to discuss dog ownership with her parents.

When she brought the subject up with her parents again, they seemed a little more positive about it than they had been at first. They were impressed that she had learned so much about dogs and their care, and they began to think that maybe a puppy would be good company for her. They promised to take her to the animal shelter that next Saturday, but only to look.

The shelter was in a large cement block building that had

been decorated with colorful pictures of cats and dogs. On the linoleum floor inside there were kitty or puppy paw prints to lead the prospective adopters to either the cat or the dog section. The dog kennel, where Molly and her parents went, was a huge room with tiers of cages, and in each was a dog or puppy. Some of the older dogs looked sad, like they knew someone had forgotten about them. The puppies were all frisky and not old enough to understand about adoption.

Molly wanted to take them all home, but of course that was impossible. When Molly looked up at her mother, she was surprised to see tears at the corners of her eyes, and her father looked unhappy as well. They said they had never thought about all the dogs and cats that needed homes, and they wished they had room for more than one.

What happened that day was amazing to Molly, and beyond her wildest dreams. They all agreed on an adorable puppy that was a cross between a golden retriever and a Siberian husky. They knew she would get big, but she would be smart and very friendly. The surprising thing was that after selecting the puppy, they went to the cat side and chose a little black kitten for Molly's mother. "After all," she said, "the puppy will need a companion while Molly is at school."

After reading Molly's story, ask your child to identify the goal and to talk about the things that Molly did to get her puppy. Ask your child to talk about how Molly showed her parents that she really wanted a dog. The ways Molly thought of to convince her parents that she could take care of a pet show her waypower. Her determination to get a puppy, shown by her persistence and desire, are illustrations of her willpower. (Look at the end of the chapter for the answers to goal questions related to Molly.)

Molly's story is one example of goal setting and the use of willpower and waypower thinking. At the end of this workbook, you will find many suggestions for stories with themes of hope in action. You can read these stories aloud to young children, or older children can read them by themselves. In chapter 10, we will show you how to use children's and adolescent's literature as a tool to enhance hope.

Tackling Everyday Goals

Identifying goals is rather easy when the objective is large or unusual. Most of the time, however, it is the everyday tasks and hurdles that call out for higher hope. Not only are these often more difficult to identify as specific goals, but your child may not be motivated to change his existing behavior. Self-talk is an important example of such a behavior. Negative self-talk maintains low hope, but it is habitual and familiar to the child and is a challenge to change.

In the last chapter, we introduced you to Caleb, who was trying to change his self-defeating messages about overeating. He felt bad about himself because of his size and told himself it was impossible to lose weight. After writing a vignette about his problem, he and his mother highlighted the negative statements he used. Then, they made a list of positive phrases that Caleb agreed to read at least ten times a day. He was also to remember, whenever possible, to use a positive statement instead of a negative, self-depreciating one when he used self-talk. Let's return to Caleb and see how he is doing, looking closely at how he is changing his behavior.

* Caleb—From Mean-Talk to Nice-Talk

Mom and I worked out a plan where I had two things to remember to do. One of them was to read a list of sentences that said good things about me, and I had to do that ten times every day. The other thing I had to do was to stop saying mean things to myself about being fat, and to say nice things instead. Mom said that if I did these things, I would start to feel better about myself, and that I would begin to believe I didn't have to be so fat.

I didn't have any trouble remembering to read the list. I put copies of it in places where I would go during the day, like the kitchen (on the refrigerator), in the family room (on the TV), and in my bathroom (on the mirror). I even taped one on the ceiling over my bed, so that when I wake up in the morning it is the first thing I see.

Remembering not to say mean things to myself was much harder than reading the list. I guess I was so used to telling myself I was fat and ugly that these thoughts just popped into my mind. Mom says that I think these mean things automatically, and I know that's true. When we go to the cafeteria for lunch, I eat a lot, but I keep telling myself how fat I am. When I'm out at recess, I keep thinking that I waddle when I run. Trying not to think these things is hard, but I will find some way to do it. I don't want to feel so bad about myself anymore.

When I told Mom about how the thoughts kept happening, we realized that I was trying to do too much all at once. We decided that I would change my mean-talk in just one or two situations first. I had to think about when I said mean things to myself the most, and I discovered it was mainly when I thought the other kids were looking at me. Those times would be at recess, at lunch, doing something in front of the class, and the worst time of all—gym class. In gym, I have to run and play basketball in front of boys who love teasing me.

I decided that I would start by trying to change my mean-talk to nice-talk in just one place first. Recess was the one I chose, because I can be by myself and think about what I am saying. For two weeks, I concentrated on saying nice things to myself at recess. I reminded myself that I am smart, and that I can do a lot of things really well. During those two weeks a funny thing happened; I started saying good things to myself at other times, too. In fact, nice-talk is getting to be a habit.

A few of the nice statements that I have been reading everyday tell me that I can lose weight. I really want to lose some weight because I want to play sports in junior high school. Mom says not to try anything drastic, but I made a big decision the other day. I asked her not to buy me any more snack foods, like potato chips, and to help me eat only three or four times a day. I also asked Mom to go for a walk with me every day in a park across town where I wouldn't see kids from my school. I'm going to lose weight, but I don't want other kids to know I am trying.

The next thing I'm going to do is sign up for wrestling. I'm going to lose a few pounds first, though, because I don't want to be called a Sumo wrestler. I know I can lose weight now, and I'm feeling better because I'm saying nice things to myself.

Changing self-defeating messages into encouraging self-talk is a common strategy for enhancing hope. Although this is a long-range goal, automatic thoughts can occur so frequently and in so many situations that they must be tackled in small parts to be changed successfully. For Caleb, changing his "mean-talk" became an everyday goal. Similarly, changing the way he ate became an everyday objective, although the long-range goal was to become fit and slimmer.

Selecting goals with your children isn't always an easy process. Frequently the goals you would like for your child are not the ones she would choose. One of the characteristics of goals that will enhance hope is selecting a target that your child *really* wants. Unless the goal is truly desired, the chances of success are limited. For that reason, we suggest that you use the Life-Domain Scales as a place to begin.

Life-Domain Goals

In chapters 3 and 4, you read about the important life areas of children and adolescents, and you used the scales to determine hope levels in each domain. As you talk with your child or teen about goal setting, refer to the hope scores on each of those scales as a way to identify some areas in need of hope enhancement. The important life domains of children between the ages of six and twelve were schoolwork, family, safety, health, play, recreation, and spirituality. The adolescent life areas were academics, family, health and fitness, and romantic relationships. Remember that any of the domains might be important for either children or adolescents, and that you can use the scales for either group.

To identify goals from life domains, you will need to spend time discussing each objective with your child. To determine which domains are the most important to him or her, as well as the ones with which there is the most and least satisfaction, we suggest that you ask your child to take these two brief scales. On the first scale, have your child assign a number showing the importance of each life area. A score of 1 = little importance, a 2 = some importance, and a 3 = a great deal of importance. On the second scale, have your child rate how satisfied he or she is with each of the domains. Again, a rating of 1 = very satisfied, a 2 = somewhat satisfied, and a 3 = not satisfied. When the ratings are completed, *select goals from the domains that are the most important but with which your child is the least satisfied.*

Life-Domain Importance and Satisfaction

1	2	3
Little Importance	**Somewhat Important**	**Very Important**

Academic/Schoolwork _____ Family _____ Safety _____

Health _____ Play and Recreation _____ Spiritual _____

Health and Fitness _____ Romantic Relationships _____

1	2	3
Very Satisfied	**Somewhat Satisfied**	**Not Satisfied**

Academic/Schoolwork _____ Family _____ Safety _____

Health _____ Play and Recreation _____ Spiritual _____

Health and Fitness _____ Romantic Relationships _____

Notice that the highest rating your child can give on the importance and dissatisfaction scales are both 3. The life domains to which your child has given a total (importance and dissatisfaction) score of 6 are the best sources for goal selection. Remember that hope-encouraging goals should be important and highly desired by your child. When a life domain is very important, yet the child is dissatisfied with his or her activities in it, goals selected from that area are more likely to be met successfully.

Here are some common problems that children experience in each of the life domains. Along with the problems are some possible goals you might suggest that will help your children to achieve more success in these areas. The goals that you and your child select will be unique to your individual situation, and the suggestions here are merely examples to show how goals relate to a child's concerns in a life domain. Remember, your child should rate the domain as an important one, and one that he or she presently finds dissatisfying. You may wish that your child would study harder, or get along better with siblings, but if those goals are not important to your child, he will not be motivated to change.

The Academic/Schoolwork Domain

Probably the most common problems in this area are that children and teens may not want to attend school, do homework, or even care about making acceptable grades. The causes of these problems can be many, from having a teacher whom your child doesn't like, finding the material uninteresting or too easy, being teased by other children, and so on. Conceiving a goal that will address your child's reluctance to go to school requires you to determine the most important reasons for this hesitance. Depending upon how long your child has disliked school, this can be a difficult problem without any ready solutions. The goals for this concern may be as wide ranging as helping your child to develop better social skills in order to get along with peers, to changing your child's classroom (different teacher), or even arranging a change of schools.

One goal for homework problems is to establish a set time and place for your child to do this work. Carrying an assignment book for each class or subject will help, and, in some cases, it may be advisable for the teacher to initial the work assigned. Such a system will insure communication in the school hope triad—child, teacher, and parents. It will be important for you to monitor the progress your child makes toward achieving all of these goals, showing that you care and are interested in his work.

When you attend parent and teacher conferences, you may learn that your child has problems that you haven't seen at home. For example, your child may be shy in school and afraid to speak up in class; at home, however, that same child is very outgoing. Setting a goal to learn to be more assertive would help such a child. Another common problem for young children is daydreaming in class. A child need not have a learning disability to have difficulty focusing their attention. It is helpful to such children to practice attending for short periods of time, slowly adding time, until the goal of a normal attention span is achieved.

If your child has poor relationships with peers, goals could include learning social skills or how to cope with teasing and bullying. For a child who is the victim of this latter type of harassment, attending school can be torture.

The Family Domain

The types of problems that are most common in this domain are arguments with parents and siblings, procrastinating on or refusing to do family chores, and distancing by your child from the rest of the family. As with the schoolwork domain, the causes of family problems can be many. One common reason that may be at the heart of many concerns, however, is that the child may be angry.

Anger can come from many sources, some real and some imagined. Sibling rivalry or perceived favoritism are common causes of anger. There also can be arguments and unhappiness between the parents that are reflected in the anger of the child. It's important that you and your child talk about the reasons he isn't getting along in the family. If you determine that your child's concerns are a result of dysfunctional family dynamics, you would be well advised to seek the help of a family therapist. Here are some goals related to anger that can help your child get along better in the family, as well as other situations in which anger is a problem.

Anger management and fair fighting are the subjects of many books and articles. These programs usually have a number of steps that a child can learn in order to control her temper. If a child is angry, however, it's important to treat the cause as well as the angry behavior. To understand the causes of anger, you will need to listen and be open to what your child tells you. Remember that feelings are not wrong, but the way they are acted out can create havoc.

Another common family domain problem is when children resist or procrastinate in doing the chores that they have been assigned. This can be both irritating and disruptive to the flow of family life. This problem is amenable, however, to the establishment of small goals. In the next chapter, where you will learn how to enhance willpower and waypower, you will see how using small steps along with reinforcement can overcome a child's resistance to chores. Each task assigned becomes a goal, as well as an opportunity for enhancing your child's hope.

The Safety Domain

If a child has indicated a low score on the satisfaction scale for the safety domain, it's important to set goals in this area. There are few places in this country where children are totally safe, and it behooves you as a parent to be certain that your child knows safety rules. Learning each rule of safety can be a goal, and your child demonstrating them to you can be a measure of achievement.

For young children, learning where to cross a street and looking both ways is very important. This can be demonstrated when you and your child take a walk. It also is important to teach your child not to talk to or go with strangers and what to do in case of fires or other accidents. There are excellent books and videos available in which young children are exposed to this information at a suitable level. Your child should be able to repeat what has been learned, so that you know the goal has been achieved. Remember that safety goals are extremely important in our fast-paced society.

The Health and Fitness Domain

As a parent of young children, you have a great deal of control over their behaviors. Regardless of how important this health domain was ranked by your child, it is an important area for them to have good habits and knowledge. Some of the goals in this area may help you as much as your child.

Children often are picky eaters, with vegetables high on the list of disliked foods. It can be frustrating for the cook to prepare foods, only to have family members turn up their noses. Many parents insist that their children join the "clean plate club," no matter how long they have to sit at the table. It's our experience that this tactic doesn't encourage children to eat correctly and only makes mealtime a more dreaded experience. Asking children to eat one or two bites is less stressful and may teach the child to try new foods without incurring anxiety.

One goal in this domain is for your child to learn how to eat so that he will develop and maintain healthy habits. To help your child work toward this goal, you will need to have clear information about nutrition, and will also have to set a good example by the foods you prepare and eat. If your meals are high in fat, sugar, and salt, no matter how good they taste, you are teaching your children poor eating habits. As is true for the other domains, there are good books on nutrition available for both you and your child.

Exercise is an important part of the health domain. Many children spend hours watching television or playing computer games instead of being physically active. This television watching will lead to poor health habits and a general lack of muscle tone and development. Goals can be set in this area that involve sports or spending more time out of doors in some form of active play. As parents, you can control television time, and it is important for you not to use the television as a baby-sitter. If we somehow were to walk into a thousand family rooms in apartments and homes across the United States, our fear is that we would find hundreds of children "plugged into" their televisions.

Helping your teenager with goals in the health domain can be challenging. Although they frequently seem very set in their ways, teens also may want to look and feel more attractive, giving you an edge in teaching them better habits. Adolescents are old enough to learn about good nutrition and exercise programs on their own. They may need your encouragement, however, to help them develop willpower and waypower thinking in this domain.

The Play and Recreation Domain

When children experience problems in this domain it often is because they don't have many friends. Goals with which you can help your children are the development of social skills and learning to play the games and sports that interest other children.

If your child is teased or bullied, it can be a very serious problem. It's important for you to find out if your child is the victim of this type of behavior. Being teased or bullied often are shameful to children, and they may not want us as parents to know what really is happening. Depending upon the seriousness of the teasing or bullying, you may need to consider changing your child's school. Bullying has become a dangerous problem in the United States and elsewhere, and one to which parents need to be alert.

The Romance Domain

This domain is primarily the province of adolescents, although youngsters are dating younger than they once did. With the onset of puberty, young people have sexual desires whether or not adults approve. This is an area where good communication between the parent and child will prevent problems and smooth the road to healthy development. We suggest that you answer relationship and sex questions openly and honestly, and indicate your willingness to discuss any concerns your child may have.

The issue of sexual orientation is an especially difficult one for parents to discuss, yet approximately one out of ten adolescents will be attracted to members of the same sex. Homosexuality is no longer considered a pathology, but many people consider it wrong. It's important for you to examine your personal beliefs about this issue and be prepared to refer your child to someone who can be objective with your child about matters of sexual orientation.

Most adolescents learn how to behave with their partners through observation and conversations with peers. While this is a valid way to learn what is appropriate to say and do, the information that your child learns may not always be accurate. Goals in this domain can include learning about STDs, learning about birth control and protection, as well as reading one of the many books written to guide young people through this difficult and sometimes confusing time of life.

Discussions of sexual issues between parent and child can be very stressful, as well as embarrassing on both sides. It may be difficult for you to hear what your child wants to disclose, but it's important for you to be willing to listen. The more willingly you listen without judgment, the more comfortable your teen will be talking with you.

The Spiritual Domain

The extent to which this domain is considered important to your child may be determined by the spiritual or religious training you have provided. If this domain is unimportant in your life, it's likely to be unimportant to your children. Children who don't receive religious education may discover that some of their friends do, and they may begin to ask you questions. While we don't advocate one position over another on this issue, it's important for you to provide some explanations to the questioning child.

Children who do receive spiritual or religious education also may have questions and concerns about their faith. You can help them achieve greater satisfaction in this domain by establishing goals such as setting times to pray, reading religious works, or learning about world religions. You also may wish to join a church or synagogue or mosk where your children can discuss their religion and related ideas with others of their age.

Goal Selection in Action

Now that you have read about some of the typical problems encountered in each of the life domains, and you have seen some of the goals that your child might target to enhance life-domain satisfaction, let's see an example of an adolescent's goal-selection process. For this vignette, we have chosen one of the most difficult concerns for parents, that of a young woman becoming sexually active.

✳ Tara—Love and Commitment

Looking back at my high school years I'm amazed that my mother was so understanding. I was able to talk to her about everything, from my college plans to whether or not to drink alcohol. Nothing challenged her as much, however, as when I decided to become sexually active. Most of my girlfriends had already had sex by the time we were seniors, but I wanted my first sexual encounter to be very special and with someone I truly loved. When I met Joe, I knew he was the one for me.

We were both eighteen and had just graduated from high school. Although we went to different schools, we knew many of the same kids, and it was at a party of mutual friends that we met. If you can believe in love at first sight, this was it. During the summer, we saw as much of each other as we could, given that we both had to work full-time. We knew that we wanted our relationship to last, and we dreaded the coming year when we would be at colleges separated by two thousand miles.

It was toward the end of the summer that Joe and I decided that we wanted to have sex. Neither of us had done it before, and we wanted it to be very special. I knew that I could talk to my mother, and even though this could be an embarrassing conversation, I worked up my courage and broached the subject. As I hoped, she was understanding and treated the issue with serious consideration. We had several long talks about the consequences of sexual activity, both the pleasures and the risks.

Mother suggested that Joe and I prepare ourselves for this event by reading a book on sexual intercourse. We went to the bookstore and I selected one that actually had pictures. This might sound "clinical" and not very spontaneous to most people, but my mother told me that, although the sex act is a natural thing, many couples really don't know how to please each other. She said that if we were going to do it, we might as well learn how to do it right.

So the first goal that Joe and I had was to read the book together and discuss the risks and consequences. Our next goal was to plan where and when we would have this experience. I knew that a lot of girls lost their virginity in the back seats of cars, or in a spare bedroom at a drunken party, and I didn't want that for me. I wanted my first time to be a special event in my life, something good to remember.

I won't tell you all the details, but I will say that it worked out the way Joe and I wanted. I will also tell you that, unusual as it may sound, we stayed together throughout college and have now been married for two years. We are both so glad that we made it a point to learn everything we could about sex and plan it out before we jumped in. It helped a great deal to have my mother to talk with, and to believe that what we were doing was right for us.

This vignette illustrates the benefit of having a parent with whom the young person can talk about important issues. The decision to become sexually active is one of the most important ones a teenager (and sometimes children) make. Without accepting and knowledgeable parental guidance, peer pressure and ignorance often cloud this decision. In Tara's case, her mother helped the couple to work out a plan to reach their goal—that of having a satisfying first sexual experience. They read a book for information, they decided on a birth control method, and they planned a time and place that would be romantic. Tara's story has an almost fairy tale ending, uncommon in this day and age. One reason for their success is that both Tara and Joe are high-hope people, and they employed hope strategies even in their most intimate encounters.

Now that you have measured the importance and satisfaction of your child's life domains, and you have seen some of the common problems that arise in these areas, you're ready to help your child make his or her list of domains, concerns, and goals. Use the sheet below, following the example taken from the story you just read about Tara and Joe.

Life Domains/Concerns/Goals

(example)

Domain	Concern	Goal
Romance	First sexual experience	To have it be good

Domain	Concern	Goal

Answers to Molly's Goal Questions

1. The goal was clear—a puppy.

2. This was a short-range goal.

3. The puppy turned out to be a big goal.

4. It was something Molly thought she could do.

5. Molly did break the goal into small steps, exercising her waypower.

6. The routes were to get information about dogs, learn how to take care of them, and demonstrate this to her parents.

7. Molly demonstrated her willpower by her determination to have a puppy and how hard she worked to get one. These things showed how much she wanted a dog.

chapter 9

Boosting Your Child's Waypower

By this point, you have learned a number of important things about your child and yourself. You have learned about the basic elements of hope—goals, waypower, and willpower—as well as how to measure them. You have examined your child's levels of hope in a number of specific domains, and you've identified areas of your child's life that can benefit from enhanced hope. You have reached back into the dusty pages of your family's past and into your own younger years. Through this detective work, you were able to create stories informed by the current levels of hope in both you and your children. In the last chapter, you learned the importance of setting goals, as well as the characteristics of those goals. These lessons aid you in building hope. Based on the information you have collected about your child's life domains, along with the satisfaction and importance attached by your child to such domains, your hope team—your child and you—has selected appropriate goals to work toward.

In this chapter, we build upon what you already know and augment your ability to help your child fulfill her dreams. You will learn techniques used by high-hope children, and you'll see more examples of young people as they search for routes and use their waypower thinking to reach their goals. To begin, let's shine our spotlight at waypower.

Visions and Plans—Waypower Perceptions

Simply put, waypwer is the *perception one has about their ability to find ways to reach their goals.* In chapter 2, you read about profiles of hope and learned that to be a fully high-hope person, you need to have a high level of both waypower and willpower. If your children have high waypower, they will be able to think of many ways to get the things they want. For low-hope children, however, it is frequently at this very point where the all too frequent stumbling blocks of life prevent them from achieving their goals. If your child has low waypower, take heart. As you will see in this chapter, learning to search for ways to reach goals is a skill that can be developed.

Notice that the description of waypower uses the word "perceived." This is a very important point for parents to understand, because they often become frustrated when their children don't see ways to solve problems. Our point here is that, although there may be a number of routes to take to achieve a goal, unless your child *perceives* herself as being able to find them, they don't exist as options for your child. Enhancing your child's waypower thinking means teaching him to perceive routes and to see herself as being capable of producing workable routes that can be used to reach the target.

Low-waypower children often think of themselves as being able to come up with only one or two ways to attain what they want. When these routes are blocked, these kids frequently become frustrated with their goal-directed thinking patterns and give up on goals. They may conclude that the goal was unreachable, or that they are incapable of reaching it. Neither conclusion may be correct, however, and both assumptions can be damaging to the child. When children give up on goals that they see other people attaining, they develop poor concepts about their own abilities to succeed. In turn, such children are increasingly reluctant to try for future goals.

In chapter 8, you learned the importance of goal selection as a tactic for enhancing hope. You were asked to help your child formulate some goals in domains that are important to them and where *their levels of satisfaction are low.* The next step in the hopeful thought process is to help your child examine his self-referential perceptions about how to reach those objectives. Even though a low-waypower child may have a tremendous desire to achieve certain goals, that child will often be stuck as a perennial nonstarter who lacks the routes to desired goals. For this reason, we first address ways to help increase your child's waypower and work on building willpower later, in chapter 10.

As your hope team—you and your child—do the exercises in this workbook, you will choose a number of small goals as stepping-stones for teaching waypower and willpower thinking. *There is one large goal, however, and that is the development of your child's hope.* This overarching goal can be described to your child as the construction of a building in their minds, with waypower being the strong foundation on which it is built. In this foundation, there are a number of smaller building blocks, and these are the strategies and techniques your child will use to increase waypower perception. With each technique, your child's waypower will become more structurally sound. Each strategy, each technique your child practices, will add floors to his or her tower of hope.

Waypower, therefore, isn't made up of the actual routes your child will take to reach goals. Rather, waypower is your child's self-referential *beliefs* about being able to produce workable pathways. Low-waypower children thus see themselves as being deficient in their ability to produce paths to desired goals, whereas high-waypower children see themselves as virtual repositories for effective routes to desired goals.

Characteristics of High-Waypower Children

How are high-hope children, who perceive themselves as being capable of envisioning many ways to get what they want, different from their low-hope counterparts? Based on research, high-waypower children use methods that can be described and learned. In this section, we share some of the techniques and strategies that we observed in our research and in our clinical practices.

Breaking Large Goals into Small Parts

Children with high waypower look not only at the larger goal, but also at the possible ways to break the goal into smaller parts. When children can see only the long-range, large goal, as is the case for low-hope children, it often seems out of reach. When the goal seems too formidable, the child is tempted to procrastinate, or, worse yet, give up altogether. Envisioning the small steps that comprise a large goal makes the endeavor seem more do-able and breaks the maladaptive cycle in the low-hope child.

As an example, consider a child who is just learning to read. She sounds out each letter at a time until she is able to say the word. Soon she can recognize a number of words and, as she adds new ones, she finds that she can read whole sentences. She may begin reading very simple books, but after a while she can read longer and more interesting works.

Asking for Help

Young children often have difficulty in thinking of ways to reach their goals. They are, after all, inexperienced "rookies" in the goal-pursuit game, and they simply cannot be expected to know as much as older children and adults.

Nevertheless, everyone sometimes needs additional information and help in discovering ways to reach their objectives. High-waypower children know how to ask for the help that they need.

Asking others who have successfully achieved the goal is an important way to increase waypower perception. High-waypower children understand that others can give them the information they need, and they have the communications skills to ask for that help. Low-waypower children, on the other hand, may be reluctant to ask for help for several reasons: they may be timid about approaching others they see as successful; they make think that asking for help is a sign of failure; or they may not know the right questions to ask. To ask for assistance in finding ways to pursue a goal, the child first must have a clear picture of the objective. Clear goals enhance the probability that the children pursuing these goals will experience hope.

It's important for parents to provide a balance between solving problems for the kids, and allowing them sufficient time to struggle for options. Your child's waypower thinking may be stunted when you consistently provide all the answers. If you refuse help, however, your child may become so frustrated that he will give up.

When we work with children in therapeutic situations, building waypower perceptions is an important factor in an overall healthy approach to life. Children often ask us what they should do and how to solve their problems. One of the answers we use, and one that you can use at home, is: "I'll help you come up with some ideas, but first, tell me all the ways you have thought of to solve this problem." At this point, it is helpful to list the ideas the child has thought about and use them to help the child in discovering additional routes to the goal.

Here is an example from a conversation between a father and his ten-year-old daughter. She is unhappy because of her brothers' seemingly endless teasing.

Father: I know that you hate being teased by your brothers, and that you want to get them to stop.

Daughter: I have to make them stop, but I don't know how. What should I do?

Father: I can think of a couple of things to try, but first, would you tell me your ideas?

Daughter: I thought about beating them up, but they're bigger than I am. I already asked them not to tease me but this only seemed to make them tease me even more. I can't think of anything else to do.

Father: Okay, those are two things. Why do you think your brothers like to tease you?

Daughter: Maybe it's because I get so mad.

Father: That's exactly what I think. It isn't very nice of them, but they really do it to get a rise out of you. Does that give you any ideas to try to get them to stop?

Daughter: I could try to not get mad. I could go in another room instead of staying and fighting.

Father: Great. Now you're thinking. I like that idea.

The goal in this situation is to have the boys stop their teasing. Initially, the daughter has only two ideas, neither of which are feasible. After the father prompts her for additional ideas and points her in a fruitful direction, she is able to perceive a plan that might work. Notice, also, how the father praised his daughter for thinking of another approach she could use to achieve her goal. It is important to show your kids that you are proud and pleased when they increase their waypower perception.

Skill Building

Another characteristic of high-waypower children is that they recognize when they may not have the necessary skills to achieve their goals—and they are prepared to learn these skills. Sometimes this requires taking a step back before they can forge ahead. Planning a course of action toward the goal and breaking the goal into smaller steps gives the child a chance to see if he or she has all of the skills required to get the job done.

You already have learned how the routine things a child does every day constitute goals, just as do the larger, unfamiliar targets. When the objective is something your child has never tried before, it's likely that new skills will have to be learned. The skill repertoire of children is much smaller than that of adults, or even adolescents, and learning to do new things is an important part of growing up. As your child plans ways to reach goals, help him or her identify what new skills need to be learned to make the goal possible. Here is a dialogue between a mother and her twelve-year-old son who wants to be in a rock band.

Son: Some of the guys are starting a band, and I really want to be part of it. I thought I could play bass guitar. It doesn't look too hard.

Mom: I see you've borrowed one. How did you plan to learn to play it?

Son: The guy I borrowed it from showed me some chords, only it's a lot harder than I thought it would be.

Mom: If you really want to learn, we can get you some lessons. You know it's going to mean you have to practice.

Son: I think I can sort of pretend to play for a while, you know, stand there and strum a little? They know I have to learn, so when I can really play with them I will. Yeah, I would like some lessons.

          (A month later)

Son: This has taken a lot more work than I thought, but listen to me play this riff, Mom.

Mom: That's terrific. You've really been practicing.

Son: The guitar teacher said that I have talent, and that it takes time for muscles to learn what to do. But I'm at the point now where I can really play with the band.

In this dialogue, the son has a goal to play in a rock band, but realizes that he will have to learn to play the guitar—a new skill for him. His mother helps him outline his plan, including taking lessons. He is diligent about practicing, and he recognizes that developing the new skill won't happen overnight. Another quality of high-hope children is that they are willing to spend the time required to learn new skills, particularly when these skills will help them reach their goals.

Being Willing to Bend

Another important characteristic of high-waypower children is that they are willing to change or alter their goals, if necessary. Children don't always understand what is feasible, and as a parent it is up to you to help them learn. Be careful, however, that you don't discourage them from having big dreams—even if you think they are unrealistic. Children thrive on fantasy, and as long as it doesn't get in the way of their everyday lives, it's quite adaptive for them to conjure their futures.

Our point is that, in the face of insurmountable obstacles, high-waypower children can alter or change their goals rather than giving up. For example, the son in the previous dialogue may initially have wanted to play a much more difficult instrument, such as a piano. Recognizing that it would take a long time to become a good enough piano player to play with a band, as a high-waypower child, he found a simpler instrument—the bass guitar.

Low-waypower children often become fixed on one goal, and when the routes to that goal are blocked, they don't perceive ways to alter the target. As a parent, it can be difficult and frustrating to convince your child to substitute one goal for another. This cannot always be done successfully, and it's important that your child doesn't feel like a failure if the original goal is abandoned. *Changing the goal is not to be confused with failure.* Even if a goal is abandoned, the child has gained valuable waypower experience along the way.

Here is a dialogue between a grandmother and her granddaughter that illustrates this point. The grandmother has been teaching the fourteen-year-old grandaughter how to sew, but the girl has selected a very complicated pattern.

Granddaughter: I'm so frustrated with this dress, Grandma. It has so many darts and seams, I don't think I'll ever get them all pieced together.

Grandmother: It's a very advanced pattern for a person who is just learning to sew. I wondered at the time if you were ready for it yet.

Granddaughter: I just feel like throwing the whole thing in the trash. But then I would feel like a failure. Do you think I'll ever learn to sew?

Grandmother: Of course you will. Let's look at what you've already learned on this dress, even though you might not be able to finish it just yet.

Granddaughter: Okay. I learned to put the pattern on the fabric, and I learned to pin it and cut it out. I even learned to use tailor's carbon to mark the darts.

Grandmother: That's a lot for a beginner. I have an idea. How would you like to put this project aside and work on something a little easier. You could make an apron, maybe.

Granddaughter: I don't want to make something dorky like an apron, but maybe I could make a skirt.

Grandmother: That sounds like a good idea. Let's put this away carefully, then I think after you've made a skirt, and maybe even a blouse, you'll be ready to finish this dress.

This dialogue illustrates several of the high-hope characteristics we have mentioned. Although the granddaughter's goal to make a dress was planned out, it simply was too complicated for her beginning level of sewing skills. Recognizing this, her grandmother helped her find a substitute sewing goal, one that would teach her the skills she needed to complete the first project. In this case, notice that the grandmother never criticized the girl's feelings about the project, but she steered her gently toward a sewing endeavor where success was more likely.

Putting all of these high-waypower characteristics together, we see children who know how to divide large goals into small, manageable parts, and can change the goal, or even abandon it, if this seems the best course of action. If the goal is dropped, high-waypower children learn lessons from the experience that will be helpful in pursuing the next goal. High-waypower children also know how to articulate goals in order to ask for assistance or information from others. If achieving the goal requires skills that high-waypower children don't have, they then will acquire the expertise rather than giving up on the goal.

Learning to Search for Ways

Each of the characteristics just examined also describes how children learn to increase their waypower perception. Here are some strategies, based upon the qualities used by high-waypower children, that you can teach your own children.

Strategy 1: The Goal Equals the Sum of Its Parts

Begin this lesson by having your child select a goal (it can be a hypothetical one) and writing it at the top of one side of a piece of paper. Under that goal, have your child list all the steps that she can think of that would be needed to achieve that goal. If you can think of some steps that they're missing, try giving hints to point your child's perceptions toward them. Once all the steps have been listed, use the other half of the page to prioritize them into the correct order so as to accomplish the goal. Here is an example of how this might look.

Building a Model Railroad

1. Get some model railroad books, decide what gauge to have.

2. At the hobby store, get plans of different layouts.

3. Decide on the place for the train (basement?).

4. At the hobby store, make lists of the needed equipment (rails, cars, glue, paint, etc.).

5. Decide on the background setting and make lists of items needed for scenery.

6. Get plywood and sawhorses for base.

7. Ask Grandpa for help in the assembly.

This child's list could continue with all the steps required for the assembly, but the first seven steps are a good start. When this little girl first envisioned her goal, she had in mind an elaborate model train, similar to one she had seen in a store window. When she began to detail the steps, she realized that it would be an elaborate process, but one that she could manage. Each of the steps she has described can also be broken down into even smaller steps. But she realizes that, with her Grandpa's help, she can do all of them as they are. By doing this exercise, she has learned the orderly steps to reach her goal.

Strategy 2: Asking for Help From Others

Many of the stories and dialogues in this book have stressed the importance of involving others. Because children have fewer resources than adults, this is especially important for them. In the United States, independence and autonomy are stressed, and children are encouraged to be self-reliant. For children to develop high-waypower perception, however, it's often necessary for them to ask for advice and assistance. Parents can encourage children to ask questions while recognizing that this isn't the same thing as doing the work for the child.

Parents also can encourage children to seek information from many other sources including teachers, librarians, and various professionals. Here is a vignette about a high school freshman who was enthralled by the weatherman on his local television station. He had dreams of reporting exciting weather on the nightly news.

✳ Franklin—Investigating a Future Career

The weather reporters whom Franklin watched every night on television always looked like they were having so much fun. They could make even the swelteringly hot days of southeastern Kansas seem interesting. But when there was a tornado—well, that was pure excitement! More than any other career Franklin had thought about, being a weatherman was the most appealing.

Franklin decided to ask his earth-science teacher, Mr. Hale, about how a person got to be a weatherman. The first thing Mr. Hale told him was to use the term "meteorologist" instead of weatherman. Mr. Hale also suggested that Franklin visit the National Weather Service regional storm-watch center located in a nearby town. After calling for an appointment, Franklin and his parents were given a tour.

The Doppler radar receptor, which looked like a giant soccer ball without the black spots, was visible for miles. The center itself was an insignificant looking cement block square sitting on top of a hill. Inside, however, it took on a science fiction quality—except that it was science fact. The main room was filled with computers, monitors, and printers punching out complicated looking statistics. As boggling as it looked, the few men who were working that afternoon were laughing and looked like they were having a wonderful time.

Franklin learned a lot that day about what he would need to do to become a meteorologist. He learned that he would have to take a lot of math and physics, and that after college he would probably need to go to graduate school. What impressed Franklin most was the way these men enjoyed the work of tracking storm systems, not the job of being on television. That day he saw a new side of meteorology—and he liked it.

If you live in a community with few resources for your child to use, getting a computer and accessing the Internet is a good plan. Although there are Web sites that are not appropriate for children, there are many that contain valuable information and ideas.

Strategy 3: Learning New Skills

With every new skill that your child learns, waypower perception increases. This is because the more your child is capable of doing, the more options he will have when it comes to pursuing goals. Parents are criticized at times for overloading their children with various after-school lessons and activities, sometimes to the point that the child has no free time. While this can be overdone, it is important to help your child acquire a variety of skills.

Groups such as Boy or Girl Scouts teach skills that range from outdoor survival to domestic arts. Sports, such as soccer, teach teamwork and the importance of physical fitness. A well-balanced program of activities will go a long way toward helping your child learn a wide range of waypower-enhancing skills.

In the process of working toward a goal, when high-waypower children discover that they lack some needed skills, they are willing to take a step back and learn whatever is necessary for them to continue. In the following vignette this skill-obtaining is illustrated.

✳ Steve—From Snowboard to Snowball

Although a number of Steve's friends were avid snowboarders, Steve had never had the opportunity to learn that sport. He was an excellent skateboarder, however, and when his parents decided to go skiing one winter, he was looking forward to the challenge. Steve had seen many videos about snowboarding and was confident that he had the balance and skill to do it well.

That first morning the slopes looked wonderfully inviting, covered with a new fall of lush snow. Steve rented a snowboard and bought a lift ticket but thought he might just as well skip the lessons. After all, how different could it be from skateboarding? He told his parents he would meet them later in the coffeehouse at the bottom of the hill.

An hour later, sitting by the large plate glass window that overlooked the slope, Steve's parents were sipping coffee. Suddenly, the crowd in the coffeehouse began to gasp and then laugh at the sight that was coming down the hill. A giant snowball with protruding arms and legs was rolling down the hill. When it reached the bottom, it stood up, shook off the snow, and took a bow to the audience pressing against the window. Steve had learned the hard way that skateboarding doesn't translate into snowboarding.

Steve

That afternoon Steve signed up for lessons. He had a new set of skills to learn and found that this sport was more like surfing than skateboarding. He had to learn to shift his balance differently and, of course, his feet were attached so he couldn't simply jump off the board. Within two days, however, Steve had learned enough to make it down the easy slope without becoming a snowball. Before the vacation was over, Steve had even done the most difficult slope of all.

Children need to learn new things constantly to continue the growth and development of their waypower thinking, yet this can become an imposing hurdle for children with low waypower. When these children encounter a task that requires a new skill, they often give up their goal rather than learn what is required to succeed. Parents can help children understand that they're not expected to know how to do everything. There is no failure in admitting that you don't know. A high-waypower child says, "I don't know how to do that, *but I can learn.*"

Strategy 4: Learning from Mistakes

Do you remember hearing your parents and teachers say, "Learn from your mistakes"? This advice is frequently given, and yet conditions are often established for children that make these wise words difficult to follow. What are these conditions? To begin with, when parents are overly critical, they make it crystal clear that making a mistake is bad. Unsure of their actions and faced with the inevitability of making mistakes, children will often attempt to cover up with a lie. Parental anger and criticism can be frightening and hurtful, and children will develop unhealthy behaviors to avoid it.

Sometimes it's hard to watch your children make mistakes, even when you know that they'll learn from them. For some children, learning by experience is the best method—if the cost of the mistake isn't too high. Here is the story of a stubborn seven-year-old girl's mistake and the calculated risk her mother took.

❋ Kathy—Spurred On to Success

Kathy had been riding horses since she was four years old and had been showing her quarter horse for two years. Even though she was only seven, she felt confident that she could handle almost any horse, certainly the two-year-old colt, Dusty, whom she was going to show that day.

It had rained hard for part of the morning, and by the time Kathy's class was announced, the arena was a muddy mess. She had been riding Dusty around the fair grounds for a while and noticed that he was slow in the muddy areas. This was Dusty's first show, and it was important for him to move immediately into the canter when the announcer called for that gait. So, against her mother's advice, Kathy put on her spurs and rode into the ring.

Everything went well for the first few minutes. Dusty walked and trotted as if he was accustomed to being ridden in front of several hundred people. When the announcer called for the canter, however, and Kathy dug in the spurs, Dusty became a different horse. He reared and he bucked, he kicked out his back legs as he put his head between his front legs. He did everything he could to get rid of Kathy.

Together, they put on quite a show for the amazed audience. Kathy's mother, saying every prayer she knew, held her breath until her daughter finally plopped into the soft mud. As Kathy stood up, her lovely red leather chaps dripping with dirt, she heard the announcer say that she would get a blue ribbon for staying on ten seconds—even though it wasn't a rodeo.

Later that evening, Kathy and her mother had a long talk about what had happened. Kathy said she really learned two lessons from that mistake. One was never to use spurs on such a young horse. The other, which was really the most important, was to listen to someone who has more horse sense and to not be so stubborn.

If you truly want your children to learn from their mistakes, then you have to accept that they are going to make them. To learn from mistakes, however, requires understanding what went wrong and why. Parents can help their children brainstorm their mistakes, looking for ways that will work in the future. These "brainstorming discussions" should be done calmly, without frustration, disappointment, or anger from anyone. This is an excellent strategy for adding to your child's waypower perceptions.

Strategy 5: Rehearsal

Once you child has routes planned, she can begin to try them on mentally. You can describe this strategy to your child as *imagining*. Children are often good at imaginary games, and this strategy uses that facility. Have your child mentally rehearse the routes to the goal that have been planned, and in this way, some stumbling blocks can be prevented. Ask your child to visualize him- or herself actually following the routes to the goal. Waypower perception is increased when alternative routes are visualized in case of roadblocks.

Another form of rehearsal is *practicing* the steps. Not every goal or task needs to be practiced, but there are times when this is a very useful strategy. For example, if one of the steps toward the accomplishment of an objective involves performing a task with which your child is uncomfortable, rehearsal is a good plan. Suppose that your son must give an oral report in front of the class in order to reach his goal of a good grade. If he is nervous about his performance, you can suggest that he give the report in front of the family until he becomes comfortable with it.

Here is an example of mental rehearsal, a skill used by high-waypower children to anticipate troubles along the route to their goals. This sixteen-year-old girl wants to get an after-school job in a dress store that specializes in vintage clothes.

✳ Sarah—The Perfect Style

Sarah knew that her parents had been "hippies" when they were younger, and she had always admired what she knew of the counter-culture. She was a little disappointed that her parents had joined the mainstream, but she benefited by living in a nice house and having her own car. She also had plenty of money for clothes, which she usually spent at a local vintage-clothing store. It was her dream to work there after school, because she thought the people who worked there were so "cool."

Sarah admired the women who worked at the store, but she was also intimated by their age and appearance. She knew they must be in college, and they looked like they had stepped out of the 1960s—just the way Sarah wanted to look. "But," she told herself, "I won't lose anything by trying."

The night before she planned to go in and ask for a job, she mentally planned what she would wear and what she would

Sarah

say. She had the perfect dress that she had actually gotten at the store. She tried several ways of asking for work and decided on the one that sounded the most mature. After she knew what she wanted to say, she practiced it until she fell asleep.

The next day, after school, she felt a little nervous as she went to the store. However, she felt prepared because she knew what she would say, and that gave her confidence. As it turned out, the manager and owner was a conservative looking businessman, not one of the women she had admired. He told her that her application looked good, and that she certainly had the perfect style for his store. He also said that he was going to have an opening in a month and that she should come back at that time. She promised she would, but she also said she would call him before that to remind him that she was going to work for him.

This is an example of a high-hope girl who knew what she wanted, and used rehearsal to build her confidence. Even though she didn't anticipate that the manager was a man, she had her speech so well rehearsed that the change made virtually no difference. She was proud of the touch she added at the end about phoning him to keep her fresh in his mind.

By now, you and your child have had a thorough description of waypower, and you know the characteristics of high-waypower children. We have given five strategies to teach your child, including practice as an essential part of enhancing waypower. Here is a list to use each time you work with your child on waypower enhancement. You can post this list in a place where your child will see it when he is considering goals.

Waypower Strategies

Do's

- Do break your long-range goals into small steps.

- Do begin pursuing your distant goal by concentrating on the first small goal.

- Do practice making different routes to your goals, and then select the best one.

- In your mind, envision what you will need to do to attain your goal.

- Do mentally visualize what you plan to do when you encounter a roadblock.

- Instead of blaming yourself, realize that you simply didn't use a workable strategy when you don't reach a goal.

- If you need a new skill to reach a goal, learn it.

- Do find out where you can get advice and guidance.

- Be willing to ask for help when you don't know how to reach a desired goal.

Don'ts

- Don't think you can achieve your big goals all at once.

- Don't hurry when you are figuring out the routes to your goal.

- Don't rush to select the first or easiest route to your goal.

- Don't get stuck thinking there is one perfect route to your goal.

- Don't stop thinking about alternate strategies when one doesn't work.

- Don't conclude that you are no good or "stupid" when your first strategy fails.

- Don't be caught off guard when one way doesn't work.

- Don't view asking for help as a sign of weakness.

chapter 10

Maximize Your Child's Willpower

In the last chapter, we described waypower and showed you strategies that will increase this type of thinking in your child. When a child increases perceptions of paths to reach goals, they become a more hopeful person. To grow fully into a high-hope person, your child also must develop willpower thinking, which is the focus of this chapter. Here you will learn how you can help your child to have more physical energy and increase his or her sense of well-being. You also will learn strategies for helping your child reduce stress that can undermine the development of high willpower.

In this chapter, we will return to the technique of changing negative self-talk into positive messages that we introduced in chapter 9. You also will learn about modeling, envisioning, and positive feedback for your child's accomplishments. Let's begin by exploring what we mean by the term "willpower."

What Is Willpower?

If you ask your children their views about willpower, you are likely to get an answer about something they don't like, or having to give up something they want. Most adults think of willpower in terms of deprivation and determination—all connotations that are more negative than positive—and this is why our children have similar views. This is assuming, of course, that your children are even familiar with the word.

"Willpower," as we use it in this book, means: *the supply of mental energy and commitment that can be drawn upon as a child pursues goals.* While the course to what the child wants is charted with waypower, it is willpower that is the engine or the driving force of hopeful thinking. Children who are high in willpower say such things as: "I can do that," "I'll do my best," and, "I'll try." High-willpower children know they can call upon their reserve of mental energy and go for their goals full steam ahead.

The willpower-raising strategies described in this chapter will require some time and commitment from your child, as well as from you. While the strategies you learned previously to enhance your child's waypower thinking require some behavioral changes, the willpower-raising techniques require somewhat more work. Learning to think differently and change one's self-talk requires time and practice. Remember that raising waypower and willpower is a goal pursuit, and accomplishing one's goals requires small steps and a full dose of patience.

Hope Is Part of Your Child's Total System

Throughout this book so far, we have addressed various aspects of your child as if they were separate. We have divided hopeful thinking into goals, willpower, and waypower, and have shown how to divide your child's life into domains. Although people can be viewed as being made up of many different parts (e.g., mind, body, emotions, spirit), we advocate a holistic view of people as complete beings. When you want to increase willpower, for example, it is helpful to think holistically about your child.

All of the separate parts of your child comprise a total system, and it is from this system that willpower is drawn. As a case in point, if your child is not physically fit, she will lack the physical energy required for everyday accomplishments and will have a hard time getting mentally fired up to work on a new goal. Similarly, if your child is listless or depressed, he will not be energized to seek new experiences or set new objectives. Many children who are sluggish or listless also are not in top shape physically. This illustrates the relationship between mind and body, and if your child is physically lethargic, her willpower also probably is at a low ebb.

High-willpower thinking cannot be forced upon a child, and it will not be attained through deprivation, punishment, or hard labor. You will help your child to heighten his or her willpower by encouraging small, manageable changes in the things he thinks and does. We will begin the exploration of willpower-enhancing strategies with techniques for developing physical energy. If your child practices these suggestions, she will gain powerful habits that will be beneficial for the rest of her life.

Energize Your Child

Your child's hope in general, and willpower more specifically, can be greatly affected by her level of physical condition. The more fit he is, the more energy he will have to work toward his goals. How do you know if your child is physically fit? There are several ways you can tell. Does your child awaken with energy and a cheerful attitude? Or, perhaps he drags around glumly while getting ready for school. If you suggest that she play outside, does she inevitably object? If he runs for a short distance, does he seem winded? These are a few of the behaviors that indicate poor fitness and a lack of physical energy.

Here is another indicator. Ask your child to think of something she would really like to do, something that is new and exciting. Is your child's reaction energetic? Perhaps you see your child excited for a moment, then overcome by feelings of listlessness and a loss of interest in the idea. If you sense a lack of enthusiasm for an activity that seemingly is quite interesting, your child may be short on physical energy. If this is the case, it will be difficult to enhance her willpower.

You already may be familiar with some of the health and fitness suggestions in this chapter, and in fact, you may use them yourself. Many parents do not consider the importance of these energy-building suggestions for their children based on the following simple thought: if they are not sick, they are physically well. The absence of actual illness, however, does not guarantee that your child actually is in excellent physical shape. Thus, increasing your child's physical energy is one of the most important steps that you can take in increasing willpower thinking.

Following are a few guidelines that will help your child improve their level of physical fitness. If your child already has one or more of these habits, then she already has an advantage for thinking willfully. Changing behaviors that have become familiar to your child can be very difficult. Even a six-year-old can be set in his ways, and old habits are hard to change. As with all goals, it will be necessary to proceed slowly and to take small steps. We would reemphasize that all significant changes take time to accomplish, and if you ask for changes that are too big, too fast, your efforts to help your child may be doomed to failure.

Spend time with your child explaining the program you are about to undertake. Although change can be difficult, if your child understands and believes that you're laying the groundwork for higher willpower, learning to think in this manner should be easier. When your child feels better and has more energy, exercise will become a pleasure. So, too, will exercising willpower.

Nourish Your Child's Hope

With parents' busy lives and the accessibility of fast foods, many children do not get a balanced diet. Problems such as obesity have become a serious concern for children, and the number of cases of Type II diabetes have grown substantially in recent years. Although obesity is obvious in a young child, the damage caused throughout the growth years by an improperly balanced diet is not readily recognizable. Indeed, the problems caused by a long-term nutritional imbalance may not occur until late adolescence or early adulthood. What is obvious in earlier childhood, however, is that such children may not have much vim and vigor.

Nutritional information is available from a number of excellent sources. The health and wellness section in bookstores can be a good source for all types of information. Look for books and brochures that specifically address childhood and adolescent needs, because adult requirements often differ.

Most children, as well as adults, in the United States rely on a diet that is high in sugars and fats and low in complex carbohydrates and good sources of protein. Many children do not care for vegetables, and it may be a hassle to get them to even try such foods. We suggest, however, that there are some battles you need to win, and having your child eat healthy foods is one of them.

Children need a variety of fruits and vegetables if they are to get the full spectrum of vitamins and minerals they need. If your child is one who just doesn't like vegetables, and you know you may be facing a "table war," concentrate on serving a vegetable that is very high in vitamins and minerals, so that your child won't have to eat much to get a benefit. Many children prefer to eat raw vegetables, such as carrot sticks, or even peas right from the freezer bag. There is no reason why a vegetable has to be cooked or eaten at specified meal times. You can provide already-cut vegetable snacks in plastic containers so that there is no preparation necessary. The point is to help your children to develop a taste for food that builds energy, and to steer them away from energy-draining, high-sugar and high-fat foods.

It will be difficult for you to instill good health habits in your child if you don't practice them yourself. Too many parents communicate a "do as I say, not as I do" message to their children, and in the case of health habits, that just won't work. If you do not currently attend to your own nutrition, you will find that you derive the same benefits as your child when you begin to eat a balanced diet and avoid sugar and fat. You will feel better, and you will have more energy to work with. Often, learning to think hopefully involves a team effort with your child, and this is but one example.

Instilling good eating habits in your children is relatively easy when they are young. Although there may be many foods they don't like, you can ask them to eat a small portion of the foods that are good for them. When children become adolescents, however, changing their eating habits is a real challenge. Once they have their own money and mobility, they have access to fast foods, sodas, and sweets, which they consume rather than the meals you prepare.

Hamburgers, fries, and sodas are almost a staple of the American adolescent's diet, as well as an important part of their social routine. Going off campus for lunch in groups is common among suburban high school students, and it would be unrealistic for parents to expect healthy eating on those occasions. So, what can you do about your adolescent's diet? Providing education and acting as a good role model, in addition to providing a healthy breakfast and dinner, may be the best that you can accomplish if good nutritional habits were not established early. As we showed in chapter 4, however, when teens recognize that their health habits affect their energy and appearance, even they can become more amenable to change.

Activate Your Child

Contrary to what many people believe, healthy activity does not produce fatigue. Rather, a good aerobic workout produces more energy. In fact, regular exercisers avoid doing their workouts just before bedtime because they know that they will feel too energetic for sleep. For a child or teen who is sedentary, it simply may not make any sense that regular exercise will increase energy—physical or mental. Furthermore, when children (or parent role models) become couch potatoes they experience a constant low level of fatigue. Their lassitude creates an attitude that physical exercise is too much work, and that it is far beyond their capabilities.

One way to get your child or adolescent out of a lethargic rut is to have them exercise and for you to exercise with them. Many families belong to health clubs that offer different types of exercise for all ages. Most YMCAs have swimming pools, exercise classes, and weight rooms available at reasonable family rates. If, however, you do not live in an area where health clubs are available, or the cost is beyond what you can afford, there are other forms of exercise in which the whole family can participate. Biking, hiking, or walking are fun activities, as are playing basketball or touch football. These latter activities require a minimum of equipment and can be done by young or old.

The key to using exercise to increase energy is to do it on a regular basis. A once-a-week, strenuous workout only causes your child to feel tired and have aching muscles. Whether the exercise is vigorous outside play, or working out in a gym or club, it should be done consistently, at least several times a week.

Involving your child in a sport is one of the best ways to insure physical exercise. Sports that include running, such as soccer or singles tennis, are excellent forms of exercise. Team sports have the added benefit of teaching social skills and cooperation, which will enhance hope and satisfaction in other life domains. We suggest that your child become involved in several types of physical activities. Cross training is good insurance against boredom. Whatever form of exercise your child selects, however, it should be enjoyable. It is virtually impossible to sustain an activity that isn't any fun.

Visit the Sandman

In your concern for your child's good health, don't overlook the importance of sleep. All people need healthy sleep, and children need more than adults. Sleep can be divided into two general stages, nonrapid eye-movement sleep (NREM) and rapid eye-movement sleep (REM). The first stage, NREM, occurs just prior to falling asleep, as well as in the earlier, lighter period of sleep. The second, REM, stage is the deepest sleep where most of the rejuvenation takes place. Researchers have shown that dreaming and thought activity are taking place during the REM deep sleep stage. REM sleep is a necessity for good health. Sleep researchers have linked the absence of REM sleep to various emotional and psychological disorders including confused thought and psychotic-like behaviors. Most children need a minimum of eight hours of good quality sleep, and adolescents may need even more. It can be challenging to help your child attain good sleep habits. In this regard, your child needs rest in bed, not in front of the television; moreover, the room should be quiet, well ventilated, and dark enough to promote sleep. Although sleep requirements vary from child to child, it's important for you, as a parent, to insist that your child obtain the minimum number of hours to insure the necessary REM sleep—usually about eight hours.

Substance Abuse

Adolescent use of alcohol, tobacco, and drugs has been decreasing over the past ten years. For many teenagers and their families, however, substance abuse continues to be a serious problem. In chapter 14, we will address this issue in more detail. But, at this point, we will highlight how substance use is a willpower-diminishing habit.

There is no question that using alcohol, tobacco, or illicit drugs has a negative effect on the mind and body. Alcohol is a depressant and will diminish the physical energy that fuels high-willpower thinking. Many people consider tobacco to be relaxing when, in fact, it is a stimulant. Moreover, the active agent in tobacco—nicotine—is a potent poison. Illicit substances, such as marijuana, also neutralize the energy that you are trying to build in your child, in addition to putting them at risk for legal problems.

Loving parents and caregivers don't want their children using alcohol, tobacco, or illicit drugs. Once parents discover that their children have been using these substances, however, they often do not know what they can do about it. Researchers have described the factors that place children at risk for developing substance abuse problems. These factors include previous or experimental experience with drugs, a dislike of and resistance to school, unstable family life, and peer influences. Poor communication with parents is a precursor for all of these risk factors. Take heart, however, for there are positive things parents can do.

Researchers have identified several protective factors that parents can use to help prevent or mitigate risk factors. These factors are built upon developing, first and foremost, good communications with your adolescent. You also can help your child or adolescent bond with the school by being active in the parent-teacher organization, serving on school committees, or chaperoning at dances. Many schools have a contract in which parents, by signing, guarantees that no alcohol will be served at parties for teens held in their homes. If your child's school does not have such a contract, suggest one. Most young people obtain alcohol, as well as a veritable "drug store" of prescription pharmaceuticals, from their own homes. Keeping them unavailable at home is a smart move.

Another protective factor is a peer group that has a positive influence on your child's life. Some psychologists believe that a child's peer group is *the* most powerful influence. We, however, take a different perspective. While it's true that friends can exert a strong influence, parents can make it a point to know these young people and to meet and discuss rules with their parents. Teens often try to convince their parents that other adults know and approve of their activities. By having good communication with the parents of your adolescent's friends, no wool will be pulled over any parent's eyes. In a community where all of the adults are looking out for the young people, it is much more difficult for alcohol, tobacco, and drugs to get a foothold.

Your Child's Total Health Picture

There is no question that your child's physical health and fitness are important parts of their willpower thinking. Your child must have a reservoir of physical energy from which to fuel the mental willpower that is needed to work for goals. Without this willpower, your child's dreams remain just fantasies. Let's review the strategies you can use to help your child develop increased willpower.

1. Slowly change your child's diet to include power-packed foods such as fruits, vegetables, whole grains, lean meats, and lowfat dairy products. Help your child decrease intake of fast foods and high-sugar and high-fat snacks.

2. Help your children add regular exercise to their lives. Exercise not only will help your child to cope more successfully with stress, but also to sleep better.

3. Be sure that your child gets enough rest. Remember that sleep requirements vary from child to child, but a minimum of eight hours is usually necessary.

4. If your child or adolescent uses alcohol, tobacco, or illicit drugs, actively help them to quit. If you cannot do this alone, seek professional assistance. The use of these substances can seriously compromise your child's future, in addition to being an illegal activity.

Remember to take small steps as you help your child institute these new and energy-producing behaviors. Changing too much, too soon, is a recipe for failure. High-hope people know this, and they plan their moves in advance, knowing that it's important to be comfortable with each step along the way. Your children may resist the changes you're asking them to make, but by making small ones over a period of time you are increasing the chances of success. Make it clear to your child that you want her to succeed.

To help you see how these strategies for increasing a child's physical energy work, we reintroduce Tiffany, whom you met in chapter 2. You will recall that Tiffany wanted to be a professional singer but lacked the willpower to pursue that goal. Tiffany found it much easier to sit by the window and daydream rather than implement the ways to reach her goal successfully.

✳ Tiffany—A Songbird Is Hatched

For months, Tiffany's parents, Karen and Phil, had listened to her talk about how she wanted to become a singer. At the same time, however, they watched as she sat in a rocking chair by the window fantasizing about the show business world. They knew she had a pleasant voice, perhaps even a good one, but without lessons and practice she would never fulfill her dream. They puzzled over whether to let her continue living in her fantasy world, or try enticing her into taking action.

Tiffany's parents decided to take a close look at all of her daily activities to see what did excite and energize her. What they found was alarming. Tiffany didn't seem to get enthused about any part of her day. In fact, she seemed to move through all of her daily activities in slow motion, like wading through mud.

Wondering if this lack of enthusiasm was normal, Karen took Tiffany to see the family doctor. After a thorough examination in which she was pronounced well, the doctor suggested that they examine her lifestyle. What foods did she eat? How much rest and exercise did she get? What were her friendships, and what were her interests?

An examination of Tiffany's lifestyle revealed things about

Tiffany

her parents' health habits, as well—things they had not paid attention to before. One of the first things they saw was that they were "meat and potatoes" people, rarely eating green vegetables or fruits. When they did eat vegetables, they usually had corn or lima beans rather than a high vitamin green, such as broccoli. Salads were often made of gelatin and whipped cream rather than lettuce or spinach. Tiffany's parents had grown up in the South where "good cooking" consisted of starchy, high-fat meals. They had not developed a taste for vegetables that were not floating in a cream or butter sauce. It was going to take some time to change their eating habits.

Another discovery that Tiffany's parents made was that none of them enjoyed exercising. Both her parents worked at desk jobs, and when they got home from their offices, they usually watched some television and then went to bed. Sometimes Tiffany's father had a couple of beers, which made it really hard for him to stay awake after dinner. Was there any way to change these poor health habits? This was a real concern for Karen and Phil.

Tiffany's parents loved her, however, and desperately wanted her to have a "good life." They recognized, painfully at first, that they were not the best role models, and that they could not expect Tiffany to change her lifestyle on her own. Clearly, this was going to have to be a family effort.

Tiffany's mother decided to learn how to cook new and healthier foods. As an added twist, she aimed to make it a mother/daughter project. It was time for Tiffany to learn to cook, and she might as well learn to fix healthful meals. After visiting the cooking section of the bookstore and buying a book filled with pictures, they took the subway downtown to the produce market. There they found tables of beautiful vegetables and fruits, some of which they had never seen. They made their purchases and, on the way home, Tiffany told her mother that she had really had fun.

There also were interesting ways that the family found to get exercise. That next Sunday, they went to the zoo and walked for hours. The following weekend, they went to the natural history museum and again walked and walked. One day, when Tiffany was daydreaming in her spot by the window, the doorbell buzzed and a voice over the intercom said there was a delivery. Much to her surprise a man delivered three brand new bikes—one for each member of the family.

From then on, Tiffany's family had fun getting their exercise together. They biked for miles every weekend, and in the summer, when it stayed light later, they biked after work. Tiffany and her mother made good meals several times a week, although they didn't give up their tasty southern dishes altogether. The whole family began to enjoy being active and getting out to see new things, one of which was the opera. After seeing *Carmen* Tiffany began taking voice lessons. Instead of dreaming that she was singing on a riverboat, she visualized herself singing arias. Not only did the family feel better, but, instead of watching television in the evening, they enjoyed listening to their songbird practice.

There are several important points to note in this story. The first is that children usually develop lifestyles very similar to their parents'. If parents do not eat well and exercise, children are not likely to learn those habits. The second point is that once the doctor had suggested that Tiffany's lassitude might be related to her lifestyle, changes were made *as a family.* Tiffany was not expected to do it alone. Tiffany's mother and father also made the new habits as fun and exciting as possible, and they didn't try to change everything at one time. They knew that there was a great deal of value in their old lifestyle, but that they would benefit from adding new habits to their lives.

Now that you have learned about some ways to increase your child's physical energy, let's look at ways to promote your child's mental willpower. In the next section, we will reexamine self-talk, visualizing, and positive feedback as ways to increase your child's reserve of mental energy.

Boosting Your Child's Mental Willpower

Earlier in the book, you learned that family legends, as well as stories from your own life, have a powerful influence on hopeful thinking. You saw how either negative or positive attitudes could be handed down through generations, conveyed through the family tales that have been told. You examined your child's hope in light of the stories that he or she created, and through this exercise, you began to discover the self-talk your child uses when tackling a goal.

In this section, we want to turn your attention to the process by which your child's willpower thinking can increase through the use of positive self-talk. In chapter 7, you met Caleb, who was attempting to gain a better self-concept, in part, through the use of positive messages. Changing negative messages into positive ones was a strategy you learned to help your child reach goals by building her willpower.

Willpower comes from the positive thoughts and feelings a child has about himself. Each time a boy tells himself that he is stupid, he diminishes his willpower. Each time a girl tells herself that she is silly or frivolous, her willpower goes down. Children need to hear and learn to make positive statements about the many parts of their lives. It's virtually impossible for a child to feel incompetent about one life domain while feeling great about the other areas of life. Thus, if children habitually use negative self-talk, the damaging effects will spill over into all areas of their lives.

Sources of Negative Self-Talk

You have seen how family and personal stories affect perspective, and you have used stories as a way to identify you child's self-talk. However, children learn to say mean and nasty things to themselves from sources other than stories. One common source of negative statements is the family. Siblings are great name callers and, as a parent, you may not have realized the powerful effect this can have on the way a child thinks about herself. Although children often appear to brush off hurtful comments, inside they may feel bruised and come to believe what has been said.

It's common in family therapy, for example, to see one child identified as the cause of the problems the family is having. What usually has happened, unfortunately, is that this child has become the scapegoat for many of the bad feelings that family members have about each other. Believing that she is the cause of the family dissention, the child then acts badly to confirm the family's convictions. This is an extreme case of internalizing destructive self-talk, but it shows how children absorb negative statements.

It's especially devastating when parents use destructive words to punish a child. Some parents use sarcasm as a way to point out mistakes, and worse yet, some parents use ridicule. Does this sound familiar to you as a parent? It is important to remember that whatever you say to your child is very likely to remain part of his self-talk. Once you have said an unkind thing, you cannot take it back. If you hear your child calling himself negative names, ask yourself if they sound familiar. Have you used those names to describe your child? If you have, explain to your child that you do not mean them and balance the negative statements with praise. It's good to tell your kids that you were wrong to behave in this manner.

Other children frequently are the sources for your child's negative self-talk. The playground can be a torturous experience for any child who is the least bit "different." Children are called names and teased for being short, tall, thin, fat, wearing braces or glasses, having an odd name, or even having red hair. Children can be exceptionally cruel to one another and, unfortunately, the names that children are called then show up in their negative self-talk. Teasing easily can turn to bullying, and this is a serious problem at schools in the United States. Children who are consistently bullied appear to have a higher incidence of suicide and surely are unhappier than children who escape bullying.

As a parent, it's difficult to know how to protect your child from teasing and bullying. Here are a few tips to start with. Good communication with your child tops the list. Unless you know what is happening to your child, what names she is being called and in what situations, you can't take preventive steps. Children often are ashamed to talk about this, believing that the names they are being called are true and that they are somehow deserving and responsible for this treatment. If you suspect that other children are victimizing your child, be a good listener, ask open-ended questions, and make it a point to learn what is happening.

Once you understand the situation, you have several recourses. If you believe the situation is relatively minor, you can teach your child how to cope with teasers. Usually learning to ignore the taunts is the best policy. If, however, you think the situation is more serious, you should consult the school counselor or psychologist, confidentially, and take whatever action that you mutually agree upon. In some cases, you may wish to place your child in a different school.

From research we know that children are the most likely to tease or bully any child who appears to be different. One step parents can take to help their children is to insure that their clothes, hair, shoes, book bag, and other accoutrements do not cause them to stand out. This can be difficult, especially for families with a limited income and a number of fast-growing children. The most expensive clothes and shoes are not necessary, but be sure that your children are neat and clean and that their clothes fit.

The point is that children can acquire negative self-talk from many sources. When children say negative things to themselves their mental energy is depleted, and they lose the confidence required for full-fledged goal pursuit.

Restructuring Your Child's Self-Talk

To help your child attain high willpower, one of the crucial ingredients of high-hope thought, it's necessary to restructure your child's self-defeating thoughts and replace them with positive statements that increase her mental energy. Here are some ways to help your child restructure thinking patterns.

1. Help your child identify negative self-talk. You can do this by having your child keep a record of what statements are said and when the statements are made. For example, your child might call himself stupid if he doesn't do well on a test. Or, your child might call herself slow when she can't score in soccer.

2. Help your child rephrase negative statements into positive ones, the way you saw Caleb and his mother do in chapter 7.

3. Help your child understand the situations in which he or she uses self-denigrating statements. Show your child that these statements have been learned, and that they do not reflect anything that is inherently "true."

4. Changing negative self-talk is a goal, and to accomplish this goal you will need to divide it into small steps. Select one or two situations in which your child can change his or her self-talk. After those have been mastered, add another one or two situations. Each time positive statements are used, willpower will be enhanced. With each successful addition of positive self-talk, subsequent changes will become easier.

5. When you hear your child self-correcting negative messages, be sure to praise such an effort. Changing habits of speech is not an easy task, and your child should receive a verbal reward, or better yet, a big hug.

So far, you have learned to help your child increase willpower through developing physical energy and changing self-talk to positive, encouraging messages. Here are a few more strategies to increase your child's reserve of positive mental energy.

Don't Underestimate the Power of Praise

A number of years ago, a well-known behavioral psychologist by the name of B. F. Skinner did a study to determine how children learn best. He compared punishment (negative reinforcement) with either ignoring the behavior or giving the child a reward (positive reinforcement). What he found was quite interesting. Children who were *rewarded* for a desirable behavior quickly learned what was expected of them. If a desirable or undesirable behavior was ignored, the child tended to stop doing it. Children who were punished for an unwanted behavior learned rather quickly not to do it, *but when the punishment was stopped, these children resumed the undesirable behavior.*

The implications of Skinner's findings are important for parents. For optimum learning, it's important to give your child ample positive reinforcement in the form of praise, literal pats on the back, and showing your pride in her accomplishments. There is a place for *appropriate* punishment in child rearing, but it should be balanced with love and understanding. Some parents expect good behavior and accomplishments from their children as a matter of course and consequently forget that these are praiseworthy endeavors. These same parents, however, may not hesitate to criticize or punish their child. This is an unbalanced situation that is likely to lead to low hope. Examine your approach to discipline. Are there changes you need to make? Each time you praise your child and show affection and pride, you are adding to his reserve of willpower.

Interest Pays Off in Higher Willpower

Busy parents often have problems finding time for their child's activities. You may have your child enrolled in various after-school classes and events so that you won't have to take time away from your own busy life. As working parents, we understand this dilemma, but we also suggest that it is shortsighted not to take an interest in your child's activities. It's important for parents to attend school functions and to be present to cheer your children on when they are participating in an event.

It isn't necessary, however, for you to be the soccer coach or the den mother for your child to know that you're interested. It *is* necessary for you to ask about the activities, to praise his or her accomplishments, and to attend events when your child's efforts are on display. It also is important for you to be nonjudgmental about your child's work. You certainly can suggest improvements, but balance criticism with praise at all times. Remember that children, even those who are beginning to look like adults (i.e., adolescents), are sensitive beings.

Participation in extracurricular activities is important for your child's development of hope. Without your support for such activities, however, it may be difficult for your child to maintain interest. Knowing that you are interested in these activities will help your child feel more confident and proud—high-willpower characteristics.

You have seen how Tiffany's family helped provide her with a foundation of wellness from which she might develop willpower. The following story about Marion illustrates how a child learned to cope with teasing children and an overly demanding father, thus giving him a chance to develop higher willpower.

❋ Marion—What's in a Name?

It was an old family name—Marion. His parents never thought about the consequences of giving a boy that name. After all, spelled with an "o," it's a boy's name. Marion was teased about his name from the very first day in school when the teacher called the roll. Whenever he had to tell new kids his name, they always snickered and made some comment about how he didn't look like a girl.

Maybe Marion could have handled the teasing if that had been all there was to it. But on top of that, his father expected him to live up to his namesake—his grandfather, who was a brilliant physicist. Marion just didn't like arithmetic, and he was even having a hard time learning his multiplication tables. His father gave him nightly math drills, but it seemed the more that he was drilled, the worse he got. Marion's conclusion was that he was just plain dumb. Unfortunately, it seemed that his father agreed.

During the fourth grade, Marion's low willpower became very evident. He quit raising his hand to volunteer answers in class, and he seemed to spend a lot of time daydreaming, even falling asleep occasionally during reading time. At recess, Marion played alone, or sat on the steps shuffling his Pokémon cards. Although Marion never had been an energetic and outgoing boy, he was noticeably changing for the worse. His teacher decided to call his parents with her concerns.

Marion's mother was very upset, but his father seemed as if he expected that Marion would be a disappointment. During an after-school conference it became evident to Marion's teacher that Marion's father was a big part of the problem. He was an impatient man, a hard-driving executive who had high expectations for Marion. Marion's mother, on the other hand, was a quiet and submissive woman who would be of little help coming to his defense.

Surprisingly, when the family was referred to a psychologist, Marion's father accepted the idea. As their therapy progressed, Marion's dad realized that his own father had been a hard taskmaster, and that his criticisms of Marion were similar to those of his father. The psychologist explained that Marion was developing an image of himself as stupid and incapable of success. Marion had internalized his father's criticisms and used them against himself when he tackled difficult problems.

Marion and his parents, with the help of the psychologist, decided on a plan to help Marion to feel more positive about himself. His parents began to praise his efforts, and his father tried very hard to be less critical and impatient. The psychologist also suggested that Marion could use his middle name—which was Alan. It would take time for the other students to forget that his first name was Marion, but eventually they would, and then the teasing would stop.

With time and a gradual change in his father's critical behavior, Marion began to feel more mental energy. He became willing to try new things and participate in class activities. His willpower increased, and he became a higher-hope child.

Here is a checklist of strategies you can use to increase your child's willpower. Keep this list handy and try to implement as many of these tools as you can. The results you will see in your child will be well worth your efforts.

Willpower Strategy Checklist

☐ Teach your child to eat and enjoy a balanced diet filled with energy-enhancing foods.

☐ Be sure that your child exercises every day.

☐ Insure that your child gets an adequate amount of good-quality sleep.

☐ Monitor your child's self-talk, and be prepared to help your child restructure negative thinking.

☐ Give ample praise and affection to your child.

☐ Take an interest in your child's activities.

☐ If you use punishment, balance it with positive feedback and love.

☐ Be patient—important and lasting changes take time.

chapter 11

Story Strategies for Raising Hope in the Early Years

So far you have learned strategies to help your child enhance the two basic elements of hope, waypower and willpower thinking. You also have learned the importance of helping your child select goals that are clear, manageable, and can be divided into small steps. Each component—goals, waypower, and willpower—has been examined separately. The story strategies that you will learn in this chapter bring all three parts of hope together in enjoyable lessons for you and your child.

How We Developed the Strategies

The technique of using stories to increase children's hope was developed through our research in public and parochial schools. We worked with children of all ages, from families of all income levels and from a variety of ethnic groups. The powerful technique we created to help those children are what we share with you now.

    Children of all ages enjoy stories. Young children love to have stories read aloud, and older children can become lost in books. As parents, we want our children to read books that will advance their knowledge and educate them about the things they may not be able to experience directly. Sometimes stories are used to make moral points, as with *Aesop's Fables*, or they may take your child on wild adventures, as with *Alice in Wonderland*. Of course, we also want our children to read books for fun—just because they enjoy them.

Stories teach children lessons in a unique manner—through the actions of the central figure, the hero or heroine. If the story is told well and is believable, the reader identifies with the character's actions and thoughts. When we considered ways to raise the hope levels of children and adolescents in our research, we reasoned that stories where the central character demonstrated high hope would be one means by which we could make hope lessons interesting and alive for children.

The members of our research group spent many hours reading stories to elementary school children and then discussing these stories using the strategies that you will be learning in this chapter. From the results of those studies, we know that such hope-enhancing lessons are effective in raising hope. Not only did the children in our studies demonstrate a rise in hope scores, but their teachers also rated significant improvements in their hope.

The strategies that you will learn in this chapter have been developed and refined since the original research. In this chapter and the next, you will be given stories of high-hope children that are suitable for different age groups. You will learn effective ways to discuss these stories with your children, showing them how to understand the stories as lessons of hope. Reading the high-hope stories is the first strategy.

The second strategy you will learn involves story completion, in which your child selects waypower- and willpower-enhancing actions for the main character. As a third strategy, your child will write a personal hope story. Using this strategy, your child has the opportunity to demonstrate an understanding of hope as it operates in his or her life.

The techniques are organized into two age levels. In this chapter, you will learn to use these strategies with children ages four or five to ages nine or ten. In chapter 12, the strategies are adapted for children ages eleven into adolescence. The techniques are similar for every age group, but the content and the amount of involvement required of the child vary. More specifically, older children work more on their own, with relatively little parental participation; younger children, on the other hand, need more of their parents' active involvement. Whatever the age of the child, however, parental encouragement is very important.

The ultimate goal in using story strategies is that you, as a parent, can increase your child's hope. As you work through this chapter, you will notice that the strategies are arranged in an order that goes from somewhat less to a more active involvement of your child. In the first strategy, you will read stories to your child, followed by a discussion. In the second strategy, your child selects action options and, in the third strategy, your child composes a personal high-hope story. Throughout this process your sense of involvement, engagement, and listening contributes to your having a more productive outcome. Remember, you are the teacher, your child is the pupil, and hope is the lesson.

Strategy One: Story Reading

For the first strategy, you will read your child the following story. Select a quiet, comfortable place where there will be no distractions. For the best learning experience, a one-parent to one-child situation is the most desirable, but you can use this strategy with more than one child. If you do that, we suggest limiting the group to no more than three children and allowing each child a chance to answer the questions at the end of the story. If one of the children is more talkative or dominant than another, be sure to allow the quieter children to answer the questions first.

When you're ready to begin reading the first story, remind your child about the things that she already has learned about hope. Here is what we said to the children in our research groups:

> Remember what you've learned about hope. Hope begins with a goal, which can be anything that you really want to do or to have. The next step is to think of ways to reach your goal. If it looks like your first way won't work, then you find other ways to get what you want. Hope also means that you keep trying to reach your goal, because you really think you can get there. You want your goal, and you are willing to work hard for it. Knowing that you can find ways to reach your goal is called waypower, and having the energy to reach it is called willpower.

Be sure to ask if your child has any questions about the meaning of hope. Next, tell your child that you are going to see if he or she can pick out the goal, the ways, and the will in the story you are about to read them. Here is the story.

✳ Tim—Unexpected Rewards

Tim Taylor loved his big brother, Josh. Josh was twelve, and he was tall, strong, and a fast runner. Tim was just six.

Josh and his friends played basketball every summer afternoon at the elementary school playground, and Tim couldn't wait to be big enough to play with them. But none of Josh's friends wanted a small, six-year-old boy on the court.

"Get out of the way, Tim! You're tripping me!" hollered Eric, Josh's best friend.

"You're too runty for basketball," shouted Michael, Tim and Josh's next-door neighbor. "Go play tag with your little friends."

Tim was crushed. More than anything, he wanted to play basketball. He went to talk with his mom, who had played basketball when she was in college.

"Mom, can you teach me to play basketball?" asked Tim.

"Honey, I don't think you're quite old enough to play basketball," said Tim's mom. "It's a sport that requires not only height, but muscles and coordination that you haven't quite developed yet. Let's find another fun game we can learn to play."

"But Mom, I want to play basketball!" Tim wailed. "Please, please, please show me how to do it! I promise I'll work really, really hard, and practice lots. I know I can learn how. I *know* I can, if you'll just teach me."

Tim's mom felt sorry for him.

"Tim, if you really want to try, I'll help you. But you need to know that it will take a lot of time and a lot of practice. You'll need to work for months to learn about basketball. Are you sure you want to spend your playtime and energy this way?"

"Oh yes," cried Tim, who was so happy that he danced around the kitchen.

The next morning, Tim's mom woke him up at six instead of seven. "If you're going to play basketball, the first thing we need to do is build stamina. So we're going to run every morning."

"What's stamina?" asked Tim.

"Stamina is the ability to play hard for a long period of time. You have to run back and forth on the court a lot in basketball, and if you don't have stamina, you won't be able to do it." Tim's mom pulled her hair back in a ponytail and put on her running shoes. "Because you're not used to running, we'll start out slowly and only go for a short distance. We'll go a little farther each day, though, and we'll run faster and faster."

Tim had fun running with his mom, and the rest of the day he kept thinking of outrunning Eric and Michael on the court.

That afternoon, Tim's mom said, "Hurry and do your chores. I have some exercises for us to do before supper." So Tim emptied the trash and unloaded the dishwasher, then he went into the living room to work out with his mom.

"If you're going to play basketball, you'll need good arm strength," she said. "You have to be able to throw the ball far and accurately. We're going to do some exercises that will help develop those arm muscles."

Tim had fun doing the arm exercises. He could picture himself shooting the ball from midcourt, right over Josh's head and right into the basket.

At supper that night, Tim was very hungry. He took lots of ham and macaroni and cheese but passed up the spinach.

Tim's mother passed the spinach back to him. "If you're going to play basketball, you need to make sure your body gets everything that it needs," she said. "You will particularly need to eat lots of fruit, vegetables, bread, milk, and meat and not so much ice cream and cookies. These are things that help build muscle, and you will need plenty of muscle."

Tim was not so happy about eating spinach, but he did. He kept thinking about how surprised Josh would be when he jumped high enough to throw over his head.

The next morning, Tim noticed that his arms and legs were sore. "That means you're building muscles," said his mom, and she had him run and do exercises anyway.

At first it was fun, but as the week dragged on, he got tired of getting up so early in the morning and tired of missing his playtime with his friends. And he was sure tired of eating spinach!

"If you want to quit, that's okay," said his mom. "There will be plenty of time to learn to play basketball when you're older."

But Tim couldn't imagine giving up his dream, so he kept running and exercising and eating spinach, even though now it was boring. After three months, his mom said, "I think we're ready to start shooting baskets. The one over the garage is too high for you, so I'll lower it until you get good at hitting the basket. Then we'll gradually raise it higher."

As with the other exercises, this was really fun for Tim at first, although he couldn't make many baskets. He tried harder and harder, and he began to get better and better. As he improved, he began to get tired of shooting baskets day after day, particularly when he thought about his friends watching their favorite TV shows.

"If you want to quit, that's okay," said his mom. "There will be plenty of time to learn to play basketball when you're older."

But Tim wanted to impress Josh so much. He kept up his exercises all through the rest of the summer, through the fall, and even through the winter and spring. He kept eating spinach and broccoli and apples and raisins and lots of bread. He went to bed early, because athletes need lots of rest. He got up early, too, so he could run with his mother. He began to feel stronger and faster.

The next summer, Tim was seven. "I'm old enough to play basketball with you now," he told Josh.

"No you're not," laughed Josh. "Look at how short you are!"

"I've been practicing all winter, and I'm really good," bragged Tim.

"I don't care how good you are," said Josh. "You're not playing basketball with my friends. Maybe you and I can just play a little here at home."

"But I want to play with your friends," pleaded Tim. "Please let me! I've worked so hard! Please at least let me try!"

"Tim *has* worked hard," their mom said. "I think it's only fair that you give him a chance."

"Oh, Mom!" groaned Josh. But he knew he had to let Tim try.

On Saturday, they all went to the elementary school playground. "Okay, guys, my little brother wants to try to play with us," said Josh. "Is that okay?"

"Sure it's okay," said Eric. "As long as he can hit a shot from the free throw line." All Josh's friends laughed. But Tim walked up to the line, carefully aimed the basketball, and sank it.

Josh's friends were stunned.

"Okay, let's see how he can play," said Michael, and they chose up teams. Tim was the last person chosen.

Early in the game, Tim darted in front of Eric and stole the ball. He dribbled down the court, but just as he was about to shoot, Michael towered over him and blocked the shot. Michael had no trouble sending the ball over Tim's outstretched arms. The ball missed the basket, and Tim's attempt at a rebound was a failure. Tim had plenty of stamina to run back and forth and plenty of agility to steal the ball and evade defenders. What he didn't have was height. He was just too short to shoot over Josh and his friends and too short to guard them. When the game ended, Tim didn't have a single basket, or block, or rebound. He felt like a failure.

"You played well, kid," Josh ruffled his hair as they walked off the court. But Tim was humiliated. He had worked so hard, but Josh was right. He was just too short.

Tim

As he walked away dejectedly, he noticed a man talking to his mom. Tim didn't feel like being sociable, so he went to the swing set to be by himself. He sat down in a swing and began drawing patterns in the sand with his toe.

"Hi, there," Tim looked up to see the man who had been talking to his mom. "I watched the game you played over there. You're pretty good."

"Yeah!" said Tim sarcastically. "No baskets, no rebounds, not even a block. I'm too little to be any good."

"Your running was great, though, and you sure know how to handle a ball. I coach football for the community league, and I was hoping I could talk you into trying out this fall. With your speed and agility, you could be a running back, or a wide receiver—maybe even a quarterback. What do you say?"

"But I'm too little to play," cried Tim. "The other guys would run all over me!"

"No, no," laughed the coach. "This is the little league. You would be playing against guys your age and your size. Could you do that?"

Tim agreed to try out for the team, even though football wasn't his first love. He had worked hard, though, and thought he might as well put his newly developed strength and skill to work. He was pleased when he became the quarterback for the Mapleton Giants. Josh and his friends, as well as Tim's parents, came to every game and cheered him on. His team won ten and lost four games that season and made it to the semifinals of the league tournament. And Tim was named his team's Most Valuable Player.

Now that you've finished reading the story to your child, here are some questions to test comprehension and understanding of hope as shown by Tim's thoughts and actions. Write down your child's answers, so that you can discuss them more easily.

1. Who was the main person in the story?

2. What was his goal? What did he want to have happen?

3. Name some of the things he did to make his goal happen.

4. What were some of the problems he faced?

5. Did he achieve his goal? What happened?

6. How did his goal change at the end of the story?

7. How did he show his willpower—that he really wanted to reach his goal?

Here are the answers we used with the children in our research groups.

1. Tim

2. He wanted to learn to play basketball and to be able to play with his brother's friends.

3. Tim ate the right foods, and ran, and did exercises to build up his strength and stamina. He also practiced shooting baskets.

4. Tim didn't like spinach, but he made himself eat it. He missed playing with his friends, and he suffered aching muscles. When he finally played, he found out that he was just too short.

5. Yes, Tim learned to play basketball, and he played with his brother's friends—although he was too small to play well.

6. Tim didn't completely achieve his goal, but when he was offered the opportunity to pursue something else, he took it. He was very successful at football.

7. Tim's willpower showed when he was able to put aside his discomfort and dislikes in order to keep working toward his goal. His mother offered him the chance to quit several times, but each time he chose to continue.

If your child gave answers that approximated our answers, then he or she has a good understanding of hope. If, however, the answers did not reflect a comprehension of the process, you will need to go over the explanation and story again. Even if your child answered all of the questions correctly, it's a good idea to repeat this process with other books and stories as a way to strengthen the understanding of hope. There is a list of excellent high-hope stories at the back of this workbook that will help in your work with your child. Look for the stories that are suitable for the age of your child and read those to continue the hope lesson you have begun here. To test your child's understanding, you can use many of the questions that applied to Tim's story.

Strategy Two: Story Completion

Using this strategy, you teach your child about waypower and willpower by having him or her select actions for the character in the story. At several critical points, your child can select either high- or low-hope behaviors for the main character. By following the story with the behavior selected, your child can see the outcome of his or her choice. Read the story, stopping in the places we have marked, and ask your child what the main character, Alexis, should do. Follow the directions that are given for each answer.

✳ **Alexis—The Easter Kitten**

Alexis lives alone with her mother because her father lives in another state and she has no brothers and sisters. She and her mother used to have a black-and-white cat with no tail whom they loved dearly. But two months ago, the cat disappeared. They put signs all over the neighborhood, but no one ever called or found their cat. They missed him because he had been part of their little family.

Alexis had an idea that she thought would make her mother happy. Easter was about a month away, and she thought it would be nice to get her mother a new kitten as a surprise. Every year for Easter, Alexis' mother spent hours making a dress for her to wear to church on Easter morning. And, even though they didn't have much money, there always were candy eggs hidden for her.

Alexis wanted to do something special for her mother, too. She thought that getting a free kitten from the animal shelter would be something she could do.

Question: *Is this a good goal? Is it something you think she can do?*
If your child says "no," the story ends there. If your child says "yes," go on reading.

Well, the first problem came when Alexis rode her bike to the shelter to see what choices she would have. The shelter people told her that to be able to adopt a cat, she would have to pay to have it neutered so that it couldn't have kittens. The adoption was only five dollars, but the neutering was thirty dollars. This was a problem because, although Alexis did have the five dollars (she had saved ten dollars from her allowance), she didn't know how she could come up with the other twenty-five dollars.

Question: *Should she give up? Should she use the five dollars to get her mother something else? Or, should she try to find a way to get the thirty more dollars?*
If your child said to give up, end the story right there. If your child suggested another gift, discuss what it would be, and then simply have Alexis give it to her mother on Easter. If your child wants Alexis to try to get the money, then keep reading.

Later that evening, Alexis began to wonder if people who leave cats at the shelter ever say they will pay for the operation if someone will adopt them. Perhaps grown cats that have already been neutered need adoption, although she thought her mother would prefer a kitten. The next day she called the shelter and found out that once in a while someone does bring in a kitten and leaves money to pay for its neutering. Alexis put her name on the list to get a kitten if one was brought in like that.

About a week later, Alexis got a call from the shelter saying that a man had brought in a little tabby kitten. He loved her, but he had dogs that didn't like cats, so he couldn't keep her. He said he was sorry that he couldn't have the tabby, but he would pay for the operation if someone would adopt her.

Alexis was very excited, but then she realized that it was still two weeks until Easter. How could she get the kitten and still make it a surprise?

Question: *Should she tell the shelter people that she can't take the kitten? Should she get the kitten and give it to her mother early? Should she try to find a way to keep it a secret, so that it can still be a surprise?*
If your child says that she shouldn't take the kitten, end the story there. Giving the kitten to her mother as an early present shows some degree of hope, in finding a kitten and solving her money problem. However, Alexis would be giving up before she has reached

her final goal, thus this is not the highest hope response. If your child wants Alexis to continue trying to reach her goal, then go on reading the story.

Alexis knew she could figure out some way to keep the kitten hidden because she really wanted to surprise her mother. Maybe she could have the next-door neighbors keep it. No, they too had a dog. How about asking her best friend to keep it? But that wouldn't work, because she was allergic to animals. She didn't know anyone else to ask.

Question: *Can your child think of any other ways that Alexis could try? Should Alexis give up? Should she go ahead and give the kitten to her mother?*

If your child wants Alexis to give up or give the kitten to her mother early, you can end the story there. If your child thinks of another way for Alexis to hide the cat, praise that suggestion and go on with the story.

Well, Alexis had a bedroom of her own in the basement of their house. If she was very careful to keep her mother upstairs, maybe she could hide the kitten in her room. It was worth a try.

The next thing she had to do was to figure out how to bring the kitten home and get it set up in her room, all before her mother came home from work. To do this, she enlisted the help of her next-door neighbor. Before picking up the kitten at the shelter, they went to the store and bought kitten chow and cat litter with the five dollar Alexis had left over. She also got a cardboard box for the litter, which she lined with paper, and borrowed two plastic margerine containers for food and water dishes. Now the kitten was all set, if only it would keep quiet.

As it turned out, hiding the kitten was kind of fun. At night, it slept under the covers with Alexis, and during the day, it stayed under her bed. She gave it lots of love and, because her mother worked all day, they had plenty of time to play together. There was only one close call. Once Alexis' mother went into her room to put some clean clothes away, but the kitten stayed out of sight.

When Easter morning came and Alexis presented her mother with the kitten, her mother was very happy. She was really proud that Alexis had gotten the kitten by herself, and that she had kept it hidden for two whole weeks.

Alexis

They laughed together at how hard it had been, and how her mother had almost discovered it.

After that, the kitten began to eat like a horse. They named it Max, because he grew into such a large cat. Because of all the care he got when he was so young, Max grew into the most loving cat there ever was.

If you completed the story with your child, you now can review the questions you asked after Tim's story. If you didn't complete this story, it may be an indication that your child may not fully understand the hope process. It will be important for you to continue asking the questions you asked them after you read the story of Tim, using additional stories. The strategy of story completion is intended to engage your child in the active decision-making process that is part of developing hope. At each juncture, choices must be make that will determine whether the character pursues the goal or quits. This exercise mirrors life experiences for your child.

Strategy Three: Story Writing

In chapter 7, we introduced your child to story writing as a way of examining his or her hope. The stories in this strategy are somewhat different, however. Here they are used to show how your child uses high-hope thinking to work for goals. At this point, you have already used a number of strategies to enhance your child's hope, and these stories are a way to bring together everything that has been learned.

Because your child is young and would probably find the act of writing a distraction from the story, use a tape recorder as you used it in chapter 7. Here are the instructions that we used with the children in our study. Try them with your own child.

> We have read two stories about children who set goals and then found ways to accomplish them. We read about Tim, who wanted to play basketball, and then we read about Alexis, who wanted to surprise her mother with a kitten for Easter. You were able to say the goals, and the different ways these children used to get what they wanted. You also were able to tell how much willpower they had for their goals by how hard they worked to achieve them.
>
> Now I would like you to tell a little story about a time when *you* wanted to do something or to get something. Tell about what the goal was and about the ways that you thought of to get what you wanted. Tell about any problems that you had while you were trying to reach your goal and how you solved them. Tell, also, about whether or not you reached your goal. How does your story end?

Your child may need some prompting in order to do this assignment. If he or she cannot immediately think of a goal, you can help by suggesting one that you have observed. You may need to tell several stories of high hope from your child's past before he or she gets the feel of this strategy. In our research groups, however, young children were able to identify a number of goals they had struggled to achieve. They told about learning to skate or ride bikes, and one child even remembered learning to walk.

The important message in this strategy is for your child to recognize that his or her life is filled with hope stories. Even young children have accomplished quite a lot, but these accomplishments may need to be put into a high-hope frame of reference before children can come to see themselves as hopeful thinkers and doers.

The following story is an adaptation of one that was told by a child who was eight years old about when he first began school. It was originally tape recorded, and it is written here with appropriate grammar and punctuation added. Notice how this child shows hopeful thinking.

✳ Domingo—New School and a New Language

My parents are from Mexico, but I was born in the U.S. When I was very little, we moved around a lot because my parents picked fruit on farms in many different places. When I was about five, I think, we moved to this town because my parents got a job in a meat-packing plant. Now we live in one place, and I have to go to school.

There are a lot of other Mexican kids in my school, and like me, most of them don't know how to speak English very well. There is a special class we go to where we learn English, but the problem is that in the regular classroom, they don't speak any Spanish. I felt lost a lot of the time, because I didn't understand much of what the teacher was saying.

For a while I didn't know what to do. My parents couldn't help me because they didn't speak English even as well as I did. The kids in my class who spoke English didn't speak Spanish, so I couldn't ask them for help. Then I had an idea of what to do.

I asked the ESL (English as a second language) teacher if she knew any older kids who had learned to speak English but also

Domingo

still spoke Spanish. She told me that she knew lots of them. She gave me some names of kids and told me where to find them. Just as school was ending that day, I went to the sixth-grade classroom to try to find a boy named Rudolfo to ask him if he would teach me English.

I found him, but he was with a few other boys who were all Anglos. When I called his name, he got angry and said his name was Rudy and not to bother him. I decided to try a girl next time, thinking that maybe girls would be nicer.

The next day I went to a fifth-grade class and met a girl named Rosa. She was very sweet, and she was also very pretty—which was okay with me. She said she would be happy to teach me what she could, because she said she knew it was hard to learn a new language. It turned out that she lived near me, so she said I could come to her house. She was busy after school taking care of her younger sisters, but since she was teaching them English, too, I could learn along with them.

I went to her house nearly every afternoon. Rosa taught us words and sentences that we didn't learn in ESL, things we needed to learn to help our parents get along. I learned how to ask for things at the grocery store, and how to talk to people who telephoned our house. Everything I learned from Rosa, and a lot of the things I learned in ESL, I tried to teach to my parents. Teaching my parents helped me learn faster, too.

Now I'm in the third grade and I speak English pretty well. The ESL teacher said that she hadn't thought about having older students who could speak English and Spanish help teach the younger ones. She said I had given her a good idea, and that the school would begin to do that all the time.

Learning to speak another language is hard, even when you are as young as I was. I feel very proud that I learned to speak English, and also proud that I had given the teacher a good idea. I know one thing, though, I'm really proud of being Mexican, and I am never going to change my name just to try to be one of the Anglo boys.

Read this story to your child and discuss the goal, waypower, and will-power Domingo demonstrated. Be sure to point out that this story was based on one told by a third-grader, and that it has been adapted to be in this book. You can "write" your child's story as well, based on what he or she tells you. After you have "written" your child's story, read it to him or her. See if your child can identify the components of hope.

These strategies—story reading, story completion, and story writing—are techniques that can be used again and again. When you read other stories to your child, whether they are about people or animals, real events or fantasy, you can usually find the components of hope. Teach your child to look for waypower and willpower in all the stories you read together. This activity gives an added boost to the many benefits of storytime. You are teaching your child to love literature, the value of reading, and you are sharing a wonderful activity together. You are also showing your child love by giving him or her the essential quality of hope.

chapter 12

Story Strategies for Older Children and Adolescents

The techniques for enhancing hope in children from ages ten or eleven into adolescence are similar to the ones you learned for younger children in the last chapter. The major differences are that these techniques are appropriate for the reading level and interests of the older group, and older kids will do more written work on the assignments. We have used these strategies with middle and high school youth and have found them to be successful in enhancing hope scores.

It's our experience that young people in the middle school age group often disclose their thoughts and feelings more easily than younger children, who may not know the right words, or adolescents, who are generally resistant to any adult intervention. For this reason, the middle years are an excellent time for parents to teach lessons of hope.

When children enter adolescence, often they are not as amenable to change as they were when they were younger. But if you have followed the strategies suggested in the preceding chapters, your adolescent already has a good grasp on the elements of hope. In that chapter, the format was geared to the cognitive abilities of younger children who need more guidance in their discovery process. Older children can be expected to have creative ideas about hopeful actions and choices. Possible answers are suggested, however, if your adolescent cannot offer any. Allow ample opportunity for answers to be given, and then suggest any alternative that your child did not present. We also suggest that you have your adolescent read one or more of the high-hope books from the list at the end of this workbook. You, too, can read the book and then discuss the hope messages you both learned. The first two strategies presented here are most appropriate for children in the middle years, but they can also be used with adolescents. The third technique, story writing, is well suited to teenagers. A high school girl wrote the story we selected to illustrate this strategy.

Strategy One: Reading the Story

Teaching lessons of hope to young children requires that their parents play a pivotal role. It was your responsibility to select, read, and then discuss stories about high-hope children. Enhancing hope in children who are in their middle years continues to require your participation, although, at this point, your child is capable of reading the stories alone. Because older children are able to pay attention better than younger children, story reading can be done in a group. For example, reading high-hope stories can become a fun family activity, with different members taking turns reading aloud. Afterwards, a family discussion of hope can be a rewarding learning experience for everyone.

Begin with the story below. Have your child read it alone or read it in a group. Have him or her answer the questions at the end of the story and then discuss the answers. We have provided a space for your child to write the answers—you may want to refer to them later for the discussion. If you read the story as a family, be sure to allow your child to give the answers first. You want to be certain that he or she understands how hope has helped the child in this story.

✱ Robin—Protector of Small Creatures

Robin is a bright, nine-year-old girl with long black hair who lives with her mother, father, and three brothers in a small town in Oklahoma. She is a member of the Creek Indian nation—her mother is Creek and her father is Creek and Cherokee. Many of Robin's cousins, aunts, and uncles also live in the town. There are lots of children for her to play with, but she has a problem that stops her from playing many of the games the others play. Robin was born with one leg shorter than the other, which causes her to limp and stops her from running fast enough to keep up with the other children.

When Robin joins her brothers and cousins in their games, they try to include her, but after a while they forget and go running off. She often feels left out and alone. She feels that no one except her dog really notices her. Even though Robin loves her family and being part of her small community, she wants something that would make her special in a good way, not just special because of her leg.

One evening Robin was trying to play hide-and-seek with her cousins down by the stream. She decided to hide in a small hole she found in a bank near the water. As soon as she started to crawl inside, she heard a hissing sound. She moved back, afraid it was a rattlesnake.

Then she realized it wasn't a rattle, but a hiss. She crept closer, using a long stick to brush aside some of the bushes, and looked inside the hole. Inside she saw a raccoon—at least she thought it looked like a raccoon. She was used to small wild animals, so she went quietly away, leaving the raccoon alone.

She had forgotten the raccoon until the next week on the way to school. From her school bus window, she saw a raccoon lying dead beside the road. She said a little prayer for the animal's spirit, as she always did when she saw an animal that had died. Later that day, Robin got to wondering if it had been the raccoon in the hole that she had almost disturbed.

In the evening when Robin got home, she went to the hole by the stream and cautiously ventured to the entrance. This time, instead of a hissing sound she heard a high mewing noise. The mewing sounded like a baby something—but what? She crept closer and closer, until she could put the stick clear inside the hole. When nothing happened to the stick, Robin cleared the brush away so that she could see inside the hole. She found two baby raccoons, very small, and now very quiet with fear. She quickly backed away from the hole—what if the mother or father returned and found her there? Yet, where were the parents? Robin realized the she didn't know much about raccoons, but she knew someone who did.

That night after dinner, Robin went to her grandfather's house and asked him what to do about those baby raccoons. Did he think their mother had been hit by a car? Where did he think the father was? Robin's grandfather said that it might be that the parents were gone, but that the raccoons were meant to be wild and should be left alone. He said that she would not know how to take care of raccoon babies, and even if she could keep them alive, what would happen to them later? Besides, he said, raccoons are pesky and get into everything.

That night Robin tossed about in her bed with thoughts of lonely baby raccoons. Before the school bus came the next morning, she went to the creek and looked in the hole. Sure enough, the baby raccoons were still there and were mewing even louder.

During the day Robin could hardly pay attention to the teacher because she was so worried about those raccoon babies. As soon as she got home, she went to the hole to look and found them there and still alone. By this time, Robin was certain that they were orphans and so she did a daring thing. She got a cardboard box, put a towel in it, and carried the raccoon babies up to her house. Her mother was in the kitchen fixing dinner, and Robin was able to slip past her up the stairs to her room. Because she had only brothers, she had a very small room all to herself, which for a while would be a good hiding place for the little raccoons.

Now that she had actually rescued the raccoons, she had to figure out what to do to keep them alive. She did another daring thing next. Robin asked her oldest cousin, Jim, who lived next door and had a car, to drive her into town to talk to the veterinarian, Dr. Smith. She confided to Jim what she was doing because she was so excited she could hardly keep still. Jim said that he would take her, but she would have to tell her family. They would hear the raccoon's noises and probably begin to smell them before too long.

Dr. Smith was nice and very helpful. He told Robin and Jim to buy some cat chow and fresh fruit and corn to feed the raccoons. He also said that raccoons could eat worms and bugs. Dr. Smith cautioned Robin that it's not a good idea to keep wild animals and that, if they lived, she could not keep them as pets. He said she would have to feed them often, and that they probably wouldn't live without their mother. But Robin was determined to do everything she could to help her raccoons grow.

At home, after she fed the babies with the food she had gotten and the bugs she had found, Robin told her family. Surprisingly, her parents were very encouraging and told her they would help her buy more food. Her mother said she would do the feeding while Robin was at school. Robin's brothers said they wished they had found those babies, but they also thought it was going to take a whole lot of work to keep them alive.

Robin did set to work, feeding each raccoon every three hours, except at night. She petted each of them and made sure they had lots of love. She often had to change the paper in their box because, like all babies, they were messy.

Word spread through the small town that Robin was trying to raise the baby raccoons. The children in her class wanted to come and see them or have her bring them to school. But she didn't want too many people around them yet because they were still young. Many people asked her how the raccoons were doing. When Jim and Robin took them back to the veterinarian for a checkup, Dr. Smith gave them free shots. He was amazed that Robin was not only keeping them alive, but also helping them grow big and healthy.

As the raccoons grew in size, they also grew in mischief. While Robin was at school one day, the raccoons climbed out of their box. They took a lot of her clothes out of the drawers and generally messed up her room. After that, Robin's parents borrowed a cage from an uncle who raised rabbits. It was certain now that the babies were growing into healthy raccoons.

Robin had a new problem: What should she do with the raccoons now that they were growing up? A lot of people wanted them for pets, but Dr. Smith and her grandfather said that grown raccoons get into too much trouble. It just isn't a good idea to try to make pets out of wild animals. Robin had an idea that she discussed with Dr. Smith. Tulsa had a children's zoo that she loved to visit, and she wondered if the raccoons could live there. Dr. Smith said that he had a friend who worked as a zoo veterinarian, and he would ask. Soon they had an answer. Yes, the children's zoo would love to have the raccoons, and when they were all grown up, they could live with the other raccoons.

Robin took the raccoons to school finally, just before they went to Tulsa, and all the children saw how big they had grown. Robin was very sad to part with her little fellows, but the day her parents and Jim drove her to Tulsa a lot of townspeople came out to wave good-bye to them.

Robin cried on the way home from the zoo, but she knew that the raccoons might not live in the wild now that they were so tame. She also knew that they would not have lived at all had it not been for her. And best of all, everyone knew that she had saved their lives, and she was now known to everyone as the girl who rescued raccoons.

Robin

As you've probably noticed, this story is longer and more complicated than the ones for younger children that you read in the last chapter. Here are some questions for your child to answer to insure that he or she understood the hope message.

1. What did Robin want to have happen? What was the goal, or goals, in this story?

   _____

   _____

2. What were some of the problems Robin had to solve in order to save the raccoons?

   _____

   _____

3. What ways did Robin think of to reach her goal?

_____

_____

4. What feelings did Robin have that kept her trying to save the raccoons?

_____

_____

5. How did Robin finally achieve her goal?

_____

_____

Here are some correct answers to the above questions. Again, because the story is for an older group of children, the answers are more complicated.

1. Robin had two main goals. She wanted to be known for something other than her limp, and she also wanted to save the baby raccoons.

2. Robin had two main problems to solve. She had to learn how to care for the raccoons, and she had to figure out what to do with them when they got older. She also had to find people to give her information and get her parent's permission to keep the raccoons.

3. When Robin took her concerns to her grandfather, Dr. Smith, Jim, and her parents, some of them encouraged her and some discouraged her. High-hope children get help when they need it, and they are not easily discouraged.

4. Robin was moved by the plight of the baby raccoons, and she wanted to save their lives. She also believed that she could do it and was persistent in her efforts.

5. Robin achieved both of her goals by raising the raccoons and by becoming known as the girl who rescued them.

The story you have just read is one of many that can teach lessons of hope. At the end of this workbook you will find a list of such stories appropriate for many ages and reading levels. Read the stories your child reads. You can formulate similar questions for discussion and turn many reading experiences into fun hope lessons.

Strategy Two: Story Completion

This story-completion exercise involves having your child read the story and then choose which alternative would show high-hope thinking. Follow the directions after each choice.

✱ Shane—Skill and Concentration through Martial Arts

Shane was the smallest and thinnest boy in the sixth grade. Not only was he small, but he was also shy. Unfortunately for Shane, his father was a large, outgoing man, who loved sports—especially basketball. In fact, it seemed to Shane that everyone he knew loved sports, either to play or to watch. Shane thought sports were okay, but he preferred to read books or play chess than go to the games.

One evening, Shane's father told him that it was time for him to play a sport, and that he was to enrolled in the community basketball league. The next day they went to the Parks and Recreation office where Shane was signed up to play on one of the teams.

For the next few months Shane's life was miserable. The practices were embarrassing, and the games were humiliating. The coach was always yelling at him, and the other team members made fun of him when he lost the ball or missed a basket. Shane couldn't throw or guard as well as the other boys, and he wasn't really interested in trying very hard. Finally, the season was over and Shane was glad to get back to his books.

Shane's father was very disappointed and kept after him to choose a sport.

Questions: *What are Shane's options at this point? Do you think he has a goal in mind yet?*

Answers: *Shane could just try to ignore his father, hoping he will give up. Or, he could try to find a sport he might enjoy. If Shane has high hope, his goal will be to try to please his father but also to please himself.*

If you think Shane should ignore his father, think about what kind of problems he will have. Ignoring his father would be a high-hope choice.

In some of the books Shane had read, the characters were good in martial arts such as karate and tae kwon do. Often the heroes won exciting battles through concentration and skill. Shane liked the idea of concentration and decided to ask for lessons in tae kwon do as his sport.

Shane's mother thought that was a good idea, and together they visited the community center where the classes were held. Surprisingly, they saw small children, both boys and girls, as well as older children and adults. All of them were practicing the graceful movements. Shane was very happy to see a boy no bigger than himself wearing a black belt over his standard white pants and top. That meant that this small boy was actually strong and quick, and had reached one of the highest levels. Shane decided that he was going to earn a black belt, too.

Questions: *What is Shane's goal now? How did he reach the decision to choose martial arts?*
Answers: *His goal is to earn a black belt in tae kwon do. He decided on martial arts through his reading. Concentration and skill are appealing to Shane.*

When Shane told his father that he had signed up for tae kwon do, the reaction was not encouraging. His father wanted him to play a team sport, as he had done. He was satisfied, however, that Shane was at least getting some physical activity.

The first few months of Shane's classes were spent learning specific sets of movements, called forms. He progressed quickly from a white to a yellow belt, and then on to an orange belt. With the orange belt, the students began to fight, or spar, with each other. Although they were not supposed to make physical contact when they hit or kicked, it sometimes happened. On one occasion, Shane had to spar with a boy who held a higher belt and was bigger than he was. The boy accidentally kicked Shane quite hard in the face, which momentarily stunned him. Shane was unable to kick or hit back, and when it was over he felt humiliated—just as he did after those awful basketball games.

On the way home in the car Shane cried, and told his mother he wanted to quit.

Questions: *What should Shane do? Should he quit, or should he try harder? Should he find another sport?*
Answers: *If you think he should quit, think about how he will feel about giving up his goal. Will he think he's a failure? Will it be harder for him to believe he can succeed at his goals in the future? If he tries another sport now, how will his experiences with basketball and martial arts influence his future success? If you think he should continue with tae kwon do and try harder, you have made the high-hope choice.*

Shane's mother was sympathetic, but she told him he could quit only after he had gone back and sparred again with the same boy. She gave him a pep talk and told him she knew he could do it.

That night, and all the next day, Shane talked to himself about being brave and facing his fears. He knew he had been able to earn three belts since he started, which was very good. He really didn't want to give up now. The next night, while he was falling asleep, he imagined himself in his white uniform with a black belt. He saw himself spinning and kicking and even breaking boards with his hands and feet. He also imagined how amazed the boys who played basketball would be when they saw the things he could do.

Questions: *How was Shane increasing his willpower to continue toward his goal? What are the ways Shane sees to achieve his goal?*

Answers: *Shane is using his imagination to see himself as successful. He is also envisioning the reward of proving to the boys who had teased him that he can do something that requires skill and strength.*

Shane knows the ways to reach his goal are to learn the forms and to practice them. He also knows that he will have to spar with others who are better than he is—he knows he will have to be brave.

For the next few days, Shane practiced his spin kicks and his hand moves, always imagining that he was sparring a bigger and older person. When it was time for his class, he was afraid but ready. He was both pleased and apprehensive when he saw that he was to spar the same boy who had beaten him so badly a few days before. When the teacher said to begin, Shane started kicking and throwing his punches as fast as a pinwheel. The other boy, who thought he would win easily, was caught by surprise. Afterwards, when they bowed to each other, he told Shane that it was a much better match. He said that Shane had fought very well.

The months were going by and Shane was earning more belts, but his father rarely mentioned tae kwon do. Shane was disappointed, but he was glad that the pressure was off for him to join a ball team. On the day that Shane was to demonstrate the forms and break a board with his hand for a blue belt, he decided to ask his father to be there. Shane's father had never seen the lessons, because they took place during the afternoon when he was at work. This meant that he would have to take part of the day off, but he said he would.

Shane

Shane was very excited that afternoon, and he kept watching the crowd of parents to see if his father was there. When it was almost time for him to perform, he scanned the crowd, but didn't see his father. Shane felt disappointed, but he also felt angry. Perhaps his frustration fueled his ability to spar, because he was tougher and more precise than he ever had been. When it came to breaking the board, Shane broke three, with no problem at all.

After the demonstration, Shane's father came up to congratulate him. He had been there all along, but Shane hadn't noticed him because he was hidden behind the video camera he was holding. That evening the family watched the video many times, and each time Shane's father told him how astonished he was at the skill required to do tae kwon do. He was especially proud of how good his son was. He said he couldn't have been more pleased if Shane had been scoring points in a basketball game.

Questions: *Did Shane achieve his goal? During the course of the story, did Shane's goal change? How do you think Shane felt at the end of the story?*

Answers: *Shane achieved his first goal, that of finding a sport that pleased both himself and his father. Although Shane still had the original goal, he also decided that he wanted to earn a black belt. During the months that his father appeared uninterested in tae kwon do, Shane continued to work hard to earn more belts.*

Shane felt tremendous pride in his accomplishments at the end of the story. He knows now that he can work hard and overcome roadblocks to achieve success.

As your child reads this story, be sure to discuss the questions and answers. Be certain that he or she understands why some answers are high hope, and others are not. Have your child also tell you the ways Shane perceived that he could use to reach his goal, and how his actions showed willpower.

The next strategy involves asking your child to write a personal story of hope.

Strategy Three: Story Writing

This technique brings together all of the knowledge your young person has gained about hope through the work you both have done in this book. The strategy of story writing works well for children in the middle school years, as well as those in high school. You can give the following instructions for story writing. They are the ones we have used in our research.

When you write your story, begin with a goal that you've recently had, whether or not you actually achieved it. Write about the ways you first envisioned that you might reach that goal, and then write about the ways that you actually tried. What problems did you encounter? What did you do about those problems? Did you ask for help or advice from anyone? If you followed through on the ways you perceived, how did you maintain your energy? Write about the things that you told yourself as you worked for the goal. What was the outcome? Did you quit? Did you change your goal? Were you successful? Whatever the outcome, write about what you learned from the experience.

Go over these instructions with your child or teen. They include a number of questions to be answered, and it will help to keep the instructions handy. Remember that spelling and punctuation are not the focus of this assignment, and if you are critical of the story, it will defeat the purpose of enhancing hope. Here is an example of a story written by a high school student.

✳ Misty—Fifteen Minutes of Fame

People look at me and they think that I'm so lucky. I have to admit that I am pretty fortunate; I have parents who love me, and they have enough money to buy me what I want. I'm also very tall and thin, and most people say I'm very pretty. But just because I have all those good things, doesn't mean I don't have goals, and that I don't have to work hard. I do.

What I've wanted since I was in junior high school was to be a model. Not just any model, but a famous model, like you see in the fashion magazines. I always thought that I had the height and the figure for it, but I wasn't sure if I was pretty enough. Also—and this was a major problem—I didn't have a clue how to get started. So there I was, seeing myself on the catwalk but not knowing how to get there.

We live in a large city, so I decided to visit a modeling agency to see what I could learn. When I called for the appointment, they told me to come in with my mother. I thought that was strange, but she and I went together one evening. During that meeting, I was told that they could probably make me a model, but that I would have to take a course first—which turned out to be very expensive. My parents said that if I wanted to do that, they would pay for it, but that they wanted me to check on the school to see if it had a good reputation.

I decided to write to some of the big agencies in New York City to ask what they thought of modeling courses and how likely they were to use a model from one of those schools. I knew I had a lot to learn, but my parents were right about finding the best school. Within a few weeks I got a letter from Elite, one of the biggest and best-known agencies. They said that the schools were good, but that very few of the girls who went to them would ever get to be top models.

This was sobering information. I almost decided to give up my dream then and there. Then I thought, maybe I won't be a supermodel, but whatever I learn will come in handy somehow. I might as well try. If I don't try, I'll never know if I could have done it.

I got enrolled in the modeling classes, which were taught two nights a week and lasted for two and a half hours at a time. There certainly was a lot to learn. It seemed like we spent days learning how to walk, sit, turn, stand, get in and out of a car, and even bend over to pick up something. I especially liked the lessons when we walked on the catwalk they had in the studio. I really felt like a model then, and everyone said I looked great.

As part of our training, we had photography sessions. I worked with a photographer who gave me some good pointers, and we put together a portfolio that looked very good. I learned makeup tricks and had my hair done the way the agency suggested. I had to buy special clothes to carry with me if I went for a modeling call, different types of underwear and all sorts of shoes. At last, they told me I was ready.

But ready for what? Weeks went by and no one called me. Finally, I went to the agency and asked them what was going on. Was I supposed to be doing something else? After that, I got a few calls to model for ads in the newspaper, but that was hardly what I had in mind. I was pretty discouraged and wondered if everything I had done was for nothing. Then I got the call that opened up a whole new world of opportunities.

Every year my agency has a contest to decide who is the best young model of that year, and I was asked to enter the contest. The competition has several parts to it, somewhat like the Miss America Pageant but not as grueling. We had to model clothes and swimsuits, and we showed our portfolios and talked about ourselves in front of the judges. There were twenty girls in the contest, several of them from my class, and everyone looked great. I didn't know if I had a chance.

I guess I did well, though, because I was selected as a runner-up for the young model of the year. But the prize, wonderful as it was, posed problems for my family and me. I was invited to go to Milan for a year to model clothes made in Italy. I knew that many supermodels had gotten their start in Italy, but I didn't know if I was prepared to quit high school and go off to live in another country where I couldn't even speak the language. What a dilemma! I wanted it, but I didn't want it.

My parents and I weighed all the pros and cons. My mother said that she would come with me if I wanted, but I knew that would be difficult for her. I thought about quitting high school, and then I thought about the type of life supermodels really have. Even if I became a huge success, how long would it last? Now that I could almost see and touch my goal, was it what I really wanted?

I thought about what to do for a week, but there was pressure from the agency for me to make a decision. When I visualized my future in a realistic, down-to-earth way, I saw myself going to college and having a career along with marriage and children. I decided that the smartest thing for me do would be to stay in school. I had so much growing up to do, and I wanted to do it with my friends and family.

I had made my dreams of becoming a model come true, at least on a small scale. I could always get local jobs to earn extra money, and I had certainly made a name for myself in our community. I decided that I could be quite satisfied with my fifteen minutes of fame.

A high school girl who had exceptionally high hope wrote this story. Most stories would not have such lofty goals, nor as many opportunities to pursue them. However, many young people do pursue and achieve outstanding successes. Among the stories that you can suggest for your teen's reading are the biographies of successful young singers, artists, composers, actors, and writers, some of which are included in the lists at the end of this book.

Most of the stories in this workbook have been about children who live in average or fortunate circumstances. What about hope for children who are less advantaged? What about children who are in trouble? The last two chapters of this workbook will describe strategies that are especially geared for these children.

chapter 13

Minority Children and Hope

Previously in this workbook, you have read a number of stories and learned many hope-enhancing strategies. If you are a member of an ethnic minority group, you may have wondered how applicable this information is to your family and, specifically, to enhancing the hope of your child. This chapter focuses on those questions and concerns.

Ethnic minorities in the United States face negative stereotypes and beliefs held by the dominant culture (Caucasian). Although social conditions, racism, oppression, and numerous other factors have a powerful influence on the development of hope, it's not possible within the scope of this book to cover them in detail. We mention only a few before proceeding to the hope-diminishing factors experienced by ethnic minority children.

As a parent who is a member of an ethnic minority group, you may have experienced some of the risk factors that have diminished your hope. Ethnic minorities in the United States tend to have lower incomes than people in the dominant culture. They also experience higher unemployment, and there are more single-parent households, often headed by women. Ethnic minorities are frequently less educated than members of the dominant culture, have poorer health and health care, and are not as well nourished. This is but a partial list, but the picture for many minority individuals is bleak. Economic conditions force many families to live in dangerous neighborhoods where the housing and schools are inadequate.

As an ethnic minority parent, you may not personally have these risk factors, or you may have one or two, but it is likely that you have acquaintances or family members whose quality of life is lowered because of them. As you work to enhance your child's hope, it is important to consider which of these factors play a role in his or her life. It is more difficult to develop hope when these risk factors are present.

Based on our research findings with minority children, it appears that in the early years, children of all ethnicities have higher hope than do the adults of their group. They believe that they will do well and that they can find ways to get what they want. As these children grow older, however, they are confronted with the reality that their ethnicity, added to their other risk factors, may make it difficult to maintain their hope and have satisfying lives.

Although ethnic minority children have higher hope than adults of their group, we have found in our research programs that they did not score as high as children of the dominant culture on measures of hope. Within minority groups, African American children scored the highest, with Hispanic children and Native American children scoring the lowest. We have not had sufficient numbers of Asian American children in our research groups to reliably determine their relative level of hope. One obvious inference based on the low hope scores of the minority children in our research groups is that they may be the damaging effects of the risk factors experienced early on.

A Word about Stereotypes

As parents who are members of minority groups, you are aware that there are both positive and negative stereotypes about your group, and that these can have a powerful effect on how your children come to view themselves. Negative stereotypes that Native Americans are lazy, or that Hispanics are dishonest, have a negative impact on all members of the group. Other stereotypes purport to be positive, such as Asian Americans being good at math, or African Americans being good dancers. Unfortunately, even positive stereotypes can be damaging, especially if they don't happen to be true for you. One of the major causes of prejudice is that it's based on an overly simple view about all members of a racial group. People who hold stereotypes about your group expect you to behave consistently within their biased view, and they are disappointed when you don't do this.

All stereotypes diminish hope because they pigeonhole behavior and limit goals. It's important to discuss with your child the different stereotypes held by the dominant culture. How does your child experience these stereotypes in his or her life? How are his or her goals limited because of others' biased and inaccurate perceptions of your ethnic group?

Stereotypes can influence a child's view of himself. In this process, called "internalization," the tragedy is that some children come to believe that the stereotypes really are true. Remember, perception is the ruler of "reality," so such self-views are like a negative psychological virus assaulting the core of a child's self-referential thinking. For example, if a young African American child lives in a community where people believe that members of his racial group are stupid, he or she also may come to believe that. Many minority children have been placed in vocational programs or in special-education classes precisely because of the unwarranted and damaging prejudices of others. Once children are in such programs, they may come to believe that they belong there.

Another aspect of stereotypes is that they can produce added and unhealthy pressure on your child to excel. Knowing that others have stereotypes, your child may push him- or herself to compensate for the false image held by peers and teachers. In such instances, children may adopt unrealistically high standards of performance to prove that they are exceptional and that the stereotypes don't fit them. Not only are such children hurting themselves by attempting to be "special," but they are perhaps unwittingly reinforcing the stereotypical view held toward others in their racial group.

In chapter 1, you were introduced to the twins, Jared and Jamal, whose parents wanted to eliminate as many of the risk factors of racism and stereotyping as possible. They chose to give their boys many opportunities and held high expectations for their achievement. While Jared and Jamal may have been breaking stereotypes in the short run, over time they may pay a high price because the added pressure may undermine their successful performance. It also is important to allow your children to be children, and too much pushing may backfire.

As a member of an ethnic group that has experienced oppression, racism, and denigration, your choices in life, and those of your child, are defined by others to a greater extent than they would be if you were Caucasian. Not only are your choices more limited, but your perception of what is available to you and your child also may be more restricted. For the majority of people born into conditions of poverty and discrimination, it's this *perception* of fewer choices that can diminish hope. For example, if you have never known anyone who has gone to college, you are likely to discourage college aspirations in your child, attempting to protect them from disappointment. As a parent, you need to become aware of the options and choices in life, so as to make sure your child knows about them. Without your encouragement, your children will not see what is available to them.

It's not right that such racial prejudice still exists in the United States, but it does. We've begun the twenty-first century, and yet the racism of two centuries ago still remains, albeit in different forms. What we have to do is to change things in the tomorrows in which your children and their children will live. There is an old saying that "Children are the expression of hope for the future." This is especially true for minority children.

As a minority parent, you are in the best position to know what threats to hope your child is going to face, because you have been there yourself. It's up to you to prepare him or her by discussing the risks openly and by using the strategies you have learned in this book. If your own hope is low, use the strategies we have discussed to raise it. There also are suggested readings in the back of this book to help you. Remember, *you cannot give your children what you do not have.*

About the Ethnic Groups

The ethnic groups we have chosen for this chapter are African American, Hispanic, Asian American, and Native Americans. We recognize that within each group there are many subgroups. For example, as an Hispanic American you could be Cuban, Mexican, Puerto Rican, Spanish, or South American. Even within these groups there are distinctions amounting to recognizable cultures. It's not possible, however, in the scope of this workbook to discuss all of the distinctions among groups that might influence hope. Rather, you will read about general stereotypes and how they can limit your child's hope. A true story will accompany the discussion of each ethnic group, illustrating a child's struggle with the effects of stereotyping.

Your assignment in this chapter is to help your child examine the assumptions others may have of him or her. Children often may be confused and unable to articulate the negative reactions they perceive that other people have toward them. You can facilitate their understanding through discussion of the stories in this book. Damaging reactions may come from their classmates, which may seem especially bewildering to your child. Likewise, the very teachers whom they admire may be the source of the prejudice. Furthermore, other adults (such as shopkeepers) may hold negative stereotypes about your ethnic group and treat your child accordingly. You probably have experienced many of these esteem-diminishing attitudes and behaviors yourself, and it's important for you to help your child recognize such prejudiced attitudes so that they do not become internalized. Below are some questions you can use to facilitate your discussion.

1. Have the stereotypes and assumptions of others limited any of the goals your child has selected?

2. Has your child had difficulty reaching any goals because people responded to her as "typical" of the ethnic group?

3. Has your child had difficulty in believing that he could reach a goal because people of his or her ethnicity are just not capable?

4. Has your child ever expressed a belief in the negative stereotypes about her group?

5. Has your child ever lost enthusiasm or energy for the goal because of the negative reactions of others about his ethnicity?

Ask your child to think about each of these questions, exploring memories of school and play experiences. It is the unfortunate probability that the older your child is, the more likely they are to have experienced examples of prejudice. Sharing your own experiences will be helpful. Remember that your child or teen may be angry about these experiences, just as you are. In terms of hope theory, any person or experience that blocks our desired goal pursuits can make us angry. But it is when we stop being angry and become accepting or resigned to the goal blockages that hope also dies. Anger can be constructive and motivating, if it is guided and used wisely. If anger is not used properly, the blocked person can become more blocked and ineffectual. As such, the hope-enhancing strategies in this book will help you to channel your child's anger in a positive, productive direction. Teach your offspring that living a successful life may be the best antidote to use on those people in our society who have prejudicial attitudes.

Native American Stereotypes

Many beliefs are held in American society about Native American culture. Some of these beliefs are negative, and many are romantic. Movies and television, where Indian people have been portrayed variously as being savage, lazy, or spiritually evolved, have shaped many of these ideas. There is a fascination with Indian rituals and spiritual artifacts, such as the medicine wheel or dream catchers, which are often seen as having an exotic "primitive" power. By holding these and other romantic views of Native American culture, most Americans do not get close enough to see the social and economic reality of many Indian people's lives, which often includes extreme poverty and a lack of educational opportunities.

If you are a Native American, you probably are very aware of the negative stereotypes held by many people. Native American people often are seen as being lazy, dishonest, and prone to problems with alcohol. Some differences in cultural values are misunderstood and exaggerated to bolster negative sterotypes. For instance, Native Americans do not traditionally value the acquisition of material goods, an idea that is at odds with the values held by most other Americans. Native American culture traditionally values cooperation and sharing, whereas for many people in American culture, acquiring things and winning are signs of success. Those who do not understand their value system often label Indian people as being lazy.

A major threat to hope in Native American children is the poverty in which many of them live. In our research measuring levels of hope, Native Americans scored the lowest of any racial group. Native American children perceive that they have limited options available for obtaining educations and careers. This desperation is reflected in a high attrition rate from school, high unemployment, low annual income, and frequent problems with alcoholism. Many Native American children live on reservations, where there are few opportunities for advanced education and employment or a social life that does not include alcohol.

Enhancing the Elements of Hope in Native American Children

What can Native American parents do to help their children to cope with these disadvantages and have happy, satisfying lives? Enhancing hope is one important way to help your children. As we discuss how each of the components of hope can be enhanced in your Native American culture, let's look again at stereotyping and its effects on your child's hope.

Discuss with your child the negative views from other people that you have experienced in your life. In all likelihood, your child is encountering the same stereotypes. If your child is quiet and rarely volunteers in class, does the teacher regard him as slow? Has your child ever been accused of stealing or lying and ever since lived under a cloud of suspicion? Has the teacher indicated that your child is lazy because she is not competitive? Many Native American children who go to school in predominately Caucasian areas are stereotyped in these ways because their teachers do not understand Native American values.

If your child has experienced such reactions, there are two important, hope-inducing actions you can. First, you can help your child understand that these prejudicial beliefs are not true simply because a significant person, such as a teacher, holds them. Second, you can take action. This requires more courage but is equally important. You can talk with your child's teacher about the customs of your ethnic group and explain how Native American values can be mis-understood by people who are unfamiliar with these customs. You can suggest readings specifically about your tribe, as well as more general material about Native American people. A reference librarian can help you find the appropriate material. Just as you have taken the time to "teach the teacher" about your tribal customs, you also should convey this heritage to your child.

As you have learned, the foundation of hope is goal setting. Many children who live in impoverished situations do not perceive many options and may not have seen examples of others who are pursuing a range of goals. This can be especially true if your family lives on a reservation or in a community that lacks opportunities for its children. In this case, it's especially important for you to increase your child's scope of possibilities—their vision of what's possible. You can do this by using the library to obtain career information and books that show high-hope Native American children.

If you don't have a library in your community, you can use television as a medium for increasing knowledge of what is possible. Your child *can* achieve many of the visions presented in the media, although such goals may appear unreachable from the vantage point of the reservation. Native American people have government-mandated financial resources for higher education available, and you can encourage your child to take advantage of these funds. Remember, the level of your hope is critical to your ability to encourage your child to see goal options. If your hope is low, do the work required to raise it so that you can con-vincingly and thoroughly impart goal-selection skills to your son or daughter.

Your level of parental hope also influences your child's waypower and will-power thinking. To increase waypower thinking, you and your child will have to be able to perceive routes to goals. If you cannot do this, you can neither encour-age nor teach your child to find ways to pursue dreams. You can increase your own waypower thinking, and thus help your child, by reading and learning about new subjects. Become an observant student of the world. Help your child survey the environment to perceive new ways to achieve goals, and don't hesitate to ask for help from others when necessary. Use all of the willpower-building techniques described in chapter 10, especially the energy-building health habits of good nutrition, rest, and exercise. If you are a drinker or a smoker, consider giving up these habits, as they sap both the physical and mental energy that you need for high willpower.

In chapters 3 and 4, you learned about life domains, one of which was the spiritual domain. Because spirituality is an integral part of the culture, and its principles of balance and wholeness are an excellent foundation for hope, we suggest that you teach your children about their spiritual heritages. If you do not have the knowledge to do this, seek out elders who can teach both you and your child.

The following story is about a ten-year-old Osage boy from a large family who saw few options for his life.

✳ Richard—Discovering His Talents

Richard and his large family lived in a mobile home on a plot of land just outside a small midwestern community. There were four children, his mother, father, and a cousin, all sharing the three-bedroom trailer that stood on cement blocks and rocked in a strong wind. Richard's parents worked at a factory in town and barely made enough money to cover their family's expenses. There was no money left over for entertainment or for many of the things that other children take for granted.

Richard and his brothers and sister spent most of their time after school watching television. Sometimes Richard went for long walks alone, preferring to explore the creeks and woods over the chatter-filled trailer. He was bored and found very little to interest him. Furthermore, when he looked ahead at his life, he only saw more of the same. It was on one of his long walks that he discovered a herd of horses on a neighbor's land. At this point, his life took a turn for the better.

Although Richard had never ridden a horse and wasn't sure he wanted to, he was fascinated by their grace and movement. Sometimes they would chase each other, tails and manes flying in the wind, and they filled Richard's heart with their beauty. Day after day, Richard returned to the pasture to watch the horses. He began to think about them as *his* horses and even brought carrots to them when he could. In turn, the horses began to accept Richard, until finally they allowed him to walk among them, stroking their manes and scratching their chins.

One day Richard went to the pasture, and the horses were gone. He was desperate to find them, and so he overcame his natural shyness and went to the barn where he thought the horses belonged. As he was about to slip inside, a man stopped him with a touch on the shoulder. Richard looked up into the face of a kind, grandfatherly man who was an Native American, like himself.

After Richard explained that he missed the horses and only wanted to see them again, the man asked him if he would like to come on a regular basis and learn to handle them properly. Richard jumped at the chance, and that began a friendship that changed his life.

Richard

In addition to learning about horses, Richard learned many things about what it meant to be a Native American from his new friend. He learned the ways of Native American spirituality, and the values that would help him stay in balance with himself and his world. Soon Richard knew he had found a purpose in life. He found that his quiet ways helped him work with the horses, and he came to see that he was on his way to a making a dream come true.

Richard worked with horses all through high school, and eventually he became an expert rider and trainer. He earned enough money to buy his first horse, and from that point on, Richard's life was filled with the satisfaction of achievement.

While Richard was not originally a high-hope child, he stumbled upon an interest that carried him along until he was able to develop hopeful thinking. The man who became his mentor taught Richard about their shared Osage heritage. In the process, Richard gained an identity he had not understood before. The combination of his Native American identity and the patience and encouragement of his mentor helped Richard to turn his life into one of high hope and success.

Asian American Stereotypes

Asian Americans belong to an ethnic group that is actually made up of many cultures. In fact, one expert has suggested that there are at least twenty-five distinct

Asian American ethnic groups in the United States. Your heritage might be Chinese, Japanese, Korean, Vietnamese, Thai, Asian Native American, or one of the many other subcultures that make up the group called "Asian" in America.

As a member of the Asian ethnic group, you probably are all too aware of the paradox of being the "model minority," while at the same time being the object of racial prejudices. The values espoused by most Asian cultures, especially the work ethic, also are those esteemed by the general culture. Hence, Asian Americans often have fared well in the United States. There are problems with this stereotype, however, because the experience of all Asian Americans has not been the same. Some people immigrated to the United States over 150 ago and, consequently, are well established in their communities. Others came very recently, fleeing war-torn countries and arriving with next to nothing.

Research on immigration has shown that a person's reasons for immigration and their past experiences have major effects on how that person will adjust and flourish. In research programs, we have found that the children of immigrants, facing language difficulties and new social expectations, score significantly lower in hope than do children from other minority groups. Many Asian American children are adjusting to the American way of life, which is likely to be very different than the lives of their parents. These children will have barriers to overcome that many other minority children do not have.

Some of the stereotypes appear to be positive—they may seem to open doors to jobs and education. We should emphasize, however, that all stereotypes are limiting to an extent and can diminish hope. For example, a common assumption about Asian American students is that they are good in the sciences, especially matters pertaining to mathematics and computers. While there are a large number of Asian American students who do select those fields, there are many who are not talented in those areas, or who are simply not interested. These students often experience pressure from teachers and parents to choose careers in line with these expectations. Given the strong value of respect and obedience to one's parents, many of these young people are destined to lead less-than-satisfying lives.

Along with the value of respect and obedience to elders, the value of conformity to the group can produce conflict and diminish hope in Asian American young people. The Caucasian-based culture in America values individuality and sees the person as the central societal unit. In Asian culture, however, the group is viewed as the focal point, and the strong expectation is that young people are to subsume their own wishes to the needs of the family or community. Thus, if a girl wanted to attend college, but her parents needed her to work in the store, she would feel compelled to do as they requested or face being a dishonorable daughter.

Although there are a number of values that distinguish Asian Americans from the dominant culture, perhaps none is as pervasive as the concept of "face." From an early age, Asian American children are instructed that the honor and pride of the family rests with their offspring's behaviors. As such, it is incumbent upon Asian children to act responsibly so as to uphold these values. Because those values are sometimes in conflict with those of the dominant culture in the United States, Asian American children may grow up with a foot in each world. To the extent that their options are limited, their hope is diminished.

Enhancing Hope in Asian American Children

There are two important actions you can take that will provide a groundwork for your child's developing hope. The first is to discuss the stereotypes your child has experienced. Use the questions provided at the beginning of this chapter as a guide. The second action is for you to examine your personal level of acculturation. Are you comfortable with the Western cultural values of individuality and personal choice? Your child will be growing up in America, and it is important for you to examine how comfortable you are with the system of values that is most widely endorsed. While it's very important for you to teach your child about her cultural heritage, you may limit available options if you insist on a strict adherence to Asian values.

Once you have examined your values, acculturation, and taken a measure of your own level of hope, it is important to discuss these issues with your child. If you can foster two-way communication, you will find that you're more effective at enhancing hope. Asian cultures are typically patriarchal and nonegalitarian, so you may be unaccustomed to very open communication with your child. In this regard, we have found in our research that high-hope people believe that there are other people who will really listen to them and give their views a fair chance.

If your family is accustomed to "top-down" communication, listening to your child will be a new experience. It may feel wrong at first, but keep in mind that it is the most effective way to develop understanding. Use the communication skills that we gave you earlier in the book. They involved asking good questions and really listening with a nonjudgmental attitude.

The hope-building strategies in this book will work well for your child once the stereotypes and assumptions have been brought to light. Remember that all stereotypes, whether negative or positive, limit goal options, as well as perceived pathways. It's important for you to free your child of these constraints.

Next, we present a story told by a seventeen-year-old girl who feels as if she is stuck in another century and longs to escape.

✳ May Ling—Out of the Shop and Into the World

There are many Chinese families who have lived for generations in San Francisco's Chinatown, and my family was one of them. When my grandparents came to this country, they leased and then eventually bought the store that my parents still have. All of the children and grandchildren have worked in the store, but I seem to be the one who is destined to take over for my parents when they are old.

I have two older brothers, but they are both in college and plan to become physicians. My parents are very proud of their accomplishments, as am I, but I constantly seem to fall short of their expectations. I don't really care for school, and I especially don't like the science courses that my brothers loved. If I had my way, I would study all kinds of art and nothing else.

I suppose it's because I'm not the scholarly sort that my parents have decided to make me a businessperson. They want me to learn all there is about the store so that I can take over when they are very old. The problem is, although I deeply respect what my parents have done, I don't want my life to be the same as the one they have led.

My friends at school tell me that I should make up my own mind and do what I want to do. I wasn't raised that way, however, and I feel ashamed when I think about disappointing my parents. I wish that they had gotten out of Chinatown and discovered that there is a world of choices out there. Perhaps it's up to me to bring my family into the twenty-first century. But it's so hard.

I thought about the different ways I could tell my parents that I didn't want to manage the store. Because my position in the family is the lowest, everything I thought of saying sounded impertinent. I knew my father would be displeased and angry. Then I decided to speak to my brothers about my situation. Though my father is the head of the family, he respects my brothers and will listen to what they say. I wasn't sure they would help me, but it was worth a try. I explained to them that I wanted to be an artist and, while I did not mind working in the store, I really wanted to go to art school instead of business college.

Surprisingly, they agreed to help me and they called a family meeting with my parents. They explained how values are different in the United States, and that I should have a chance to do what I want with my life. They said that just because I wanted to be an artist instead of a shopkeeper did not mean I was bringing shame upon the family.

My parents reluctantly agreed that I could begin studying painting after school at the

May Ling

community center. They want me to work in the store as a way to pay for my classes, but I don't mind that. It feels like I have been set free, and my artwork shows this new attitude. My teacher says I have talent, so I am very happy with my potential future.

In May Ling's story, we see how her goals were limited by her parent's strict adherence to their traditional Asian cultural values. She had formulated a goal, but her waypower was diminished by her own vacillation between independence and her filial duty. She wrestled with her strong desire to be an artist, which conflicted with her father's expectations. In her mind, she tried various ways to tell him what she wanted to do, but the way she chose to overcome her father's resistance was to work through her brothers.

Hispanic Stereotypes

If you are Hispanic, your cultural origin could be Mexican, Cuban, Central or South American, Spanish, or Puerto Rican. The stereotypes held by the dominant culture, however, may not distinguish between the values of each subcultural group, and this can be a great cause of frustration. Furthermore, commonly held stereotypes regarding Hispanics are often negative.

The length of time that you and your family have been in this country may make a difference in how closely you identify with your Hispanic cultural roots. If, for example, your family is of Mexican descent and has lived in California for generations, you may not consider yourselves to be very different from the majority Anglo culture. On the other hand, if your family has immigrated recently, you may still be immersed in the food, music, and language of your native country.

What are some of the stereotypes of the Hispanic culture that are limiting? Many Anglos believe that Hispanics are lazy, do not want to learn English, are dishonest, and that they do not value education. The basis for these stereotypes may be that many Hispanics, as with all immigrant groups who come here to make a better life, often come with very meager resources. Furthermore, in part because of poverty and a need to work, there is a high dropout rate from school among Mexican youth.

Most people who immigrate to a new country move into communities where there are others of their racial and ethnic group. This is a comfortable situation, enabling families to be able to help each other. The drawback is that adults often fail to learn English, relying on their children to speak for them. As we can see in the story of Domingo (chapter 11), learning to speak for their parents is a responsibility many Hispanic children must undertake.

How do stereotypes held about Hispanics diminish your child's hope? When others hold negative beliefs about your child's potential for success, it will be more difficult for him or her to reach goals. There will be more roadblocks on the pathway to achievement, and it may be harder for your child to envision solutions to these problems. Furthermore, it may be more difficult for your child to maintain the energy it takes to achieve goals in the face of the negative beliefs of others.

Enhancing Hope in Hispanic Children

Examining the negative beliefs that your child has encountered is the best place to begin. You must assess the damage that the beliefs of others may have caused in terms of your child's restricted goals, waypower, and willpower. Use your own experiences as a springboard from which to examine the negative stereotypes to which your child is subjected. You can recount particular events in your childhood, when you were confronted with prejudice, and share how those events make you feel and what you did.

Increase your vision for what is possible for your child. If you didn't finish high school, realize that not only can your child complete school, but that he or she can attend college. Think beyond your own experience. Let your vision wander outside of your community. Encourage your child to try new goals and praise him or her for the efforts. If there are certain goals that are only open to boys or to girls in your culture, try to eliminate such gender stereotypes within your own family group. The world your child is in today is different than it was when you were young, and it's important for you to widen your sights so that you can encourage your child's dreams and nurture hope.

The next story is about a young boy whose family recently immigrated to the United States from Mexico.

✳ Miguel—A Fair Exchange

Miguel came to San Diego from Mexico when he was seven years old. His father was the first to come to the States to find work, because their family in Mexico was very poor. Next, Miguel's mother was able to get a job in San Diego, and then both of his parents were sending money for their children's support. While his parents were working in California, Miguel and his sister lived with their grandmother in a small village in Mexico. Although the small town was very poor, Miguel loved living with so many people he knew and so many other members of his family.

One day a letter came from his parents saying that they had just had another baby, and the family would be reunited. The trip to San Diego in their father's old car was fun, and Miguel saw parts of Mexico he had never seen. Everything was strange and exciting—a wonderful adventure for Miguel and his sister.

Miguel was amazed when they reached San Diego; he had never seen such a large city. At first the houses were large and had beautiful shrubs and flowers, but as they got closer to where Miguel's parents lived, the houses were much smaller and not so nice. When they finally pulled up in front of their new home, Miguel was a little disappointed. The house was very small and made of stucco painted a faded pink. The yard had no grass, only dirt and a few weedy flowers. Nevertheless, the whole family was together now, and their lives were bound to be better.

As Miguel's father began to unpack the car, a number of children from the neighborhood gathered around. It seemed to Miguel that they were all talking at once and he couldn't understand anything they said. Most of the children had been born in the United States, and all of them spoke English. Big tears formed in Miguel's eyes as he realized how much he had to learn, and that it wasn't going to be easy. A girl named Maria, who was about his age and spoke Spanish, told him that he would have to learn English for school the next year.

Miguel and Maria became friends, and because it was summer, they had a lot of time to play. They always spoke Spanish, however, and so did Miguel's parents. As the summer wore on, Miguel started to wonder how he was going to learn to speak English and be ready for school in the fall. He decided to come up with a plan. Because Maria could speak both languages, Miguel knew he also could learn to do this. Maybe Maria could give him English lessons, like the ones that she got in school.

When he suggested this idea to Maria, she was not very enthusiastic. She liked the games they played and teaching him English sounded too much like school. Miguel thought about that and decided to offer to teach Maria something in exchange. Even though he was very young, he had been known in his small Mexican town for his dancing ability. At fiestas he performed the *jarabe tapatillo* along with the local mariachi band and always got lots of applause. He thought that Maria might like to learn to dance.

She said that learning to dance would be fun, and so they agreed that for two hours every morning they would study English, and for two hours every afternoon they would practice dancing. Miguel got out the castanets he used—the wooden clappers he wore on his fingers to keep time with his tapping feet. They found a Mexican music station on the radio, and the two began to exchange their lessons.

Miguel found that learning English wasn't so hard after all. He picked up the words quickly, and before long he was chattering away with Maria and the other children in a combination of English and Spanish they called "Spanglish." Maria loved the dance lessons and, although she didn't learn to play the castanets, she did become an adept dancer.

School went well for Miguel that next year. His teacher said that he was speaking English very well for someone who had been in the

United States for such a short time. Miguel and Maria continued their dancing, adding many new dances, and in the spring they were asked to perform for the Cinco de Mayo fiesta. Miguel's mother made them both costumes; Maria's had a full, ruffled skirt that swished when she moved, and Miguel wore tight black pants and a shirt with full sleeves.

Their performance was perfect, and they even had their pictures in the newspaper. All of this was wonderful for Miguel, but what he liked most was that, even though he felt like a real Californian, he could still keep his treasured Mexican culture.

At first, Miguel was overwhelmed by all of the things he would have to learn in the United States. He had moved from a small and comfortable community to one of the largest cities in the world. Everything was different and challenging. Miguel was a high-hope child, however, and he selected one thing to learn first—English. He showed his high waypower by offering dance lessons in exchange for English lessons, and his willpower was demonstrated by the systematic manner in which both children went about learning new things. Their efforts paid off in their eventual success in both dancing and English.

African American Stereotypes

In the past and continuing into the present, negative stereotypes about African American men, women, and children have been prevalent among the majority White culture. If you are an African American, you are probably very familiar with a number of these stereotypes. Many of the commonly held beliefs about African Americans are negative in nature, depicting African Americans as being lazy or prone to committing crimes. Other beliefs are neutral, such as the ideas that African Americans have rhythm or are especially good dancers. Examples of seemingly positive stereotypes are that African Americans are good athletes, or that Black women are the strength of the family. What is important to realize is that even neutral or positive stereotypes are limiting. When people are stereotyped by society, their individuality is lost, and they come to be viewed through one narrow lens.

One of the most damaging aspects of stereotypes on growing children is that kids can come to believe they are what others expect them to be. If an African American child is exuberant and energetic in the classroom, and the teacher expects Black children to be troublemakers, that child is likely to be referred to special education classes for a behavior disorder. Similarly, when your child goes into a store, the shopkeeper may assume that he or she is planning to steal and start following your child around the store. Growing up with stereotypes such as these can make it difficult for African American children to develop positive images of themselves.

Enhancing Hope in African American Children

In addition to the strategies you learned previously in this workbook, there are other actions you can take to enhance your child's hope and improve his or her self-esteem. Begin by having an open discussion with your child about the discrimination he or she has experienced, being sure to share your own experiences. These discussions are certain to evoke emotions, and these are natural under such unfair circumstances. It's important to understand these feelings, and not to allow them to become so strong and preoccupying that they undermine positive, high-hope thoughts.

Another important action you can take is to provide your child with books and videos about high-achieving African American figures. Over the past twenty years, many movies have been made that depict the struggle for equality and the bravery of Black men and women. Become active in Black History Month celebrations and learn more about your heritage and how it shaped the development of the United States. There are truly high-hope individuals to be found there, and they will serve as excellent role models for your growing children.

Another action you can take is to learn about the opportunities that exist to help your child get a good education. For a number of years, the federal government has funded grant programs to insure that young African American men and women have equal access to college educations. Do not allow your child to be given a second-class primary and secondary education. Keep track of what your child is learning and request that he or she be placed in a precollege tract. Even if you do not have a college education, your interest will help your child succeed. Education is the most dependable route to achievement in American society. The following story illustrates this point.

✳ Michelle—A Quest for a Better Life

When I was in junior high school, I was at the top of my class, even though I didn't have a whole lot of time to study. You see, my father had moved to another state and my mother worked two jobs to support my two younger brothers and me. When I got home from school, I had to baby-sit, do laundry, fix the meals, and see to it that my brothers did their homework and had their baths.

When I look back on it, that was a lot of responsibility for a twelve-year-old, but I guess I grew up fast. I was able to do my own homework, and I made good grades. What I didn't get to do was to hang out with friends, so by the time I got to high school, I was desperate for a little fun.

The first couple of months in high school, I met a lot of cool kids. I got a boyfriend and learned about sex. I even tried marijuana but drew the line at crack, even though some of my friends used it. I liked being popular, but there was a nagging feeling that I wasn't doing the right thing. For one thing, I couldn't tell my mother about the sex and drugs, because I knew she would be really mad. When I went to church on Sunday, I felt guilty because I knew the people I loved and had known all my life would be disappointed in me.

What I decided to do took a lot of courage. I knew that I wanted to make something of my life and not be stuck in the housing projects, so I decided to pay more attention to my schoolwork and stop hanging out so much with my friends. These so-called friends of mine were really angry when I stopped doing things with them, and my boyfriend dumped me right away. That hurt a lot, but in another way, I felt better. I felt more like I was on the right track for the things I wanted.

I started making better grades again, and I started doing the things that I thought would help me get into college. I worked on the school paper, and I joined the debate club. During the second year I was elected to the student council, and I chaired the committee for Black History Month. While gathering information about famous Black men and women, I started to feel pride in my heritage and who I was. I started to see myself as a person who could do important and meaningful things.

That year I was admitted to Howard University and was given a grant that covers all of my expenses. I know that I will have a better life than a lot of the people I used to hang around with, and I won't have the struggles my mother has had. I plan to help her out when I can, and I will certainly help my brothers go to college. I am so glad that I decided to find ways to stand by my own values and that I worked hard in school. I developed pride in myself and pride in my culture.

Michelle

Michelle faced the dangers shared by many young men and women living in disadvantaged areas. The two major rites of passage for many youth who feel disenfranchised are to deal drugs or to have children. Both of these actions limit opportunities for future success. As parents, it's vital to encourage your children to make high-hope choices and not ones that will limit their options. Stay involved with your children's lives, know what they are doing and who their friends are. Even though you may be busy with your own life, and may often find yourself struggling to make ends meet, your children are your best investment for the future.

The story of Michelle illustrates a high-hope girl who was able to stay out of trouble. What about the children who don't make such wise choices? What about the children whose troubles have been caused by forces outside of themselves? What can parents do to increase the hope in these children? The next chapter addresses these concerns.

chapter 14

Hope for Children in Trouble

You've worked hard to give your child a good life. You've tried to be a good parent, and then you find that your child has gotten into serious trouble. Perhaps your child is using drugs, has gotten pregnant, is skipping school, or is in trouble with the law. Discovering that your child has a serious problem is one of the worst experiences a concerned parent can have. You feel angry at your child's behavior, yet at the same time you're afraid of the consequences for the future. How can this have happened to your child? Where did you go wrong? Will it happen again? How can things be made right again? All of these questions flood your mind as you realize that you must cope with a child in trouble—*your* child in trouble.

This book is filled with strategies to raise your child's hope. The stories you have read have been about average children with normal concerns rather than children in serious trouble. In this chapter we will introduce you to two children with problems of a greater magnitude than the children you have previously met. There are many serious pitfalls waiting for children and adolescents, but we have selected drug abuse and truancy as our focus. These are two problems that are destructive to a child's future and difficult for parents to handle. They also are common problems found in children of all ethnic groups and at all socioeconomic levels. Furthermore, such problems not only can be found in children in bad living situations, but also in kids living in caring families.

We recognize that there are many other problems that concern parents, such as eating disorders, ADHD (attention deficit and hyperactivity), serious legal trouble, and sexual promiscuity. It is not within the scope of this book to give these grave problems the attention that they deserve. If your child or teen has one or more of these problems, while we strongly recommend that you use the hope-enhancing strategies you have learned in this book, we also urge you to consult a mental-health professional.

Troubled Children—Troubled Parents

How do children develop serious problems? Nearly every specialist in child development has an answer to this question, but as varied as those answers are, they agree on one point: *Children are not born "bad."* Neither are children born "good," although each of us carries in our genes a propensity for certain dispositional characteristics. Some infants are more reactive to stimulation, others are calm; still other babies may be cranky or cheerful. If you are a parent with several children, you know how different each one is by the time he or she is one day old. Yet the infant is, to an extent, a blank slate ready and waiting for the lessons she will learn. It is from those lessons that children become who they are, and it is from what they learn that serious problems develop.

Obviously, the role of parents is crucial in the life of a growing child. Children look to parents to set limits, provide structure, and to model correct behavior and values. This is an especially imposing challenge in the world of today. With nearly one half of all marriages ending in divorce, there are more single-parent families than ever before in our nation's history. We would draw your attention to one important result of such divorces: there is less parent time available to help children grow. When parents cannot or do not set and monitor guidelines for their children, the message is that no one cares. In seeking structure and role models, children often turn to their peers who may be as misguided and confused as they.

Some psychologists believe that the peer group is primarily responsible for the formation of a child's behavior. While peers do provide a very important influence, especially in the adolescent years, parents can have an influence on whom their children select as friends by insuring that they meet kids who have the positive values of the parents. For example, one way to help your child meet positive peers is to enroll him or her in groups such as Boy or Girl Scouts, 4-H, Bluebirds, or other similar organizations. Your children will meet others with similar interests through lessons such as tennis, or dance. Playing on soccer or Little League teams is another good way to have your children meet new friends. In addition to providing a wholesome peer group, these activities are interesting, fun, and teach values that will stay with your child throughout life.

If you live in an inner city where many of the opportunities just described do not exist, we suggest that you seek out the Boys and Girls Clubs of America, the YMCA or YWCA, Big Brothers or Big Sisters organizations. Don't forget the importance of your church. As we have seen from research, young people who are active in their church are less likely to get into serious trouble.

We also advocate your involvement in as many aspects of your child's life as is feasible. Being an active parent takes time, and we know that for single parents, or for families where both parents work, time is scarce. If this is your situation, you may not have the time to chauffeur children to and from lessons or attend many of their activities. There are, however, many ways you can be active in your children's lives. For example, there are many activities that are held on weekends and in the evenings, precisely because so many parents work during the week. Seek these out and become active along with your child. You will both enjoy the time together.

In suggesting that you make time for your children's activities, we do not intend to make you feel guilty. In order to have a good relationship with your children, however, you'll need to devote time and energy beyond that used in earning a living to support them. It is a fact that children who have good relationships with their parents have fewer and less serious problems than children who don't have such positive relationships. Throughout this book, we have stressed the need for open communication between you and your child. If you don't have that, you will have much more difficulty in teaching your child to use hope-building strategies.

Communicating with Children in Trouble

Once your child has a serious problem, you may think that it's too late to develop good communication. Many parents are frustrated and confused about what to do. They may blame themselves, thinking that if they had shown more interest, spent more time, or provided stricter rules, then their child would not be in trouble. Other parents, in their anger, blame the child. Neither stance is helpful when communication with your child is the goal. Children need to take responsibility for their choices and actions, but they also need to understand how they got into trouble. If your child is able to talk to you and knows that you will listen, you can teach him what can be learned from the predicament.

Emotions can run high when you learn that your child is in trouble. You will probably be frightened, angry, sad, baffled, and generally upset. Most parents see their child's behavior as a reflection of their own competence, and it is humiliating when their children's problems become public. Even though you are upset, it is important for you to be able to talk with your child calmly and without rancor. Most children expect their parents to be angry under these circumstances and are prepared for a fight. If you are reasonable and can remain unruffled, you may be able to take them by surprise and stand a good chance of having a meaningful conversation about the incident. Listen to your child with an open mind. Find out what happened from her perspective, and help her understand how she made the choices that got her into the situation.

Some parents make a black-and-white assumption: their children always are innocent, or they always are guilty. When parents have the attitude that their children can do nothing wrong, they are not seeing the kids realistically. Any young person, no matter how good the family, can get into trouble. When parents refuse to acknowledge that their child has done something wrong, the child knows that he is not being seen as a real person. Some parents assume the worst—that their child is always guilty. In this case, the child is not being seen as an individual, and also is likely to take on those negative characteristics that are automatically assumed to apply to him. When children are treated "as if" they are bad, they will begin to believe they are bad and act in bad ways. This process of internalization of other's beliefs that you learned about in the previous chapter can be an insidious influence on your child.

If you are a parent who believes that your child is usually guilty, examine your reasons for taking this position. Perhaps you have been raised with a "spare the rod, spoil the child" philosophy. This biblical stance is based on the philosophy that children are innately bad. The underlying belief is that children will always get into trouble if left to their own devices, and that they absolutely need the threat of punishment to keep them in line. This approach to child rearing was widely accepted until the 1950s, when Dr. Spock introduced a child-centered approach in his book *Baby and Child Care*. Unfortunately, many parents are still influenced by the centuries-old belief that children are bad and, consequently, do not establish relationships built on mutual trust and respect.

No matter how serious the problem your child presents, good communication and a good relationship will help. Don't give up on your child, even if you are frustrated and angry; it's never too late to use the communication techniques you learned earlier in this book. The parent-child bond is strong, and *your children need you to be there for them, especially when they have big problems.*

Next, you will learn about two common yet serious troubles experienced by children and their parents. For each problem, in addition to ideas about how you can use hope strategies to help your children cope, you also will read a story about a young person who is dealing with that particular concern. Let's begin with drug use and abuse.

Children Who Use Mind-Altering Drugs

What Are Drugs?

Many parents don't have experience with recreational drugs, and have inadequate or false information about what they are and what they do. The scope of this book does not include presenting a thorough compendium of that information, but there are excellent sources available. Check the Suggested Reading section of this book for some of these resources. Mind-altering drugs can be legal or illegal, and they can be ingested through the mouth, skin, nose, or lungs. The only substance that is legal for young people, aside from drugs prescribed for them, is caffeine in the form of sodas, coffee and tea, chocolate, and over-the-counter caffeine pills. If there is any doubt that caffeine is a drug, try to eliminate it and notice the reaction. You will become sluggish and develop headaches. These are withdrawal symptoms, the severity of which indicates the extent of the addiction.

The illegal drugs used by young people are many. Alcohol and tobacco, while legal for adults only, are the most common drugs used by youngsters. Every year the government conducts studies to monitor the extent to which children and adolescents use these and other drugs. Although the statistics indicate that use has declined, alcohol and tobacco still remain a serious problem for young people.

Marijuana, which is illegal for everyone, is the next most frequently used substance. It can be smoked in a pipe or made into a cigarette. It can even be baked into cookies or brownies and ingested through the stomach. The use of marijuana has declined somewhat, but it continues to be a popular drug among young people of all socioeconomic and ethnic groups.

Other illegal substances are cocaine, and its derivative crack, designer drugs such as MDMA or "extasy," and various stimulants or depressants. Heroine and opium are occasionally used but are less common. Young children sometimes use inhalants, such as glue, gasoline, aerosols, or solvents, because these substances are readily available. Inhalants, however, do far more damage to the central nervous system than almost any other drug. If you suspect that your child is using these, get professional help immediately.

Ironically, alcohol and tobacco, which are legal for adults in this country, are two of the most damaging drugs available. These also are the ones most commonly used by children and adolescents, precisely because they are more available. Many parents believe that if they allow their children to smoke, or even to have an occasional drink, that will prevent them from moving on to "harder" drugs. This has been shown to be a fallacy. Alcohol and tobacco are called "gateway" drugs, because their use is a precursor to the use of other substances.

Many professionals in the substance-abuse field believe that parents should give their children an unequivocal "no" about using any drugs. At the same time, parents need to be able to discuss drugs with their children in an open and enlightened way. Many parents have no personal experience with mind-altering substances and may give misleading or frightening information in order to prevent their children from experimenting. Most young people, however, know what is fact and what is not, and offering exaggerated information only destroys your credibility. Make it a point to get accurate information before you have a discussion about drugs with your child.

What Is Use and What Is Abuse?

One definition of drug abuse is *the ingestion of a drug to the extent that it impairs the user's well-being*. This is a good definition, although it does imply that there is a level of use that might be considered acceptable—not a belief held by many parents. Indeed, there is no level of illegal drug use by children and adolescents that can be considered acceptable, and parents have an obligation to make that clear. On the other hand, if you find that your child has experimented with drugs, it is counterproductive for a good parent-child relationship to automatically assume that she is a drug abuser. Learn the myths and facts about youthful drug use and learn to distinguish use from abuse.

Setting Guidelines and Rules

If your children are quite young, setting rules is relatively easy. Although they may argue with you, it's easier to monitor their behavior when they are young than when they are older and more mobile. It's important for you to stick to your rules and not make exceptions. Before you make any rule, however, be certain that it is something that you believe and with which you can live. If you vacillate or are unsure about whether your rule is reasonable, your child will spot your hesitancy and challenge your authority.

If your child is older or an adolescent, and you have not established rules and guidelines for living, it will be more difficult to do so. Furthermore, if you are a very permissive parent, both you and your child will be unused to discipline and enforcing the rules will be difficult at first. Children need structure in their lives, however, and sanctions against substance use are realistic rules to set. Establish rules that can and will be followed. If your child is young and has never experimented with substances, it is reasonable to expect abstinence. If your child is older and has already experimented with or regularly uses one or more drugs, your rules are just as important, but it will require time for your child to adapt to the new structure. Setting rules when you have not done so before requires patience and understanding. Your child will resist, and a psychological tug-of-war can ensue. If harsh punishment is your mode of rule enforcement, you should be aware that the result could be deceitfulness on the part of your child. Children frequently resort to lies in order to avoid what they perceive to be unfair or even frightening consequences. A less threatening but productive consequence could be the use of time-outs or grounding.

If your child or teen is using substances on a regular basis, you will want to consult a professional about drug use. Family or individual counseling may be required to solve the problem. Follow all the suggestions made by the counselor or psychologist, and in addition, you can use the hope-enhancing strategies that follow.

Hope Strategies for Prevention

Earlier in this book, we introduced the concept of risk and prevention factors. Researchers who were studying youthful substance abusers originally identified these factors. Certain conditions were present more often for young people who became involved with drugs than for young people who abstained. By employing these prevention factors, you can lessen the chances that your child will use drugs; moreover, by using prevention approaches, you are providing a good foundation for hope-enhancing strategies.

We have stressed good communication throughout this book, and not surprisingly, this is the most effective prevention technique you can use. When your child has good relationships with other family members, she is less likely to be negatively influenced by peers. You may wish to review the strategies for enhancing hope in the family domain, especially if your child appears to be distancing him- or herself, as often happens when children become involved with drugs.

Being involved in school is another important prevention factor that has a curative effect on the problems discussed in this chapter. A child has bonded with the school when he or she enjoys school, rarely misses, and takes part in extracurricular activities. As a parent, you can play an active role in helping your child to bond by becoming involved in school events, e.g., you can sponsor school clubs or chaperone at dances. If your children are young and you have the time, you can be a classroom aide. These activities allow you to observe your kids outside the family and get to know their friends.

Researchers have shown that children and teens who take part in positive extracurricular activities are less likely to use drugs than young people with time on their hands. Boredom is often given as a reason why young people begin experimenting with substances. You can help prevent boredom by enrolling your child in after-school activities, with you taking an active part. If your adolescent seems to have a large amount of free time, you might suggest that she get an after-school job. Young people who hold jobs are also less likely to become involved with drugs.

If your child or teen is already a substance user, the process of hopeful thinking can be used to facilitate his quitting. Once a young person has decided to stop using, the goal becomes abstention. This can be broken down into smaller goals, such as eliminating one substance at a time (if he is a polydrug user), or abstaining in one situation at a time.

There are a number of effective means for treating drug use. Your child can learn refusal skills—appropriate ways to say no. Substituting other activities that are fun and exciting is another effective way to treat drug problems. Participating in a treatment program may be the most effective way your child can quit substance use, even though you as a parent may see it as a last resort.

Willpower, as the term is commonly used, is usually thought to be the most important part of abstention. This definition of willpower, however, relies only on the child's strength of character and implies that he or she must "go it alone." Willpower thinking, as we use it in this book, is enhanced by both waypower and setting realistic, small goals. Parents can help in developing hopeful thinking in such a way that their children do not feel alone with the problem. To enhance your child or teen's willpower to achieve the abstention goal, pay special attention to the suggestions for developing good health and fitness habits. Drugs sap a user's physical and mental energy, and it may take some months for your child to rebuild his or her mind and body.

The following story is about a young man whose occasional experimentation led to frequent use. Through the use of hope-building strategies, he was able to make healthier choices and avoid serious trouble.

✳ Quinn—Learning to Say No

Some people think that you only find kids who use drugs in the ghetto. From my experience, they are *so* wrong. I go to one of the best high schools in the city, and my family lives in a good neighborhood, yet I have many friends who use drugs. Not just alcohol and tobacco; the people I know use crack and speed and a lot of other things. Of course, marijuana is everywhere. You can even smell it in the boy's bathroom at school.

I got into drugs fast once I started using marijuana. It was the cool thing to do, and the people I liked to hang out with all did them. My parents didn't have a clue about what was happening, they were off in their own worlds, making lots of money. They did notice that I was changing my style, however, when I grew my hair into shoulder-length dreadlocks.

Your life changes when you use drugs. At first it's fun and you think you're cooler than the other kids. After you get over the thrill of doing something risky, though, you're just tired all the time and you lose interest in the things you used to like. I quit going to French club, my grades fell, and I dropped out of the track team. My parents didn't pick up on what was happening to me, mostly because I avoided spending time with them.

I would probably still be using drugs if I hadn't gotten arrested. A policeman pulled my car over when I ran a red light, and I guess he

Quinn

searched my car because he thought I looked like a drug user with my long hair. It didn't take long to find the bag of marijuana, and then my world came crashing down.

The first person I had to deal with was my dad. I expected him to be furious with me and yell all the way home, but instead he was quiet. It seemed like he was thinking really hard about what had happened. My mother also was calm, and together we all sat down for a family discussion. When they asked me about my drug use, they really listened to what I had to say, and they said they were disappointed, rather than really mad. Their disappointment was harder to take than if they had yelled at me; then I could have yelled back.

We talked about a lot of things that day. We talked about my grades, my interests, the risks I was taking of getting into serious trouble, and they told me I had to stop using drugs. That was hard to hear, and I needed to think about it for a while. I knew I could continue to hang out with my friends and still use drugs, because I had gotten very good at bluffing. On the other hand, I was running the risk of getting arrested and going to jail. Some of my friends had already spent time in treatment programs and doing community service. I didn't want to have something like that on my record.

The thing that helped me decide to quit drugs was thinking about my future and what kind of a person I wanted to be. I didn't know what I wanted to be when I grew up, but I knew I didn't want to become a criminal. Those were risks I didn't want to take with my future. My parents trust and respect was also important to me, and I was certainly on the verge of losing that.

People say that your peer group is what influences you to use drugs. I know that in my case that was true, but I really liked my friends and I didn't want to give them up. I decided that I was going to hang out with them, but tell them I was going "straight edge" (abstaining). They said that was cool and didn't seem to mind if I didn't smoke when they did. A strange thing happened though. When I wasn't high, and they were, I didn't think they were so much fun to be around—actually, they were kind of boring. Once in a while I would get high again, but then I thought about how my parents were working with me to help me quit, and I felt really bad.

One of the ways my parents were helping me was to encourage me to get back into running, even if I had lost my place on the track team. My father even went to the health club with me, and we lifted weights. We started eating breakfast and dinner together and stopped eating so much fast food. I could see that my parents were changing some things about their lives to help me stay off drugs, and that made me want to try even harder.

Eventually, I started hanging around with a new group of kids who did more interesting things than take drugs. I joined a snow boarding/skiing club at school and took a winter trip. I learned to skateboard, and I found out you can get into lots of trouble with that, too—but that's another story. Sometimes I wish I could still get high and sit around with my old friends, but for the most part, I am much happier now that I have succeeded in quitting drugs.

Quinn used some hope-building strategies as he worked toward his goal of quitting drugs. He decided to keep his old friends for a while, which meant that he was not changing everything at once. He gradually moved away from that peer group and the situations in which he had used drugs and pursued a new set of interests. His parents helped him by maintaining a calm attitude. They also made some changes in their own lives and focused more interest and attention on Quinn.

The next problem is common to many young people—a dislike and avoidance of school. Truancy (skipping school) is often associated with drug use, but it can occur in the absence of any other serious concern.

Children with School-Related Problems

What Are School Troubles?

School-related troubles range from a simple dislike of school to more serious truancy. There are many reasons why your child may want to avoid going to school, not the least of which is the stress that nearly all children experience. From the very first day, school can be a frightening experience. Your child must meet many new children, figure out and obey new rules, and perform many tasks she has never done before. If English is not your child's first language, or if a dialect of English is spoken in your home, he also must struggle to be understood.

Some of the problems children encounter at school are the result of poor social relationships. Being teased or bullied makes school a nightmare experience for children and can have serious, negative effects on their budding self-esteem. Earlier in the book we discussed the school domain as an important part of children's lives. We gave you suggestions to help raise your child's hope in this area, and you might wish to review those now.

What about the child who refuses to go to school and who is truant? In most states, a child must attend school until the age of sixteen, at which point some young people quit. Researchers suggest that children who skip school are more likely to drop out prior to graduation than those who attend regularly. If you want your child to graduate from high school and go to college, which is the surest route to success in this country, it's important that you take truancy seriously.

As we have mentioned, skipping school can be associated with other problems, notably drug use. Failure to bond with school is a known risk factor for drug abuse, just as successful bonding is a prevention factor. Problems in adolescence can be like an iceberg; one problem, such as skipping school, may indicate the presence of many others. If your child or teen is skipping school, you will need to confront the issue with the same firm yet calm approach you use with other difficult issues. In the course of your discussion, you can ask your child about other problem behaviors, using the skills you have learned of openness, acceptance, and listening. Once again, a good relationship with your child will go far in helping you solve the problem together.

Hope Strategies for School Problems

For children below the age of sixteen, attending school is not optional—they are required to go. As a parent, you are held responsible if your child does not comply with this law, and it is one rule you should insist that he or she obey. Once this is clearly understood, the goal for your child is to attend school on a regular basis. One way to make this goal less imposing is to have your child think about it as one day at a time, rather than years and years of going to school. Have your child focus on only the day ahead and plan activities that would be fun for that day.

To help your child increase school waypower, find out what is the hardest for him or her. Perhaps it's getting up and getting ready to go in the morning. Have your child think of things that would make that part of the day easier. One way could be having a special food for breakfast or putting out clothes the night before to make dressing easier. If the problems center on some part of the school day, discover what's going on then and brainstorm possible solutions. Your child might need tutoring or may need to make friends; the solutions will depend on the nature of the problem. The important thing is that you are willing to listen, to understand, and to help your child find ways to solve the problems.

As your child develops more of an interest in school, her energy and enthusiasm (willpower) will increase. Be sure that your child starts the day with a nutritious breakfast that includes a high protein food, a complex carbohydrate, and fruit. Cereal alone is usually not sufficient to maintain a high level of energy until lunch. Any meal that is mainly sugar will raise energy fast but will leave the child in a slump by midmorning. A better breakfast would be eggs or meat, toast, milk, and juice. The protein in this meal will sustain your child.

If you discover that your young person who is skipping school has any of the other problems we have mentioned, you can use all of the hope-building strategies you have learned, but also we recommend that you seek professional counseling. It is important to remain caring and open, but, at the same time, you must stress the seriousness of your child's behavior and the implications for their future. In the next story, we illustrate how skipping school became a destructive habit, and how hope-enhancing strategies worked to get this girl back in school.

❋ Shasha—Getting Back on Track

I was a pretty good student in elementary school, but in junior high I started to slack off a little. I had a boyfriend and a lot of friends, and it was so much more fun to hang out at the mall than to do my homework. By the time I got to high school, my grades had dropped and I decided that, since I didn't like school, I just wouldn't go very often.

You might think I would get caught, but I didn't—at least not for a long time. You see, my parents both went to work before I had to leave for school, and it was so easy to pretend that I was getting ready to go. Then, as soon as I heard the car leaving, I would go back to bed for a few more hours of sleep. When I finally got up, I watched television or read magazines for a while, then my friends and I got together at one of our houses.

I usually didn't skip more than two or three days each week. I made sure that I had a note written in what looked like my mother's handwriting to give the attendance office, and it was months before anyone bothered to check with my folks. Finally, the assistant principal called my mother at work. She said she was concerned because I was sick so often, and she thought perhaps I needed to see a doctor.

Of course my mother was totally confused and alarmed. When she came home from work that night, she and my father confronted me with what I had done wrong. My father was really angry and said that he had trusted me and was bitterly disappointed. My mother was better about it. She said that when she was a teenager she didn't like school either, and that she had even skipped a few times. I was pretty surprised to hear that because I always thought she was Miss Perfect. I had never even thought of my mother as a teenager.

She calmed my father down, and then they both asked me a lot of questions about why I didn't like school. I really couldn't tell them any specific thing, it was just that skipping had become easier than going. In the beginning, it was just a day or two here and there, and it never seemed like it mattered very much. As skipping became easier, I did it more often, until suddenly I had missed so much that it looked like I would fail a lot of my classes.

Shasha

Mom asked me what else I did when I was skipping school and hanging out with my friends. I knew she wondered if I was using any drugs, so I told her that sometimes I smoked cigarettes and had a drink. One of my friends liked to raid her parent's liquor cabinet, and it was always easy to get cigarettes.

My mother accepted this calmly, even though my father wasn't quite so cool about it. Mom said that she had been known to do that sort of thing when she was in high school, and finally she got my father to admit that he had done it, too.

With my parents confessions, I didn't feel like such a bad person. In fact, I felt pretty normal. My parents told me, though, that I had to start going to school, and that if I skipped again they were going to take some very serious action. They might even send me to boarding school for the next few years!

After that discussion, I knew I had to straighten myself out. I decided to start by telling my friends that I wasn't going to skip anymore and not to ask me to join them. My next step was to find out if I could make up the homework and tests that I had missed. I discovered something that made me look forward to school, and that was having pretty clothes to wear. Each night I laid out an outfit that would look great so that in the morning I would look forward to getting dressed.

My father still had trouble trusting me, and I knew that I would have to rebuild his trust in me slowly. He started driving me to school and watching until I had walked into the building—as if I couldn't walk right out the other side. But after a few months, he stopped watching me and even talked about getting me a car of my own. Wow!

I'm back on track now, and going to school isn't so bad. I can't say I like all my classes, but there is usually something interesting about each of them. Sometimes it's just looking at the cute boys, but that gets me through.

The turning point for Shasha was when her parents told her that they had done some of the same things she was doing. Children rarely think their parents understand what's going on in their lives, let alone that they have had the same experiences. Sasha's relationship with her parents improved because there was mutual understanding based on honest communication.

Shasha used hopeful thinking when she identified steps to her goal, such as telling her friends not to ask her to skip. She used her waypower when she thought about the different things she could do to make attending school easier, such as getting caught up with homework and tests and selecting her clothes for the next day. Shasha knew that at one time in her life she had enjoyed school, and had gone every day. Because she had done it before, she knew she could do it again—which was her willpower thinking in operation.

In addition to going to school every day, Shasha found that she wanted to regain her father's trust. Proving herself trustworthy was important, and every day that Shasha went to school she took one more step along the path toward achieving that goal.

In this chapter, we have discussed two problems that are common to children and adolescents. Both of these concerns have serious consequences, and if not corrected, they could threaten your children's futures. Although there are many problems that confront children and their parents, the two we have selected for this chapter can serve as models for hope-enhancing solutions that can be used with other concerns.

Throughout this book we have emphasized the importance of your relationship with your child. The hope-enhancing strategies you have learned will work best if you have honest and open communication about all of the concerns your child may have. As you work with your child to learn hopeful thinking, you will establish a common ground of love and caring that will lead both of you into greater life fulfillment. *Have a wonderful journey!*

A Final Word

As psychologists and parents, we know the value of the special relationship you have with your children. You will have noticed that in nearly every chapter we have emphasized this relationship and the many ways that you can enhance it. The bottom line is this: *If you cannot communicate with your children, you cannot teach them hope.*

You also will have noticed that we have focused a major portion of this book on you and your hope. We believe that you cannot give your child what you do not have. While you are altruistically and lovingly instilling hope in your children, you also will be raising your own hope. Everyone wins.

The process of developing hope is about expanding possibilities for your children—more and higher goals, more ways to reach these goals, and more energy to pursue them. We have seen these hope-instilling strategies work, and we want you to see living proof in the lives of your own children.

As we have noted earlier in this book, there is a saying that "children are our hope for the future." These words only hold true, however, if such children themselves are hopeful. It is perhaps our ultimate privilege and task as parents, therefore, to see that our children learn to think hopefully. This is our contribution to a better tomorrow, and this book is dedicated to that possibility.

Suggested Reading

Books for Helping Children with Scholastic, Athletic, and Social Skills

Athletics

Beyond X's and O's: What Generic Parents, Volunteer Coaches and Teachers Can Learn About Generic Kids and All of the Sports They Play. Jack Hutslar, Ph.D. Wooten Printing Company, Inc. Welcome, NC. 1985.
A manual aimed at helping children succeed at sports. Examines problems with current sports models, attitudes, and programs. Suggests a more helpful philosophy to adopt for children.

The Growing Child In Competitive Sport. Geof Gleeson, Editor. Hodder & Stoughton, London. 1986.
Coaches tackle the physiological, psychological, and sociological problems of overtraining, and relate such problems to the development of musicians and actors, as well.

Joy and Sadness in Children's Sports. Rainer Martes. Human Kinetics Publishers. Champaign, Il. 1978.
Focuses on nonschool sports, examines the good and bad points of sports for children from preschool to fourteen years old.

Let's Play Together: Cooperative Games for All Ages. Mildred Masheder. Green Print, London, England. 1989.
Collection of over 300 games and sports that teach cooperation over competition. Also suited for children with disabilities.

Scholastics

Awakening Your Child's Natural Genius: Enhancing Curiosity, Creativity, and Learning Ability. Thomas Armstrong, Ph.D. Putnam Publishing, New York, NY. 1990.
Over 300 practical suggestions and activities showing how parents can play a pivotal role in helping their child realize their gifts. Describes how parents can encourage their child's school to provide the types of experiences all children need in order to develop their inborn drive to learn and create. Includes resources.

Family Matters: Why Homeschooling Makes Sense. David Guterson. Harcourt Brace & Company, Orlando, FL. 1992.
A high school English teacher affirms the powerful role of the family in a child's education.

How Children Learn. John Hold. Dell/Seymour Lawrence, New York, NY. 1983.
Explores ways children learn and examines the process of learning to talk, read, count, and create. Shows how to nurture and encourage children's natural abilities.

How to Maximize Your Child's Learning Ability: A Complete Guide to Choosing and Using the Best Games, Toys, Activities, Learning Aids and Tactics for Your Child. Lauren Bradway & Barbara Albers Hill. Avery Publishing Group, Inc., Garden City Park, NY. 1993
Helps parents identify child's particular learning style and offers advice on selecting toys, activities, and learning strategies to best use this style to improve learning.

How to Teach your Child: Things to Know from Kindergarten Through Grade Six. Veltisezar B. Bautista. Bookhaus Publishers, Farmington Hills, MI. 1992
Aids parents in home teaching and school supplementation by presenting effective teaching methods, reviews of skills, and evaluation guides.

Is the Left Brain Always Right: A Guide to Whole Child Development. Clare Cherry, Douglas Godwin, & Jesse Staples. Fearon Teacher Aids, Belmont, CA. 1989.
Explains different hemispheric functions, presents tests for assessing hemispheric dominance, and includes developmental activities that are best suited for each.

School Savvy: Everything You Need to Know to Guide Your Child Through Today's Schools. Diane Harrington & Laurette Young. Noonday Press, New York, NY. 1993.
Offers an in-depth look at how schools work and provides ways that parents can be involved at many levels—from helping their children to advocating for changes in the entire system.

Teach Your Child How to Think. Edward de Bono. Viking, New York, NY. 1992.
Examples, exercises, games, and drawings teach the difference between intelligence and thinking. Provides a step-by-step method for helping children develop clear and constructive thinking.

Social Skills

Getting Your Kids to Say NO in the 90's When You Said Yes in the 60's. Victor Strasburger, M.D. Simon & Schuster, New York, NY. 1993.

Describes difficulties of being a teenager in the '90s by addressing issues including impact of divorce and single parenting, drug use and sex, and media influences. Presents latest research and advice to help parents be more compassionate, understanding, and effective.

How to Develop Your Children's Creativity. Reynold Bean. Price Stren Sloan, Inc. Los Angeles, CA. 1992.
Helps teach children to become more flexible and adaptive thinkers, as well as how to express themselves in socially acceptable ways.

Let's Play Together: Cooperative Games for All Ages. Mildred Masheder. Green Print, London, England. 1989.
Collection of over 300 games and sports that teach cooperation over competition. Also suited for children with disabilities. (See also Sports)

Playground Politics: Understanding the Emotional Life of Your School-Age Child. Stanley I. Greenspan, M.D., & Jacqueline Salmon. Merloyd Lawrence, Reading, MA. 1993.
Helps parents deal with the typical issues that arise from school interactions: aggression, rivalry, vulnerable self-esteem, late blooming, talents, learning disabilities, problems with reality and fantasy, and early sexuality.

Children's Books on Hope-Related Issues

Abuse

A Family That Fights. Sharon Chesler Bernstein. Albert Whitman & Co., Morton Grove, IL. 1991.
Henry, the oldest child, struggles with his father's abusiveness toward the whole family.

Don't Hurt Me, Mama. Muriel Stanek. Albert Whitman & Co., Niles, IL 1983.
Offers possible solutions and a positive conclusion for a young girl who is abused by her mother.

Adoption

Adoption Is for Always. Linda Walvoord Girard. Albert Whitman & Co., Niles, IL 1985.
Explores the confusion and upsetting emotions a little girl feels when she discovers that she is adopted.

Happy Adoption Day. John McCutcheon & Julie Paschkis. Little Brown, Boston, Mass. 1996.
The love and joy of new parents watching their adopted child grow is described. An adoption-day celebration is held each year.

How I Was Adopted. Joanna Cole. Morrow Junior Books, New York, NY. 1995.
The message is that adoption is just one way of making a family, and that the love in an adoptive family is the same as in any family. Thus, family is shown to be about love and spirit, not blood ties or genetics.

My Real Family. Emily Arnold McCully. Bromndeer Press, Orlando, FL. 1994.
A child bear thinks that she is adopted after hearing that her family is adopting a sheep. She runs away in order to find her "real parents," but returns home and realizes she has "real parents."

Tell Me Again About the Night I Was Born. Jamie Lee Curtis. HarperCollins Publishers, New York, NY. 1996
A young girl has her parents retell the cherished family story about her birth and adoption.

Affection

The Original Warm Fuzzy Tale. Claude Steiner. Jalmar Press, Rolling Hills Estates, CA. 1977.
Presents a story analogous to everyday life that encourages children to give as many "warm fuzzies" (loving thoughts and gestures) as possible.

Alcohol/Drugs

I Wish Daddy Didn't Drink So Much. Judith Vigna. Albert Whitman & Co., Niles, IL 1988.
Describes how a little girl, with her mom's help, learns to keep her father's problem drinking from ruining her life.

What's "Drunk" Mama? Al-Anon Publications. New York, NY. 1977.
Examines a young girl's feelings about her father's alcoholism and the negative effects it has on her family.

When a Family Is In Trouble. Marge Heegaard. Woodland Press, Minneapolis, MN. 1993.
In a workbook format, children are helped through the trauma of a parent's chemical dependency.

When Someone In the Family Drinks Too Much. Richard C. Langsen. Dial Books for Young Readers, New York, NY. 1996.
In simple terms, children are shown how to recognize alcoholism and its effects on the entire family. Ways to cope and where to get outside help also are addressed.

Anger

I Was So Mad. Mercer Mayer. Western Publishing, Racine, WI. 1983.
Describes a boy "critter," who is mad because he keeps getting into trouble. Story teaches anger control and resolution.

That Makes Me Angry! Anthony Best. Western Publishing, Racine, WI 1989.
Shows how lack of communication can make people angry at each other. Bert and Ernie work out a communication problem without getting into a fight.

Arguing

Every Kid's Guide to Handling Family Arguments. Joy Berry. Children's Press, Chicago, IL. 1987.
Explores family fighting and teaches that arguing can be healthy, and that both good and bad can come out of it.

Every Kid's Guide to Handling Fights with Brothers or Sisters. Joy Berry. Children's Press, Chicago, IL. 1987.
Gives useful tips on how to handle brothers and sisters when they do things that upset a child.

Asthma (see also Physical Illness)

All About Asthma. William & Vivian Ostrow. Whitman & Co., Morton Grove, IL. 1989.
The young narrator describes life with asthma, explaining its causes and symptoms and discussing ways to control it.

Attachment (see also Love and Unconditional Love)

I Love My Family. Wade Hudson. Scholastic, New York, NY. 1993.
An African American family's annual reunion teaches the similarity of experiences among families of different races, including good family relations, love and respect for elders, and strong values.

The Runaway Bunny. Margaret Wise Brown. HarperCollins, New York, NY. 1982.
Bunny learns that his mom loves him so much that she will follow him anywhere, even if he runs away.

Comparisons (see also Self-Acceptance)

Hard to Be Six. Arnold Adoff. Lothrop, Lee and Shepard Books, New York, NY. 1991.
A little boy compares himself to his sisters and wants to be older, like them. His grandmother makes him realize it's good to be young and tells him, "Take time slow, make life count, pass love on."

Communication (see also Arguing)

Every Kid's Guide to Understanding Parents. Joy Berry. Children's Press, Chicago, IL 1987.
Helps children identify with different kinds of parents and suggests steps for getting along with parents.

Yes, I Can Say No. Manuel J. Smith. Arbor House, New York, NY. 1986.
Gives strategies to help children respond assertively to peer pressure, compliments, criticism, and other forms of communication.

Confidence and Self-Esteem

The Good Luck Pony. Elizabeth Koda-Callan. Workman Pub., New York, NY. 1993.
A little girl finds the courage to ride when her mother gives her a tiny golden pony that radiates self-confidence.

100 Ways to Enhance Self-Concept in the Classroom. Jack Canfield & Harold C. Wells. Prentice-Hall, Englewood Cliffs, NJ 1976.
Contains exercises to help teachers improve the child's confidence and self-esteem in a nonjudgmental environment.

Crying

I Am Not a Crybaby. Norma Simon. Albert Whitman & Co., Niles, IL. 1989.
Gives reasons why people cry (e.g., a sad cry when one is hurt or a happy cry at a wedding) and stresses that one is never too old to cry.

Death

The Accident. Carol Carrick. Seabury Press, New York, NY. 1976.
Explores a young boy's feelings when his dog dies.

Coping with Death and Grief. Marge Heegaard. Woodland Press, Minneapolis, MN. 1990.
Many stories touch upon young people's grief and the facts about death.

Everett Anderson's Goodbye. Lucille Clifton. Holt, Rinehart & Winston. New York, NY. 1983.
Illustrates the stages of grief and how a boy passes through them after his father dies.

Gentle Willow: A Story for Children About Dying. Joyce C. Mills. Magination Press, New York, NY. 1993.
Amanda is upset that she is going to lose her friend, Gentle Willow, but the Tree Wizards help her to understand that her memories are gifts from her friend and that there are special ways of saying good-bye.

Help for the Hard Times, Getting Through Loss. Earl Hipp. Hazelden, Center City, Minnesota. 1995.
Answers questions of eleven-to-seventeen-year-old children about loss. Offers a guide for handling crisis, emotions, and responsibilities.

Someday a Tree. Eve Bunting. Clarion Books, New York, NY. 1993.
A young girl, her parents, and their neighbors try to save an old oak tree that is poisoned by pollution. The girl finally discovers a solution that restores her hope.

The Ugly Menorah. Marissa Moss. Farrar Straus Giroux, New York, NY. 1996.
A young girl struggles with her grandpa's death. She has a menorah for Hanukkah, but it is ugly and hard to look at. When grandma lights the candles, grandpa's presence is felt.

When Bad Things Happen to Good People. Harold S. Kushner. Schocken Books, New York, NY. 1981.
Written by a man dealing with the pain of a terminally ill child. Helps the person to find the strength and hope to carry on.

When Grandpa Came to Stay. Judith Caseley. Greenwillow Books, New York, NY. 1996.
Because Benny's grandmother died, his grandfather comes for a visit. Benny doesn't understand much about death, but he and his grandfather talk about it and learn to cope.

When I Die, Will I Get Better? Joeri & Piet Breebaart. Peter Bedrick Books, New York, NY. 1993.
A six-year-old boy tries to come to terms with the death of his younger brother by creating a story about rabbit brothers that closely parallels his own experiences.

When Someone Dies. Sharon Greelee. Peachtree Publishers, Atlanta, GA. 1992.
Suggestions are made for surviving the changes and remembering the good times when a loved one dies.

Determination

The Day the Dark Clouds Came. Phylliss Adams. Modern Press, Cleveland, OH. 1986.
A little robin uses hope, effort, and determination to overcome her fear of failure.

The Evergreen Wood: An Adaptation of the Pilgrim's Progress for Children. Alan & Linda Parry. Oliver Nelson, Nashville, TN. 1992.
After a long and arduous journey, Christopher Mouse reaches the Evergreen Wood, where all the animals live in peace and safety.

Horton Hatches the Egg. Dr. Seuss. Random House, New York, NY. 1940.
The story of an elephant who is loyal, dedicated, and determined to keep his word, no matter what happens.

Kids Can Succeed: 51 Tips for Real Life from One Kid to Another. Daryl Bernstein. Bod Adams Inc., Holbrook, MA. 1993.
Tips for teens include goal setting, maintaining a positive outlook, and trying different approaches to solve a problem.

Left By Themselves. Charles Paul May. Scholastic Book Services, New York, NY. 1982.
Family members are rescued and their lives are saved because of their strong determination and love for each other.

The Little Engine That Could. Watty Piper. Platt & Munk, New York, NY. 1976.
After a train filled with toys breaks down, several other trains refuse to help. Finally, a little blue engine comes along and, with determination and encouragement, gets the toys to the children on the other side.

Diabetes (see also Physical Illness)

Even Little Kids Get Diabetes. Connie White Pirner. Whitman & Co., Morton Grove, IL. 1991.
A two-year-old finds out that she has diabetes but learns that she is still a regular kid.

Sarah and Puffle: A Story for Children About Diabetes. Linnea Mulder, R. N. Magination Press, New York, NY. 1992.

Upset by the restrictions imposed by her diabetes, Sarah dreams about a talking sheep who helps her accept her condition.

Shoot for the Hoop. Matt Christopher. Little, Brown and Company, New York, NY. 1995.

When diagnosed with diabetes, Rusty's parents tell him to quit playing basketball. Rusty is determined to persuade his parents to let him continue to play, and overcomes many obstacles so that he can.

Disabilities (see also Learning Disabilities)

About Handicaps. Sara Bonnett Stein. Walker & Co., New York, NY. 1974.

A boy who is frightened of others' disabilities learns that people who are different can be good friends.

Howie Helps Himself. Joan Fassler. Albert Whitman & Co., Morton Grove, IL. 1975.

Young Howie learns how to interact with others about his physical disability. The story also shows how anxiety toward people with disabilites can be reduced.

I Have a Sister, My Sister Is Deaf. Jeanne Whitehouse Peterson. Harper Trophy, New York, NY. 1977.

Explains what it's like to be deaf to young readers. Sisters learn to handle their differences and to overlook disabilities so as to make their relationship stronger.

Little Tree: A True Story For Children with Serious Medical Problems. Joyce C. Mills, Ph.D. Magination Press, New York, NY. 1992.

Although she is saddened when a storm has taken some of her branches, Little Tree draws strength and happiness from the knowledge that she still has a strong trunk, deep roots, and a beautiful heart.

My Friend Leslie: The Story of a Handicapped Child. Maxine Rosenberg & George Ancona. Lothrop, Lee & Shepard Books. New York, NY. 1983.

Shows child with multiple disabilities and how she is accepted in various school settings.

Someone Special Just Like You. Tricia Brown. Henry Holt and Company, New York, NY. 1984.

Children with disabilities learn that all kids have the same wishes, joys, and desires, even though they may not see, hear, speak, or walk the same way.

A Very Special Critter. Gina and Mercer Mayer. Western Publishing, New York, NY. 1992.

The first day at school for a little boy in a wheelchair is scary for him and the other children. Gives positive examples of relating to a child with a disability and seeing similarities rather than differences.

Divorce and Stepfamilies

Daddy Doesn't Live Here Anymore. Betty Boegehold. Western Publishing, Racine, WI. 1985.
A little girl named Casey deals with the fact that her dad still loves her, even though he is divorcing her mom.

Dinosaurs Divorce. Laurene Krasny Brown and Marc Brown. Little, Brown and Company, Canada. 1977.
Tells of dinosaurs getting divorced and describes tough situations to which young readers can relate. Positive ways of handling the difficulties of divorce are approached by using humor and lively examples.

Helping Children of Divorce. Susan Arnsberg Diamond. Schocken Books, New York, NY. 1985.
Helps teachers, school officials, and divorced parents to better understand and assist children whose parents are divorced.

Let's Talk About Stepfamilies. Angela Grunsell. Gloucester Press, New York, NY. 1990.
Answers questions young people have when experiencing new additions to their home. Debunks myths such as the "wicked stepmother."

Living with a Single Parent. Maxine B. Rosenberg. Bradbury Press, Macmillan Publishing Inc. New York, NY 10022. 1992.
A collection of firsthand stories by adolescents living with single parents.

My Mother's House, My Father's House. C. B. Christiansen. Macmillan Publishing Co., New York, NY. 1989.
A young girl talks through the difficulties of living in two different houses after her parent's divorce.

When a Parent Marries Again: Children Can Deal with Family Change. Marge Heegaard. Woodland Press, Minneapolis, MN. 1991.
Helps process grief surrounding death of a parent and the emotions following remarriage. Includes illustrations that the reader draws.

When Mom and Dad Separate. Marge Heegaard. Woodland Press, Minneapolis, MN. 1990.
Through a workbook format, children are shown how to deal with their feelings about separation or divorce.

Where Do I Belong? Buff Bradley. Addison Wesley, Reading, MA. 1992.
Helps eight-to-twelve-year-old children to deal with stepfamilies. Touches on divorce and living through it, being a stepchild, and so on.

Why Are We Getting a Divorce? Peter Mayle. Harmony Books, New York, NY. 1988.
Explains adjustment to living with one parent and how to overcome the loss and hurt that children of divorced parents experience.

Domestic Violence (see also Abuse)

Something Is Wrong at My House. Diane Davis. Parenting Press, Seattle, WA. 1984.

Focuses upon children from violent and nonviolent homes giving them permission to have feelings and to make decisions about how they wish to act upon those feelings.

Environment

Alejandro's Gift. Richard E. Albert. Chronicle Books, San Francisco, CA. 1994.
Teaching environmental awareness, the main character, Alejandro, explores different climates and environments. He finds hope in his adventure to the desert.

The Boy Who Didn't Believe in Spring. Lucille Clifton. Dutton Children's Books, New
   York, NY. 1993.
King Shabazz was a little boy who did not believe that spring was coming. He did not see the blooming flowers, the chirping birds, or smell the fresh air. But one day he found a nest of unhatched bird's eggs, and then he believed that spring had arrived.

Epilepsy (see also Physical Illness)

Lee, the Rabbit with Epilepsy. Deborah Moss. Woodbine House, Kensington, MD. 1989.
Lee is diagnosed with epilepsy, but medicine to control her seizures reduces her worries, and she learns she can still lead a normal life.

Fear

Hildilid's Night. Cheli Duran Ryan. Alladin Paperbacks Book, New York, NY. 1996.
Hildilid hates the night, but no matter how much she tosses and turns, the darkness does not go away. Finally, her fear lessens when she realizes that the sun always rises the next morning.

Scared Silly! Mark Brown. Little, Brown and Company Limited, Canada. 1994.
Spooky poems, riddles, jokes, and stories help young readers to laugh at the things of which they are scared.

Sometimes I'm Afraid. Jane Watson, Werner Switzer, Robert E. Hirschberg, & J. Cotter.
   Crown Publishers, New York, NY. 1986.
A young boy, afraid in many different situations, deals with his fear and gives reasons why he becomes afraid.

What's Under My Bed? James Stevenson. Puffin Books, New York, NY. 1983.
Mary Ann and Louise spend the night at their grandparent's house, but they are afraid. Grandpa tells them he, too, used to be scared when he was their age, and this makes them feel better.

Friendship

Caleb's Friend. Eric Jon Nones. Farrar, Straus, & Giroux. New York, NY. 1993.
When a storm threatens, Caleb and his friend learn that even if they cannot be together, they will never be truly apart.

Friends Forever: Six Stories Celebrating the Joys of Friendship. Debbie Butcher Wiersma &
   Veveca Gustafson. Western Publishing, Racine, WI. 1992.
Stories about friendship are brought to life through various characters.

Little Mouse's Rescue. Ariane Chottin. Adapted by Patricia Jensen. Reader's Digest Kids, Pleasantville, NY. 1990.
A little mouse sneaks into a farm kitchen for a feast that is guarded by two cats. Her friends come to rescue her, and the power of friendship is revealed.

Pinky and Rex Go to Camp. James Howe. Avon Books, New York, NY. 1993.
By sharing his fear of going to camp, Pinky finds support from his best friend and ends up having a great time.

Goals

Grover's 10 Terrific Ways to Help Our Wonderful World. Anna Ross. Random House, New York, NY. 1992.
Using the philosophy that the world takes care of us and, in return, we must take care of the world, Grover gives a list of things (e.g., plant a tree, do not waste, recycle) that children are capable of doing.

Hector's New Sneakers. Amanda Vesey. Penguin Books, New York, NY. 1993.
Explains children's feelings about fitting in and having the "right" things. Hector's parents cannot afford the sneakers he wants, and he learns that he can be happy without them.

The Man Who Had No Dream. Adelaide Holl. Random House, New York, NY. 1969.
Story explains the importance of having goals and dreams. A rich, idle, and unhappy man finds a way to be useful and live a happy life.

Oh, the Places You'll Go. Dr. Seuss. Random House, New York, NY. 1990.
Shows the ups and downs that one might encounter in the future. Encourages the reader to persevere and find the success that lies within.

Oh, the Thinks You Can Think. Dr. Seuss. Random House, New York, NY. 1975.
Colorful pictures and silly rhymes encourage use of imagination. Introduces the reader to creative ways of thinking.

When I Grow Up. Mercer Mayer. Western Publishing, New York, NY. 1991.
A little girl dreams of the different things she might be when she grows up, such as a mountain climber, lion tamer, or a famous doctor. Exposes both boys and girls to nontraditional roles.

Health and Nutrition

American Academy of Pediatrics Official Complete Home Reference. William H. Dietz & Loraine Stern, M.D., Eds. Villard, New York. 1999.
A complete compendium of nutritional information from birth to young adulthood

Every Kid's Guide to Nutrition and Health Care. Joy Berry. Children's Press, Chicago, IL. 1987.
Teaches about maintaining a healthy lifestyle by exercising, eating nutritious food, and adhering to bodily requirements. Gives tips on hygiene and wearing appropriate clothing.

What About Me? When Brothers and Sisters Get Sick. Allan Peterkin. Magination Press, New York, NY. 1992.
Laura experiences conflicting emotions when her brother becomes seriously ill. Includes suggestions for parents to help.

Hospitals

Going to the Hospital. Fred Rodgers. Putnam's, New York, NY. 1988.
Describes what happens during a stay in the hospital, including some of the common forms of medical treatment.

Individual Differences and Cooperation

Crow Boy. Taro Yashima. Viking, New York, NY. 1983.
A young boy is taunted by classmates because he seems strange and quiet. With a teacher's support, the boy opens up to his classmates and gains acceptance and respect.

If We Were All the Same. Fred Rodgers. Random House, New York, NY. 1987.
Lady Elaine visits the Purple Planet where everybody looks and lives the same. When these Purple Planet people visit Lady Elaine's world, they are impressed with how everything is different and decide to change their world to also have differences.

The Mixed Up Cameleon. Eric Carle. HarperCollins, New York, NY. 1975.
A chameleon goes to the zoo and wishes he could be like the other animals. When this wish is granted, he realizes he's better when he's authentically himself.

Old Henry. Joan W. Blos. William Morrow & Co. New York NY. 1987.
Shows how different kinds of people learn to get along.

The Rag Coat. Lauren Mills. Little Brown, Waltham MA. 1991.
Minna proudly wears her new coat made of clothing scraps to school, where the other children laugh at her until she tells them stories behind the scraps.

The Ugly Duckling. Marianna Mayer. MacMillan, New York NY. 1987.
An ugly duckling spends an unhappy year ostracized by the other animals before she grows into a beautiful swan.

We're Different, We're the Same. Bobbi Jane Kates. Random House, New York, NY. 1992.
Explores the physical and emotional similarities and differences among people and stresses that it is natural for people to be different.

Learning Disabilities

Sixth Grade Can Really Kill You. Barthe DeClements. Viking Penguin, Santa Barbara, CA. 1985.
Helen, a child with a reading disability, struggles with her disability by acting up in school. This story has a hopeful conclusion.

Trouble with School: A Family Story About Learning Disabilities. Kathryn & Allison Boe-
sel Dunn. Woodbine House, Inc. Rockville, MD. 1993.
A dual narrative between mother and daughter shows both perspectives about the
struggles with the daughter's learning disability.

Listening (see also Communication)

Nobody's Perfect, Not Even My Mother. Norma Simon. Albert Whitman & Co., Chicago,
IL. 1981.
Lets children know that it's okay not to be perfect. Suggests that no one is perfect,
and that everyone is good at something.

Oh, Bother! No One's Listening! Betty Birney. Western Publishing, Racine, WI. 1991.
Winnie the Pooh and friends plan a party, but it doesn't turn out very well because
no one listened when Rabbit read the list of what everyone was to bring. Christopher
Robin explains how good listening can help.

Love (see also Unconditional Love)

Guess How Much I Love You? Sam McBratney. Candlewick Press, Boston, MA. 1994.
A mother rabbit shows everlasting love for her little son.

Hope. Randy Houk. The Benefactory, Inc., Fairfield, CT. 1995.
A caring family finds an injured pig and nurses it back to health at their family farm.
Love and patience bring the pig back to good health.

Moving

Home of the Bayou. G. Brian Karas. Simon and Schuster Books, New York, NY. 1996.
A young cowboy learns how to deal with moving to a new place.

The Lotus Seed. Sherry Garland. Harcourt Brace Jovanovitch. San Diego, CA. 1993.
A young Vietnamese girl saves a lotus seed and carries it with her everywhere in
order to remember a brave emperor and the homeland she has to flee.

My Friend William Moved Away. Martha Whitmore Hickman. Abingdon, Nashville,
TN. 1979.
Helps children understand that even though friends move away, there will be new
friends.

Things You Need to Know Before You Move. Lisa Ann Marsoli. Silver Burdett, Morris-
town, NY. 1985.
Prepares young people for the anticipated changes that come with a move.

Obstacles

Alexander and the Terrible, Horrible, No Good, Very Bad Day. Judith Versed. Aladdin
Paperbacks, New York, NY. 1987.
From having a bad hair day to eating lima beans, everything is going wrong for Alex-
ander. His mother gives him hope for a better tomorrow.

I Had Trouble in Getting to Solla Sollew. Dr. Seuss. Random House, New York, NY. 1963.

Troubles happen to the character on each page. The goal is to find a man who can teach how to overcome these obstacles.

Into the Deep Forest with Henry David Thoreau. Jim Murphy. Clarion Books, New York, NY. 1995.

Thoreau and two companions struggle through the Maine wilderness. As they travel through hardships, details and beautiful sites of the untouched forests are described.

Parent Travel

Traveling Again, Dad? Michael Lorelli. Publishers Desing Service, Traverse City, MI. 1996.

Addresses how some families live with a parent who must be away from home because of work. Suggestions are made for dealing with this issue in a positive way.

Parental Relations

Understanding Parents. Joy Berry. Children's Press, Sebastopol, CA. 1987.

Suggests that there are many different types of parents, and that parents love their children and want what is best for them.

Something Is Wrong at My House. Diane Davis. Parenting Press, Seattle, WA. 1984.

Explores a boy's feelings about his parents' fighting and gives good solutions.

Physical Illness

When Someone Has a Very Serious Illness. Marge Heegaard. Woodland Press, Minneapolis, MN. 1992.

Children are helped to deal with their feelings about serious illness using a workbook format.

Planning (see also Problem Solving)

Every Kid's Guide to Using Time Wisely. Joy Berry. Living Skills Press, Sebastopol, CA. 1987.

Gives advice for managing time effectively.

The Kid's Guide to Social Action. Barbara Lewis. Free Spirit Publishing. Minneapolis, MN. 1991.

Encourages the use of surrounding resources to create petitions, surveys, and letters to make an impact on society. Contains stories that inspire and promote social awareness.

Prejudice and Race Issues

Abby. Jeannette Caines. Harper and Row, New York, NY. 1973.

The challenges of an adopted black girl living with white parents are described.

Black Is Brown Is Tan. Arnold Adoff. Harper and Row Publishers, San Francisco, CA. 1973.

Two young boys are brought up by a white father and a black mother. They like it, because the things around them are black or white.

The Lily Cupboard. Shulamith Levey Oppenheim. HarperCollins, New York, NY. 1992.

A young Jewish girl during WW II learns that there are many heroes for her.

Living in Two Worlds. George Ancona. Lothrop, Lee & Shepard Books. New York, NY. 1986.

Mixed-race children talk about themselves, including feelings and special challenges they face in belonging to two cultures.

Yo! Yes? Chris Raschka. Orchard Books, New York, NY. 1993.

Two lonely characters, one black and one white, meet on the street and become friends.

Problem Solving (see also Planning)

The Book of Think. Marilyn Burns. Little, Brown, and Co., Boston, MA. 1976.

Offers a variety of problem-solving strategies and approaches, as well as practice exercises.

Did I Ever Tell You How Lucky You Are? Dr. Seuss. Random House, New York, NY. 1973.

Puts problems in perspective by using humor. Shows that one can be happy with what one has.

Every Kid's Guide to Decision Making and Problem Solving. Joy Berry. Children's Press, Chicago, IL. 1987.

Fosters understanding of what a decision is and why people make decisions. Outlines decision-making steps.

Every Kid's Guide to Responding to Danger. Joy Berry. Living Skills Press, Sebastopol, CA. 1987.

Presents situations that could harm a child, as well as how to avoid or handle those dangerous situations.

Fall Out. Gudrun Pausewang. Penguin Books, New York, NY. 1994.

There is a leak at the nuclear power station near fourteen-year-old Janna's house. Janna is left alone to look after her little brother and must make difficult decisions about what to do.

The Story of Little Babaji. Helen Bannerman. HarperCollins Publishers, USA. 1996.

An Indian boy has his new clothes stolen by wild tigers in the jungle. Babaji overcomes his fear of wild animals in order to get back his clothes.

Remarriage of Parent

When a Parent Marries Again. Marge Heegaard. Woodland Press, Minneapolis, MN. 1993.

In workbook format, children are taught how to deal with their feelings about stepfamilies.

School

Starting School. Janet and Allen Ahlberg. Puffin Books, New York, NY. 1990.
Preschoolers are shown that school is exciting and fun, and a place where friendships can start.

Self-Acceptance (see also Comparisons)

I Hate Being Gifted. Patricia Hermes. Minstrel Book, New York, NY. 1990.
A teen girl is accepted into a gifted program, but she begins to lose friends because they are jealous. She learns to deal with self-acceptance and peer pressure.

I Wish I Were a Butterfly. James Howe. Harcourt, Brace, Jovanovich, Orlando, FL. 1987.
A cricket who is unhappy with his appearance learns to accept himself. Encourages children to look at and accept what they have.

The King's Equal. Katherine Paterson. HarperCollins, New York, NY. 1992.
In order to wear the crown of the kingdom, an arrogant young prince must find an equal in his bride. Instead, he finds someone far better than he.

Least of All. Carol Purdy. Aladdin Books, New York, NY. 1993.
A little girl in a big farm family teaches herself how to read using the Bible and shares this knowledge with her brothers, parents, and grandmother during a long, cold Vermont winter.

Separation and Independence

All by Myself. Mercer Mayer. Western Publishing, New York, NY. 1983.
A little boy "critter" finds that there are some things he can do by himself, and that it's okay to ask for help with other things.

Shyness

How Come You're So Shy? Leone Castell Anderson. A Golden Book. Western Publishing, Racine, WI. 1987.
Two girls who are both shy learn to talk to each other and become friends.

Very Shy. Barbara Shook Hazen. Human Sciences Press. New York, NY. 1982.
Nancy asks her dad to help her get over her shyness and then follows his suggestions.

Sibling Relationships (see also Arguing)

Your Best Friend, Kate. Pat Brisson. Alladin Books, New York, NY. 1992.
Kate's letters to her best friend show how much she loves her brother, even though she fights with him.

Small Physical Size (see also Comparisons)

Little Puppy Saves the Day. Muriel Pepin adapted by Patricia Jensen. Reader's Digest Kids Books. 1992.

A little puppy is made fun of by the other farm animals because he is so small, but he proves his worth when he rescues a lost chick.

Staying Alone

All Alone After School. Muriel Stanek. Albert Whitman & Co., Niles, IL. 1985.
A boy talks about the things that he does after school while he's alone at home.

Suicide

When Living Hurts. Sol Gordon. Union of American Hebrew Congregations, New York, NY. 1985.
Explores suicide by showing how to deal with feelings such as anger, depression, and peer pressure. Also addresses questions about God and the purpose of life.

Traumatic Experiences

Every Kid's Guide to Coping with Childhood Traumas. Joy Berry. Children's Press, Chicago, IL. 1988.
Gives children specific terms to help in understanding their feelings related to various traumas. Also gives specific suggestions for dealing with their traumas.

Good Answers to Tough Questions About Traumatic Experiences. Joy Berry. Children's Press, Chicago, IL. 1990.
Defines traumas that children may encounter and explains the steps to overcoming the related negative feelings. Shows how positive things can come out of negative experiences.

When Something Terrible Happens. Marge Heegaard. Woodland Press, Minneapolis, MN. 1992.
In a workbook format, children are helped to deal with their feelings about traumatic events.

When Something Terrible Happens: Children Can Learn to Cope with Grief. Marge Heegaard. Woodland Press, Minneapolis, MN. 1991.
Helps process reactions to traumatic events with illustrations that the reader draws.

Travel

We're Taking an Airplane Trip. Dinah L. Moche. Western Publishing Co., Racine, WI. 1982.
Elizabeth and her younger brother are flying alone for the first time. Anxious and excited, they have a wonderful experience.

Unconditional Love (see also Love)

Mama, Do You Love Me? Barbara M. Joose. Chronicle Books, San Francisco, CA. 1991.
A daughter questions her mother's love to see if it is conditional or unconditional. The story shows the special love that exists between a parent and child.

Working Moms

That Terrible Thing That Happened at Our House. Stan Bernstein. Parent's Magazine Press, New York, NY. 1987.
A young girl feels bad when her mother goes back to work, but the family learns to handle this new situation.

More New Harbinger Titles

MAKING HOPE HAPPEN

From the authors of *The Great Big Book of Hope,* this powerful program shows adult readers how to break old self-defeating habits, learn new ways of thinking about themselves, and develop the willpower to say "Yes, I can" and the waypower to overcome roadblocks and find new routes to their goals.

Item HOPE $14.95

HELPING YOUR ANXIOUS CHILD

Anxiety in childhood can result in tremendous personal suffering—and it often goes untreated, in part because parents don't know where to turn. This book offers valuable practical advice to help parents understand their child's anxiety and the options for dealing with it, with or without a therapist's help.

Item HAC $12.95

WHY CAN'T I BE THE PARENT I WANT TO BE?

This breakthrough guide helps parents recognize and challenge the deeply held beliefs, or schemas, that lead to problematic parenting styles.

Item PRNT $12.95

UNDERSTANDING YOUR CHILD'S SEXUAL BEHAVIOR

Puts parents' minds at ease by showing them how to differentiate between worrisome and natural or healthy behavior and freeing them from misconceptions about sexual abuse.

Item CSB $12.95

FROM SABOTAGE TO SUCCESS

Real-life examples, exercises, and action plans help you identify self-defeating behaviors and learn how skills such as positive self-talk, visualization, goal setting, and risk taking can help you break down the barriers that keep you from reaching your life's true potential.

Item SBTG $14.95

Call toll-free 1-800-748-6273 to order. Have your Visa or Mastercard number ready. Or send a check for the titles you want to New Harbinger Publications, 5674 Shattuck Avenue, Oakland, CA 94609. Include $3.80 for the first book and 75¢ for each additional book to cover shipping and handling. (California residents please include appropriate sales tax.) Allow four to six weeks for delivery.

Prices subject to change without notice.

Some Other New Harbinger Self-Help Titles

Multiple Chemical Sensitivity: A Survival Guide, $16.95
Dancing Naked, $14.95
Why Are We Still Fighting, $15.95
From Sabotage to Success, $14.95
Parkinson's Disease and the Art of Moving, $15.95
A Survivor's Guide to Breast Cancer, $13.95
Men, Women, and Prostate Cancer, $15.95
Make Every Session Count: Getting the Most Out of Your Brief Therapy, $10.95
Virtual Addiction, $12.95
After the Breakup, $13.95
Why Can't I Be the Parent I Want to Be?, $12.95
The Secret Message of Shame, $13.95
The OCD Workbook, $18.95
Tapping Your Inner Strength, $13.95
Binge No More, $14.95
When to Forgive, $12.95
Practical Dreaming, $12.95
Healthy Baby, Toxic World, $15.95
Making Hope Happen, $14.95
I'll Take Care of You, $12.95
Survivor Guilt, $14.95
Children Changed by Trauma, $13.95
Understanding Your Child's Sexual Behavior, $12.95
The Self-Esteem Companion, $10.95
The Gay and Lesbian Self-Esteem Book, $13.95
Making the Big Move, $13.95
How to Survive and Thrive in an Empty Nest, $13.95
Living Well with a Hidden Disability, $15.95
Overcoming Repetitive Motion Injuries the Rossiter Way, $15.95
What to Tell the Kids About Your Divorce, $13.95
The Divorce Book, Second Edition, $15.95
Claiming Your Creative Self: True Stories from the Everyday Lives of Women, $15.95
Six Keys to Creating the Life You Desire, $19.95
Taking Control of TMJ, $13.95
What You Need to Know About Alzheimer's, $15.95
Winning Against Relapse: A Workbook of Action Plans for Recurring Health and Emotional Problems, $14.95
Facing 30: Women Talk About Constructing a Real Life and Other Scary Rites of Passage, $12.95
The Worry Control Workbook, $15.95
Wanting What You Have: A Self-Discovery Workbook, $18.95
When Perfect Isn't Good Enough: Strategies for Coping with Perfectionism, $13.95
Earning Your Own Respect: A Handbook of Personal Responsibility, $12.95
High on Stress: A Woman's Guide to Optimizing the Stress in Her Life, $13.95
Infidelity: A Survival Guide, $13.95
Stop Walking on Eggshells, $14.95
Consumer's Guide to Psychiatric Drugs, $16.95
The Fibromyalgia Advocate: Getting the Support You Need to Cope with Fibromyalgia and Myofascial Pain, $18.95
Healing Fear: New Approaches to Overcoming Anxiety, $16.95
Working Anger: Preventing and Resolving Conflict on the Job, $12.95
Sex Smart: How Your Childhood Shaped Your Sexual Life and What to Do About It, $14.95
You Can Free Yourself From Alcohol & Drugs, $13.95
Amongst Ourselves: A Self-Help Guide to Living with Dissociative Identity Disorder, $14.95
Healthy Living with Diabetes, $13.95
Dr. Carl Robinson's Basic Baby Care, $10.95
Better Boundries: Owning and Treasuring Your Life, $13.95
Goodbye Good Girl, $12.95
Fibromyalgia & Chronic Myofascial Pain Syndrome, $19.95
The Depression Workbook: Living With Depression and Manic Depression, $17.95
Self-Esteem, Second Edition, $13.95
Angry All the Time: An Emergency Guide to Anger Control, $12.95
When Anger Hurts, $13.95
Perimenopause, $16.95
The Relaxation & Stress Reduction Workbook, Fourth Edition, $17.95
The Anxiety & Phobia Workbook, Second Edition, $18.95
I Can't Get Over It, A Handbook for Trauma Survivors, Second Edition, $16.95
Messages: The Communication Skills Workbook, Second Edition, $15.95
Thoughts & Feelings, Second Edition, $18.95
Depression: How It Happens, How It's Healed, $14.95
The Deadly Diet, Second Edition, $14.95
The Power of Two, $15.95
Living Without Depression & Manic Depression: A Workbook for Maintaining Mood Stability, $18.95
Couple Skills: Making Your Relationship Work, $14.95

Call **toll free, 1-800-748-6273,** or log on to our online bookstore at **www.newharbinger.com** to order. Have your Visa or Mastercard number ready. Or send a check for the titles you want to New Harbinger Publications, Inc., 5674 Shattuck Ave., Oakland, CA 94609. Include $3.80 for the first book and 75¢ for each additional book, to cover shipping and handling. (California residents please include appropriate sales tax.) Allow two to five weeks for delivery.

Prices subject to change without notice.